Human
Dynamics

W9-BEF-040

Human Dynamics

**A New Framework for
Understanding People and
Realizing the Potential in
Our Organizations**

Sandra Seagal & David Horne

PEGASUS
COMMUNICATIONS

PEGASUS COMMUNICATIONS, INC. WALTHAM

Human Dynamics: A New Framework for Understanding People and Realizing the
Potential in Our Organizations by Sandra Seagal and David Horne
Copyright © 1997 by Sandra Seagal and David Horne

All rights reserved. No part of this book may be reproduced or transmitted
by any form or by any means, electronic or mechanical, including photocopying and
recording, or by any information or storage retrieval system,
without written permission from the publisher.

Permission to reprint previously published material can be found on pp. 326–327.
Photo and illustration credits can be found on pp. 328–329.
Book and jacket design by Judy Walker.
Originally published in hardcover (ISBN 1-883823-06-4).

HUMAN DYNAMICS™ is a trademark and service mark for
a system of **Human Dynamics International** ®

PERSONALITY DYNAMICS℠ is a service mark for a form of analysis
provided as part of the HUMAN DYNAMICS™ system.
PERSONALITY DYNAMICS℠ is also a term used for each of the systemic patterns
of human functioning identified in the HUMAN DYNAMICS™ system.

**For more information about Human Dynamics,
see the additional resources page at the back of this book.**

Library of Congress Cataloging-in-Publication Data

Seagal, Sandra, 1928-
    Human dynamics: a new framework for understanding people and
realizing the potential in our organizations / Sandra Seagal & David
Horne. — 1st ed.
        p. cm.
    Includes index.
    ISBN 1-883823-07-2 (softcover).
    1. Communication in organizations. 2. Diversity in the workplace.
3. Multiculturalism. 4. Interpersonal relations. I. Horne, David,
1931-   . II. Title.
HD30.3.S4   1997
658.3—dc20

                                                96-22826
                                                CIP

PEGASUS
COMMUNICATIONS

Pegasus Communications, Inc.
One Moody Street
Waltham, MA 02453-5339
(781) 398-9700, Fax (781) 894-7175
www.pegasuscom.com

5297

♻ Printed on recycled paper
Printed in Canada
First edition
03 02 01 00   10 9 8 7 6 5

To our parents, Genevieve and Irving Kerner,
and Mabel and Ted Horne, who fully believed in us;
our children, Eve, Debra, and Ronald, in whom we fully believe;
and our first grandchild, Max Ollivier (born March 18, 1996),
and all his generation and the generations to come,
for whom our work is really undertaken.

Many heartfelt thanks to:

Linda O'Toole, our long-term friend and collaborator, whose deep capacities, remarkable creativity, and fine sensibilities have contributed so much to nurturing and shaping the work of Human Dynamics and inform every page of this book.

The L.A. group, who willingly helped lay down the first template for this work.

The Ph.D. group, who ventured into uncharted waters.

Berit and Bert Bergström, who came forward on Swedish soil as loving and meticulous caretakers of this work.

David Goldman, a good friend and generous supporter.

Dani Kropf, who knows about friendships and building, and to the group he has gathered to seed this work in Israel.

Sharon Rosen, whose beauty of spirit graces this work.

Glenn Pridham, whose visionary capacity created the first 10-year plan for Human Dynamics, at London Life Insurance Company in Canada.

Peter Senge, who believed in us from the beginning and has given his full support.

Susan Booth, whose life has been generously given in support of this work since 1983!

John Haggerty, who coined the term "benevolent virus" in relation to Human Dynamics, and who spreads it with "infectious" enthusiasm.

Don and Leta Cormier, dear friends and colleagues whose consistent efforts support this work.

Chris Strutt, whose persistence, devotion, and intelligent strategies have opened so many doors.

Julie Morath, who beautifully models the emotional-subjective personality dynamic in its full maturity.

Penny O'Malley, who steadfastly gives her "all" in applying Human Dynamics as a new paradigm for healthcare.

David Marsing, a practical visionary who uses this work in building and sustaining conscious community at Intel.

Shelly Siskind, whose visionary capacity and open heart helped open Canada to Human Dynamics.

Sue Gillespie, whose devotion knows no end.

Roger Peters, who uses the forum of business to bring hope to young people.

Joan Loudon, whose qualities of gentleness and strength have helped move this work forward.

Fred Herr, formerly of Ford Motor Company, our first mentor in the world of business. A good friend and wonderful exemplar of the executive who cares.

Gunnar Wessman, whose sensitivity of spirit and capacity to initiate supported our entry into Sweden.

Sören Gyll, who offered us our first business opportunity in Sweden with the words, "If you shoot in the dark, you're bound to hit something! Good luck!"

Bob Barkley, Jr., Bob McClure, and Ed Robran, three dedicated champions of educational innovation who have given us their guidance and support.

Joanne and Walt Kerfoot, educators who have solidly supported Human Dynamics since 1981 and whose energies are part of the living context of this work.

Georgi Gentry, who has helped through thick and thin and brings wonderful skills to our programs for parents.

Dr. Harry Kingston, who sees the implications of this work in the medical field and who opens doors.

Erlinda and Claude Teisinger, fine coaches in the arenas of education and business.

Rita and Bill Cleary, good friends, whose vision is aligned with ours.

Henry and Georgia Greenberg, for all their kindness and support over the years.

Blair Taylor, John Blasig, and Jean Rutherford, who saw the value of this work and were willing to put their efforts into creating our first CD-ROM.

Lisa and Richard Lang, fellow pioneers and travelers along the way.

Annie Muller, a real teacher and beautiful spirit, whose inspiration, love, and deep wisdom bless those who cross her path.

Martin Muller, whose pioneering spirit and remarkable gifts profoundly changed our lives.

Our staff, in particular, Helen, Georgi, Jennifer, and Eve, whose love of this work is reflected in the quality of their daily efforts.

Kellie Wardman O'Reilly, Bea Mah Holland, Daniel Kim, Colleen Lannon, Laurie Johnson, Linda Flynn, and all the others at Pegasus Communications—thank you so much!

A *special thanks* to **Kellie Wardman O'Reilly,** who has truly been midwife to this book—for her intelligence, warmth, and collaborative skills which have contributed so much to the life and clarity of this new work!

Judy Walker, whose flexibility and artistic capacities are evident in the design and layout of this book.

All of the **Human Dynamics facilitators,** who work with patience and dedication to bring the life and substance of this work wherever there are ears to hear and eyes to see.

Every participant in every Human Dynamics seminar. *Without you, there would be no book.*

Table of Contents

Introduction to Human Dynamics

The Five Personality Dynamics

Human Dynamics in Action

Illustrations

The Need to Understand One Another

by
Peter M.
Senge

Years ago, before diversity became an almost faddish concern for managers everywhere, a wise older gentleman, John Bemis, helped me see the deep connections between the coming "systems age" and the need to understand differences in people. "Understanding a system," John observed, "means understanding the people who make up that system. And those people are all different."

John's comment seems more and more prescient as our world becomes increasingly interconnected. Events in one place can literally echo around the world in a matter of hours or even minutes. Formerly secure enclaves of homogeneity can no longer live in isolation from one another. Gradually, we realize more and more that our lives are affected by many people who are different from us. The "systems age," as John pointed out, is really, in more personal terms, "the age of diversity."

So it should come as no surprise that, today, societies everywhere in the world are struggling with how to live harmoniously with difference. Few are succeeding. Corporations endeavoring to become more "global" are finding that what globalism means in personal terms is working across cultural boundaries. Private- and public-sector organizations alike are wrestling with increasingly diverse workforces; in many regions, groups previously labeled "minorities" in the United States now constitute majorities.

But the challenge of understanding diversity does not apply just to cultural, ethnic, or racial diversity. Within organizations, there are many diverse subcultures, such as the functional "silos" or "chimneys" that divide manufacturing, sales, marketing, and research. Often, little real understanding, empathy, and cooperation exist between such subcultures. The solution everywhere is to reorganize into "teams" that transcend these traditional boundaries. The goal is to get people working more closely together to serve customers and improve cross-functional processes. But a team is only really

Understanding a system means understanding the people who make up that system. And those people are all different.

a team, as opposed to a "team" merely in name, when people begin to understand one another and learn how to work productively together. In the old hierarchical model, the name of the game was "do your job and please the boss." Now it's about working and learning with people whose experience, education, gender, and professional affiliation all differ. So the age of teams is also the age of diversity.

The challenge is made more difficult by a history of ignoring or avoiding differences. Most businesses, especially in their management ranks, have long resembled private clubs where the members all elected others like themselves. Workers everywhere have been lumped together and dealt with as if their individual differences were unimportant. Our schools have typically offered a standardized product, implicitly assuming that all students learn alike.

But diversity could just as well represent an opportunity as a problem. Difference is the wellspring of innovation. People who see the world differently have fresh ideas and see new possibilities.

Starting 30 or so years ago, the U.S. government, whose own organizations had been equally blind to diversity, began to address the situation by issuing new mandates. The result has been a raft of "equal opportunity" regulations that work to no one's satisfaction. The flaws lie not in the details of the legislation but in the simple fact that efforts by centralized authorities—be they the federal government, corporate top management, or boards of education—are doomed to have low leverage when what is required is *personal* change. Central authorities cannot mandate shifts in people's thinking. When they attempt to do so, deep change is unlikely, and indeed problems can get worse.

But diversity could just as well represent an opportunity as a problem. Difference is the wellspring of innovation. People who see the world differently have fresh ideas and see new possibilities. The United States, drawing on its diverse religious, ethnic, and racial character, is one of the most innovative societies in the world, at least in regard to technology and business. Difference is what makes life challenging and surprising. Although predictability may afford comfort, it also stultifies creativity and imagination. Qualities we value deeply, like harmony and beauty, spring from diversity—a rainbow is far more beautiful than a single color, and a chorus moves us with the blend of its different voices.

Obviously, the problem is not difference or diversity itself. The real issues are personal: does difference frighten us, threaten us, or intrigue us?

Despite the discomfort we may feel, those differences that we embrace and appreciate make our lives richer. The challenge comes in trying to understand difference and to work with it productively.

Of Categories and People

The real problems start in our own minds—recognizing differences *requires* making distinctions. The problem is that most distinctions we invoke regarding people are based on inherited assumptions and unexamined stereotypes. Distinctions such as cultural, gender, or professional stereotypes then become the bases for automatic judgments and evaluations, which then reinforce the stereotypes.

Often, these stereotypes are invoked under stress, making the judgments all the more rigid and unexamined. In this way, beliefs have a way of becoming reality. There is an old Zen teaching story: "A man who lost his ax immediately suspected his neighbor's son. When he looked at the boy, the boy looked like a thief, talked like a thief, and walked like a thief. Then, one day, the man found his ax in his own field. He noticed that the boy no longer looked like a thief, talked like a thief, or walked like a thief."

The basic problems here are twofold: (1) most categories we invoke, especially under stress, are inherently evaluative, and (2) we tend to invoke and act on these categories automatically, with little awareness of how these assumptions are actually driving our perceptions and actions.

Understanding these problems, many theorists have advocated explicit, non-judgmental sets of distinctions for understanding differences. Some of these have become well known and widely used. Today there are literally dozens of such category systems being taught to educators, managers, and other professionals interested in dealing with difference more effectively. Using such approaches, we can come to appreciate the different ways that people learn, solve problems, and interact with others.

But although all of these can be useful, I have always been somewhat uneasy with the "categorization systems" I have been taught. Part of me always rebelled against the feeling of being "put into a box." I also worried about just embedding another set of categories to be invoked automatically. What about this approach, I wondered, will make us more aware of how we invoke categories in thinking about ourselves and each other? I also invariably found it difficult to learn and remember the new labels and meanings. So, I faced a dilemma. On the one hand, I had difficulty remembering the terms and meanings so that I could use them, but I also feared remembering them so well that I would use them unconsciously.

Human Dynamics

Given my apprehension about category systems, the first thing that surprised me when Sandra Seagal and David Horne introduced me to Human Dynamics some five years ago was that *I liked it*. It felt comfortable, although I had no idea why. Even before I understood it fully, it was compelling—it made deep sense. It seemed much more than just another category system.

As I listened and watched, I began to see how deeply Sandra and David appreciated each of the distinct "personality dynamics." Each person was almost like a fine wine to them—they savored each individual's ways of thinking, tone of voice, cadence of speech, use of language, quality of expression, and movement of eyes and hands. They seemed equally curious about and respectful of everyone.

One of the foundational strengths of Human Dynamics, I now realize, is that the differences among the personality dynamics are truly a source of richness to be celebrated and appreciated, without *any* implicit judgment.

At that moment, I understood one of my past difficulties with category systems. In learning most of the theories, I *did* form judgments. I did think it was better to be one kind of person rather than another. I was secretly proud of the way I was. My old habits of judgment and evaluation were subtly reinforced. But as I learned Human Dynamics, nothing like that happened. One of the foundational strengths of Human Dynamics, I now realize, is that the differences among the personality dynamics are truly a source of richness to be celebrated and appreciated, without *any* implicit judgment.

Over time, I have come to understand and value two more special features of Human Dynamics. First, once I understood the basic Human Dynamics distinctions and had reflected on their meaning for me, I never had to work to remember them. I don't think I could ever forget them now if I tried. Over the years, I have come to recognize this as a hallmark of deep insight. We are exposed to many ideas, theories, models, and improvement strategies, yet few of them stick because few make deep intuitive sense. But occasionally we are introduced to something that leads to a deep sense of recognition—a kind of rediscovery rather than learning something entirely new. It is important to live with this sort of rediscovery over time, to continue to apply and test it, to see whether it makes deeper and deeper sense. If such ideas stand the test of time, the result is an ongoing process of ever-expanding insight rather than a continual effort to remember what we were supposed to have learned. Human Dynamics has been like that for me. I can think of only a handful of ideas that I can say that about.

Second, the Human Dynamics approach is inherently developmental. Rather than sticking people in a box and saying, "This is how you are," it illuminates our distinctive patterns of growth and change. Each personality dynamic is seen as a whole system, evolving in particular ways. There is a kind of "metatheory" underlying Human Dynamics: that all human beings are questing for wholeness. But our developmental paths, our ways of integrating the "physical," "emotional," and "mental" dimensions, vary. Understanding the "developmental continuum" for each personality dynamic is very different from being "stuck in a box." It leads to seeing each of us as a *process* rather than a *thing*. As I have come to appreciate this, and as my working knowledge of Human Dynamics has deepened, I am gradually seeing more new and unexpected aspects of myself and others. I think I am becoming more curious, more open to surprise. Perhaps this is the key to a system that actually makes us *more* rather than less conscious in our dealings with each other.

The Coming Knowledge Era

In a mere 30 years, Singapore has become a leading economic power in southern Asia. Recently, I asked some visitors from Singapore to what they attributed their country's dramatic rise. The visitors responded simply, "You have to realize that we have nothing—only ourselves." With no natural resources and with modest endowments of physical and financial capital, the people of Singapore realized that the country's only real asset was its people. They thus invested accordingly in their education system and in a host of related social infrastructures aimed at safe, healthy living conditions and economic opportunity for all members of their society. This simple realization that people are our only real asset illustrates the core of what will probably determine which countries and which organizations will thrive in the 21st century.

This simple realization that people are our only real asset illustrates the core of what will probably determine which countries and which organizations will thrive in the 21st century.

Today, we hear much talk about "the knowledge-based economy" and about knowledge and learning as the key competitive advantage in business. What we often don't realize is that behind such statements is a simple mandate: we must understand people better and more deeply than ever before, and must therefore embed in our institutions a continual curiosity to understand ourselves and each other. During the industrial age, people were fundamentally one type of resource, "standing in reserve" to support an organization's needs. Businesses saw themselves as producing products from input resources—raw materials, energy, capital, and labor (more recently renamed "human resources"). At some basic level, all resources were indistinguishable, simply means to realize profit opportunities. The industrial age thus required only rudimentary understanding of human nature, because most workers served essentially as interchangeable parts.

In the future, understanding the diversity of human functioning will play a central role in the success and sustainability of both organizations and societies. This is why I expect Human Dynamics to exert a profound impact in the coming years.

But the knowledge era will require much more sophistication in understanding one another. Knowledge matters only when it is embodied in people. Knowledge is only generated by people. Moreover, knowledge sitting in books on a shelf has no direct impact on families, companies, or societies. It only matters when people *do* something with it. So, if knowledge and learning are indeed becoming a key source of competitive advantage, the industrial-age view of people will have to change. In the future, understanding the diversity of human functioning will play a central role in the success and sustainability of both organizations and societies. Nothing less will suffice if businesses are to thrive, if schools are to offer genuine opportunities for growth and learning for all children, and if societies throughout the world are to be peaceful and nurture a sense of community and belonging for all.

This is why I expect Human Dynamics to exert a profound impact in the coming years. It offers a simple, elegant, and powerful framework for understanding the diversity of human functioning and for realizing its potential—a framework that, from my own experience, promises to be effective across all cultures no matter how different they may be. Few tools will be more essential in the challenging years ahead.

What Is Human Dynamics?

Human Dynamics is a body of work based on investigations undertaken since 1979, involving more than 40,000 people representing over 25 cultures. It identifies and documents inherent distinctions in the functioning of people *as whole systems*. These distinctions in human functioning are more fundamental than age, race, culture, or gender. They can be identified even in infancy. Their existence can be scientifically validated.

Nine distinct human systems have been identified; five of which greatly predominate in Western cultures and are the focus of this book. Each system is composed of basic organizing principles—mental, emotional, and physical. These have both a quantitative (personal) and a qualitative (transpersonal) dimension.

Human Dynamics programs based on these new understandings are being applied in the fields of business, education, parenting, healthcare, and cross-cultural bridge building.

How Is Human Dynamics Different From Other Ways of Viewing People?

Human Dynamics is not a typology. Human Dynamics identifies fundamental structures (the hard-wiring) that underlie distinctions in the functioning of people as whole systems and describes the processes and functions of these systems. These distinct human systems are self-organizing and capable of infinite development.

People identify their system ("personality dynamic") through a process of self-discovery. There is no pencil-and-paper test. People are trained to identify the personality dynamics of others through heightened awareness and sensitive listening and observation.

How Has Human Dynamics Been Applied in Organizations?

- Team Functioning
- Teaching and Learning
- Valuing and Leveraging Diversity
- Change Management
- Building Conscious Community
- Personal/Leadership Development
- Health Maintenance
- Cross-Cultural Bridge Building

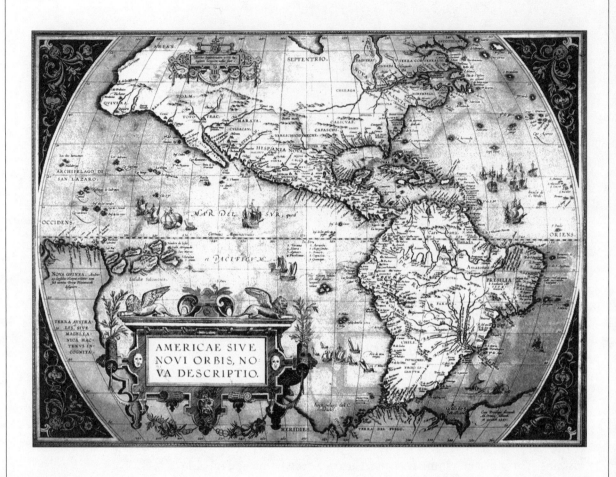

Mapping Your Learning

We ask the reader to begin this book by reading the Foreword and Chapter 1. Proceeding from there, however, are options. A central theme of Human Dynamics is that we all need to take into account the distinctly different ways in which people naturally function and learn. In accordance with this principle, therefore, we suggest some alternatives for beginning to read this book. Here are some examples:

- Some people want to understand rather quickly the relevance of the learning to their personal lives, and they also want to feel a sense of **personal connection** with their "instructor." If this is your preference, you might start with Chapter 2, *"Patterns and Promises,"* and then go on to Chapter 4, *"Five Brief Portraits."*

- Others are more stimulated by knowing early on what is **new** in the learning and what its implications are for the **future**. If this is your preference, you might like to start with Chapters 2 and 3, *"Patterns and Promises,"* and *"Basic Principles: A New Paradigm,"* and then jump to Chapter 13, *"Visions: Looking Ahead."*

- Others like to begin with a certain amount of **context**, and then gain an understanding of the **practical utility** of the learning. If you prefer to begin this way, you might try reading Chapter 2, *"Patterns and Promises,"* first, move on to Chapter 11, *"Organizational Applications,"* and then return to Chapter 3, *"Basic Principles: A New Paradigm."*

- Some people like to begin any new learning by gaining an **overview** of the subject and the basic **structure** of its presentation. If your learning begins this way, you will probably prefer the sequence given in the book: start with Chapter 2, *"Patterns and Promises,"* and continue with Chapter 3, *"Basic Principles: A New Paradigm."*

- Finally, some people prefer to begin by gaining an understanding of the basic nature and the **purpose** of the learning and then seeing its **practical applications**. If your learning begins this way, you might start with Chapter 3, *"Basic Principles: A New Paradigm,"* and continue with Chapter 11, *"Organizational Applications,"* before returning to Chapter 2.

There is general agreement that people learn differently. This has direct application for the "order" in which different people may prefer to begin reading this book.

Part I:
Introduction to
Human Dynamics

The first chapter in this book, "Effecting Change Within a Structured Organization," tells a story of Human Dynamics' contribution to breakthrough performance at Intel Corporation. This story was originally part of a keynote presentation given by David Marsing, vice president/general manager, Assembly Test Manufacturing, at a conference sponsored by the Massachusetts Institute of Technology's Sloan School of Management for the Center for Organizational Learning.

Chapter 2, "Patterns and Promises," introduces a foundational framework for the art and practice of personal, interpersonal, and transpersonal mastery, and discusses how an organization's ability to thrive will depend largely on its capacity to develop and leverage its primary asset—its people. The chapter continues by sharing the experience that catalyzed this work and its subsequent development. In this chapter, "Patterns" refers to the fundamental patterning that characterizes each of the five human systems that are the focus of this book. "Promises" refers to the opportunity offered by this new knowledge for greater realization of our individual and collective human potential.

Chapter 3, "Basic Principles: A New Paradigm," presents the basic principles and underlying structures that form the human systems we describe. We define three universal principles—mental, emotional, and physical—and describe their combination to form nine distinct systems of human functioning ("personality dynamics"). We also identify five predominant personality dynamics, which are the focus of this book.

Finally, Chapter 4, "Five Brief Portraits," provides thumbnail sketches of the five personality dynamics. These brief portraits are designed to give a sense of the essential distinctions among the personality dynamic groups, and make possible quick comparisons among them.

Effecting Change Within a Structured Organization

This book has a dual purpose. The first is to present the body of work that we term "Human Dynamics"—new findings about the systemic functioning of people and their potential for development, both individually and in their collective interactions. The second purpose is to show how understanding these differences in people is crucial for enhancing organizational functioning and success. For this, we draw on our experience introducing the Human Dynamics programs into organizations.

When we use the term *organizations*, we usually think of groups of people organized for work, and indeed most of the examples given here about the applications of Human Dynamics are drawn from our experiences and those of our trainers in the world of business. However, everything that we say about business applies equally to every other human interaction. The information given here applies as much to the "organization" of the individual, the couple, the family, the school, and the community as it does to corporations or any other kind of organization.

In light of the focus on organizational applications, it seems appropriate to begin by sharing a story told by David Marsing, who is vice president/general manager, Assembly Test Manufacturing, at Intel Corporation. In the pages that follow, he tells of gaining a powerful new insight into the centrality of the human wealth in the organizational community, and relates how he applied this new understanding to generate breakthrough performance at Intel's Fab 11 plant. In this Fab 11 story, he acknowledges Human Dynamics as "the most important cornerstone" in developing community consciousness and obtaining outstanding individual and team performance.

by
David
Marsing

I have been managing Fab 11, the Intel factory outside Albuquerque, New Mexico, for the last three years. We started the facility as a design project in 1992, and I was the first employee. Since then, Fab 11 has grown rather dramatically—by the end of 1996, the facility will employ two thousand people plus one thousand outside contractors. In addition, about another thousand Intel people support the facility directly with a variety of services. It is the world's largest semiconductor fab; and by December 1996, its finished product revenue rate will be greater than one million dollars per hour.

To generate that high revenue rate, we have had to do a lot of planning. We clearly had to hit results that the company expected, and to do this we have integrated a lot of new ideas, structures, systems, and processes in this facility. I was also after a second principle—to really build and create value—value in the workforce, value within each individual, value in terms of productivity and capability of the physical assets, and value in our relationships with the community.

In order to meet this objective of building value into the workforce, we introduced many trainings at Fab 11—good trainings. And they helped a lot. But Human Dynamics was very different. It is a body of work that goes way beyond the tools that we had used before. In fact, it has become the most important cornerstone in the development of the Fab 11 work environment.

To really appreciate this story, it is important to understand some of the context. The New Mexico culture is a fascinating one. The cultures represented in the largest numbers are—in chronological order of their arrival—the Native Americans, the Hispanic population that has been there since the 1590s, and the Caucasians who arrived only in the last 100 years or so.

Because about 45 percent of our employees are Hispanic, family is very important. You don't talk about work without talking about family, extended family, and the other people who are affected by any decision that you make. There is tremendous power in that kind of cultural norm and its integration into a business organization. I somehow missed that class in business school—but a number of my employees have helped me remain aware of these relationships.

In the period of time since we started this factory, 212 children were born to the families of those people who are part of the workforce, 93 marriages and 18 divorces have occurred, and 17 people have died. More important than the actual figures, however, is that there is a sense at Fab 11 that everybody cares about what is going on with everybody. We try to communicate that it is a community. And it includes more than the people who work there, because they are supported by a huge network of other people. So we constantly remind ourselves that this is a community within a community; and we respect and appreciate that.

Another interesting dimension of the culture we have created is the idea of assumed ownership. If you see a problem that nobody really owns, you're the one who sees it, so you own it. If it is a long-term issue, you quickly reorganize, reform teams, and put an appropriate structure in place. If it is a short-term issue, then everyone is expected to take care of it. We really try to create an environment where people live that kind of philosophy.

Personally, I've been with Intel at a variety of locations for the last 15 years. I started off in Oregon and was then in Livermore, Santa Clara, Phoenix, Albuquerque, and now, Malaysia. I've worked in seven factories in my career, in almost every function. And I did this intentionally—I really wanted to know how the whole thing operated. Most people don't really want to do this—they prefer to stay in engineering, or manufacturing, or whatever area they're comfortable with. But I spent a lot of time rotating through all the different functions. Not that I wanted to be an expert, but I wanted the ability to communicate with the people who were experts. I've managed four factories for Intel—and each one's been a little bit bigger, more challenging, and also more fun.

Some years ago, when I was managing another fab, Fab 9, I ended up being in critical physical health. I had been in this new factory for about a month. It was having serious problems—we were throwing away about half the material we were producing due to a variety of equipment reliability problems. This was right at the time that Intel was making all kinds of marketing announcements about shipping a new generation of microprocessor around the world. I was hellbent on turning it around as quickly as possible and getting it to the level at which I had run other factories. In trying to do that without people knowing about the kinds of systems we had used in other factories, I put so much pressure on myself that after a month I had a heart attack. I knew exactly what behavior triggered it and how I ended up lying on a gurney with the sensation that an elephant was trying to sit on my chest.

As it happened, I was fortunate. I didn't do any real damage to my heart. But afterward, the doctor came in and suggested that I needed to reflect on whether having this kind of career was really a smart thing. When I asked if he could be more specific, he said, "Yes. I wouldn't do the job that you are doing anymore." Well, I spent about two to three months recovering from this episode, and I spent a lot of time thinking about it. I considered doing forestry and sitting in a watchtower, or being a librarian in a library that isn't used very much. But on an intuitive level, I had the sense that I could continue my work *without* this kind of pressure and, in fact, *get even better results*. I didn't know how I was going to do it but I just knew at a gut level that it was possible, and that the approach I had been taking and the system I was in would have to be changed.

I began to focus on the balance between work and personal life and the integration of these two realities. I think one of the biggest things I realized coming back to work was that I had antennae I never had before. And these antennae were picking up signals from people all around me who were having a difficult time at work. They were doing their jobs, but they were in pain—emotionally, spiritually, and physically. People were just grinding themselves up—they were on the same treadmill I had been on. I had never been aware of that before, never realized to what degree the people around me were really suffering. That was a big eye-opener.

I asked myself what it would take to create an environment where people had a balanced approach to work and their personal lives, and where we could get breakthrough performance at the same time.

I asked myself what it would take to create an environment where people had a balanced approach to work and their personal lives, and where we could get breakthrough performance at the same time. And I mean breakthrough performance at the personal level, breakthrough performance at the group level, and breakthrough performance with traditional work indicators.

I figured achieving this was worth a try. So I began to work at creating an environment where the emphasis was on the people themselves. For example, we began a process of understanding who was really on the team. We had limited mental models—"That's an engineering manager, she's our finance manager, he's a training manager." But we didn't know who was *really* there. We would work with each other but we didn't know the composition of the teams in terms of their different attributes, strengths, and weaknesses.

We brought in some consultants who helped us see the different types of people and the composition of our team. And that was pretty fascinating, because one of the things that we learned right away was that we were an unusually diverse group of people. So we began to understand why we were having communication problems. I would say "green" and someone would hear "yellow." This was the first clue that I had about distinctions in people.

Today, we have seven trained Human Dynamics facilitators who provide classes every other week. The Human Dynamics material has been phenomenal. It has created an awareness and a knowledge at the individual and group levels that is remarkable. Through this training, individuals learn about their unique capacities and strengths, which is very important if they want to understand their contribution to a team. You learn how different people process information, communicate, learn, and solve problems. And it's not that one way is better or worse; it's just different. And you appreciate how people have some very distinct attributes that can be leveraged in an extremely creative way when they are put together. Everything you learn applies to more effective team functioning.

The Human Dynamics material has been phenomenal. It has created an awareness and a knowledge at the individual and group levels that is remarkable. You learn how different people process information, communicate, learn, and solve problems. And it's not that one way is better or worse; it's just different.

For example, there's a four-day Human Dynamics program that includes an exercise in which teams of diverse "personality dynamics" focus on a real company issue. After a number of sessions, we started videotaping each group's project summaries, because the degree of creativity and fun they had, the depth they went into, and the utility of their results were incredible. Even though people got frustrated in each of these teams at some point, they also had an opportunity to experience what a diverse team can do given the proper training. And as they practiced more and more, they began to really make use of the strengths that the different people have.

Human Dynamics is also a developmental system. This is where the other tools we worked with had not provided much help. What are our capacities and how do we develop? Human Dynamics offers key tools and practices toward this end. One of them is to intentionally create teams of diversely functioning people. We have found that when we do that, we get the most creative results, and we get a better product.

We have also offered the seminars to spouses to help the quality of family relationships, and we have used Human Dynamics in relation to the local community in other ways. For example, we maintain a continual dialogue with the community about environmental issues. On one occasion, when we were having difficulties agreeing and passions were rising, we pulled together part of my staff and people from the community and collectively went through a Human Dynamics seminar. It was one of the most intense experiences I have ever had. We worked with communication preferences and teamwork issues and slowly came to realize that we were all shooting for the same thing. We just had very different perspectives and different ways of going about it. That seminar did more to level the playing field in understanding each other than anything we had tried with this group. It laid the groundwork for future conversations and inquiry.

What is the biggest thing I have learned from my experiment? Once you are at a certain level of technical capability, you continue to drill those skills; but then the emphasis ought to be about 90 percent on ways of developing individuals, teams, and groups as a whole. If you do this, the outcomes you get are fundamentally a by-product of the group working well together. Actually, once the skills, capabilities, and knowledge of what people had to do in their jobs were there, we got better results *not* focusing on the task but focusing on how people work together.

Once you are at a certain level of technical capability, once the skills, capabilities, and knowledge of what people had to do in their jobs were there, we got better results *not* focusing on the task but focusing on how people work together.

At Intel, we have used the Total Preventive Maintenance (TPM) model, which looks at the theoretical capabilities of tools or systems and how to increase their performance in actuality. So we wondered, what if you ask yourselves the same kinds of questions about the human dimension? What is the potential of a human being and the potential of relationships among humans? What values can be leveraged in terms of human well-being and accomplishment?

It seems to me that the limits to the potential are simply our mental models of what is possible. It was actually a result of our using the

Human Dynamics work as a vehicle that we created a platform for interesting dialogue around human potential. We began talking about how we need to start relooking at the way we are dealing with each other, the constraints that we have put on ourselves, and our whole construct of what people are capable of doing—what their potential really is. Human Dynamics has thus had the most profound impact on team performance that we have ever had in our environment.

My background in martial arts has also provided the basis for some of my thinking. My particular training was so orthodox that there were only two belts—a white belt and a black belt. The basis for this system was the belief that you had to perform each move 10,000 times to be able to do them accurately and without thinking. And then you begin to do combinations of moves 10,000 times. If you have the diligence to stick with it and work through some of the physical ailments that occur from not doing these moves correctly, or from being frequently used by your instructor as an example of what not to do, you begin to develop a basis of consistent performance. It becomes automatic and hard-wired— you have physically and biologically altered your nervous system and your brain. We have used this principle a lot in our personal leadership trainings. We may not be hitting the 10,000 mark, but we are certainly emphasizing practice.

One of the bottom-line results of our work and our philosophy has been capital avoidance of over one billion dollars for the company. Our performance eliminated the need for an additional factory. Also, we are operating at about 70 percent of the cost that we originally targeted. Through the work that the teams have done using these tools, right now they are operating as the best running factory in the Intel system any way you measure it, including all indicators. This is a brand new group of people, who had never worked together, with only one person who had previously functioned at the current level of responsibility. I would pit them against anybody in the industry right now! That's the result that we got from using these tools.

> **Human Dynamics has had the most profound impact on team performance that we have ever had in our environment. One of the bottom-line results of our work and our philosophy is capital avoidance of over one billion dollars for the company. Also, we are operating at about 70 percent of the cost that we originally targeted.**

Patterns and Promises

The urge to pursue excellence and mastery is a fundamental impulse in the human psyche. We see this drive expressed in a multitude of forms—in scientific achievement, technological development, athletics, and the arts. Yet pursuit of mastery of *ourselves* as consciously evolving people has generally been neglected. We have placed spaceships on the moon, created the information superhighway, and produced countless supports for our physical comfort—yet in our collective endeavors and basic interactions with one another, we so often seem to fail. Perhaps the problem is that although we have understood that resolving complex issues requires collaboration, we have neither recognized the need for conscious training in interdependent living nor had a framework for understanding our individual and collective human functioning.

> **We have placed spaceships on the moon, created the information superhighway, and produced countless supports for our physical comfort—yet in our collective endeavors and basic interactions with one another, we so often seem to fail.**

The body of work that we term Human Dynamics provides such a framework. It offers a dramatic expansion in our understanding of ourselves both as individuals and in our interactions with one another. It also offers a rigorous training in the art and practice of personal, interpersonal, and transpersonal mastery.

The findings of Human Dynamics reflect a profound interconnectedness and underlying order in the way people across the globe are individually and collectively "designed." We identify fundamental principles common to all humanity, which form distinct patterns in the way human beings are intrinsically "organized." These distinct patterns of functioning, which we term "personality dynamics," transcend race and culture, characterize males and females equally, and are observable at all age levels—including infancy.

Each personality dynamic constitutes a distinct system of mental, emotional, and physical interplay, and is characterized by the unique ways in which its members process information, communicate, relate to others, learn, problem-solve, maintain health, and become stressed. Each personality dynamic is also characterized by its distinct path of potentially infinite development. All of these diverse "ways of being" are of equal value—anyone of any personality dynamic may be more or less intelligent, compassionate, capable, or gifted. But they differ markedly in *how* they function.

These very different ways of functioning are in dynamic interaction wherever people come together. They exist in every boardroom, in every department, in every office, and on every factory floor. They are represented on every management or project team and are present in every classroom and healthcare facility. They exist in families and among the participants in international negotiations. They are at play everywhere that people interact.

Lack of awareness of these systemic differences in people has led to much misunderstanding, conflict, and failure—failure in relationships, failure in teaching and learning, and failure in teamwork and collaboration. For example, Peter Senge has asked, "How can a team of committed managers with individual IQs above 120 have a collective IQ of 63?"[1] One answer is certainly that team members typically do not understand and appreciate their differences. When we are conscious of these differences—when we recognize, respect, and *understand* them—we can make better connections with one another, work together more effectively, learn and teach successfully, leverage our own and each other's diverse gifts and affinities, and consciously foster our individual and collective development. A business trainer or teacher understanding the differences can tailor his or her teaching to meet the learning and developmental needs of every student. *Aware* families can appreciate the complementary value of their differences and use their knowledge to enjoy greater harmony and strengthen their relationships. And a committed and *conscious* team of managers can function synergistically with a collective IQ far beyond 120!

The distinct patterns in the functioning of people that we will be sharing—their inherent capacities, needs, languages, function on teams, path of development, path to wellness, etc.—can be taught explicitly, even to children. This is the more quantitative aspect of the Human Dynamics work,

---

[1] *The Fifth Discipline: The Art & Practice of the Learning Organization* (Doubleday, 1990).

in itself a lot for people to internalize and to apply.

But there is a more qualitative dimension. We continually receive feedback that exposure to Human Dynamics is generative—it initiates not only a process of continual learning about people, but also the development of finer sensibilities and more empathic values. Implicit within the work are the directives: listen—observe—respect—appreciate—be open—inquire—know yourself—understand others—let go of judgment—be authentic—collaborate—care—forgive.

This is the underlying direction and purpose of this work: *to enhance the quality of life that people individually and collectively express.*

If we think of the distinct human systems that we identify as the instruments of an orchestra, we could say that Human Dynamics trains us to recognize the capacities inherent in our different instruments and to develop our skills in playing them, so that we can make extraordinary music together. This is more than an organizational need; it is a human need.

The Beginnings of Human Dynamics

People have asked us where this work has come from. Our answer is by way of a simple story. It goes like this:

Before there was botany or botanists, there was nature. One day, a person who was to become a botanist looked carefully at the moss and discovered that while all the moss looked alike *at first*, there actually were many varieties. And slowly, the field of botany and botanists emerged.

But the botanists never *created* nature. And it is within this context that the work called Human Dynamics was developed. Just as botanists never created nature, we never created these human systems. They have existed for a long time. We have merely had the privilege of becoming aware of them, investigating them, and sharing our findings with others.

The Human Dynamics body of work presented in this book is not derived from a theoretical construct. We did not sit down one day and say, "Let's produce a theory for how human beings function." Rather, this work is the result of a long journey of discovery involving years of direct experience, intuitive leaps, and systematic investigation.

However, as with many such journeys, this one did have a precise starting point, an unusual event that happened to one of the authors, Sandra

listen

observe

respect

appreciate

be open

inquire

know yourself

understand others

let go of judgment

be authentic

collaborate

care

forgive

Seagal, in 1979. The event was quite simple, but because Sandra paid attention to it, she found herself embarked upon an extraordinary adventure, a voyage filled with new and rich discoveries about the mental, emotional, physical, and spiritual processes of people, and with inspiring experiments in shaping this new knowledge to our common good.

Sandra's Story

In 1979, when I was working as a psychotherapist in private practice, one of my clients asked me one day to see her daughter, Caroline, who was having difficulty in school. Caroline was nine years old, articulate, and very self-aware for her age. As we began to talk, it became clear that she was not so much interested in engaging in a dialogue as in having me listen to her.

As she talked about her experiences in school, and I listened, something unusual happened. For a period which was probably brief yet seemed timeless, I was no longer aware of Caroline's words. Instead, I heard only her voice, within which I clearly detected three different sounds. While one sound was clear, the other two seemed discordant.

As I became aware of the three sounds, certain understandings became evident to me that I hadn't known before. They were as follows:

- Science had linked frequencies in sound and light to the human body.
- The highest of these frequencies or vibrations, in both sound and light, are associated with the head, the lowest with the limbs.
- A new way of assessing and developing balance and harmony in people was going to be developed.
- This new assessment would be based on an understanding of the three sounds I was hearing in the child's voice.
- It was possible to "diagnose" or evaluate the functioning of people through a sensitive listening process.
- Two of the three sounds were related to a personal identity, and one was connected to a deeper, more transpersonal, spiritual identity.

I then returned to hearing Caroline speaking as I normally would.

When the session ended, I sat quietly for a long time to ponder my experience. I knew that the experience was real and not a dream or fantasy, and that it had enormous significance. I had no idea what the three sounds represented, but I did know that I had to find out.

For the following six weeks, I felt extraordinarily energized. I was fully awake for twenty-two hours a day. My attention was riveted on the sounds of people's voices, which I continued to hear in a new way. It was as if I had been catapulted into an ultra-sensitive attunement to these sounds. Although I was aware of language, I found myself also registering the voices as pure sound—like music—and the different qualities in the music captivated me.

In addition to having a heightened sensitivity to sound, I found that I could do much more work after my experience with Caroline than I could before. On the surface, my life went on as usual, but I realized that in fact I was functioning at an entirely new level of capability. It was as if the outcome of the original experience and the responsibility associated with it would require the efforts of a more developed person.

Within this six-week period, I came to realize that this new exploration could not be done alone. So I gathered a group of friends—psychologists, artists, and educators—told them about my experience, and asked whether they were willing to involve themselves in doctoral programs to investigate the three sounds. Their responses amazed me—eight of them agreed. They seemed delighted at the prospect of new discovery, and so we began an exploration together that would last approximately two years.

During the first six months, we listened to many adults and children and tried to further discriminate the three sounds and understand their meaning. We, ourselves, were like children entering a new environment, wide-eyed, open-minded, looking, listening, sensing, and speculating, but with no authorities to provide guidance.

Gradually, it became clear to me that the three sounds were high, middle, and low frequencies, which I could distinguish even though they were operating simultaneously. And then, through a long process of trial and error, I made the connection that the frequencies were related to the speaker's mental, emotional, and physical functioning. Consistently, the high frequency expressed the mental function; the middle frequency the emotional function; and the lowest frequency, the physical function. This was the first major breakthrough.

As we listened to all kinds of people—babies babbling; individuals speaking foreign languages; men, women, and children of all ages and ethnic backgrounds conversing—I became increasingly aware that the three sounds formed distinct patterns in their voices. Moreover, these patterns paralleled distinct patterns in their behavior and processes. Different patterns in the way high, middle, and low frequencies interacted in people's voices reflected the different patterns in the way their mental, emotional, and physical elements interacted. Recognizing these distinct patterns in sound and functioning was the second major breakthrough.

In time, I grew increasingly sensitive to a wide range of nuances in voices. I tracked rhythm, modulation, articulation, psycho-acoustic placement of the voice, volume, tempo, melodic contour, texture, quality—and recognized that all of these, and more, provided extraordinarily accurate information about the speaker. Clearly, I thought, I had to teach others how to use this remarkable tool for more empathic and discriminating listening. So in 1981, I created weekly classes, which drew hundreds of people. We undertook many different listening experiments. As one example, we interviewed identical twins, young women from South America. The two women looked almost exactly alike and sounded almost exactly the same, and yet I could distinguish subtle differences in their voices. I remember saying to them, "Isn't it true that while the two of you are alike in many ways, you (pointing to one of them) are a little more *this* way in how you think and behave, while you (pointing to the other) are a little more *that* way?" They laughed in astonishment and asked, "How could you possibly know that?" I knew because I was now able to associate the nuances in their voices with specific nuances in their mental, emotional, and physical functioning. We were beginning to identify not only basic themes in human functioning, but also individual variations on these themes.

Buckminster Fuller

Our work began to receive support from some members of the scientific community. For example, the late Buckminster Fuller was greatly intrigued by our findings and encouraged us to continue our research. He was particularly interested in our experience that the distinguishing patterns could be recognized in the babbles of babies. He had long believed that all babies everywhere initially produce similar sounds, and he saw in that a harmony that he believed was humanity's birthright and part of the natural order of the universe. In fact, he asked me on two public platforms to promise him that I would continue my exploration.

We also began some research prompted by the following letter from the chairperson of the Communications Arts and Sciences department at the University of Southern California.

April 30, 1981

DEAR MS. SEAGAL:

I have recently read the article by Dr. H.S. Hayre entitled, "Pattern Recognition Applied to Speech Spectrum for Personality Parameter Detection," in which he indicated his results are highly correlated with the Seagal parameters which are derived from clinical interviews. I am very anxious to know more about your work and the results you find in your own research.

The voice is a very complex biological phenomenon which impacts every aspect of our social and psychological behavior. As a professor and researcher in the field of communication arts and sciences, I am intrigued with the unlimited possibilities that could be forthcoming as your work is validated by acoustical scientific investigation. In addition to serving as chairperson of this department at the University of Southern California, I am also director of the Speech Communications Research Laboratory in Los Angeles. I would greatly welcome the opportunity to work with you on correlating your results with our acoustic findings. Our laboratory is equipped with both analog and digital equipment for the analysis and synthesis of speech. We do basic research in the speech sciences and are particularly interested in man-machine interaction by voice. Your work could have a tremendous impact on business, education, and social interactions.

I look forward to hearing from you, if you are interested in collaborative efforts.

Sincerely yours,

JUNE E. SHOUP, PH.D.
CHAIRPERSON, COMMUNICATION ARTS AND SCIENCES
UNIVERSITY OF SOUTHERN CALIFORNIA

This letter led to my collaborating in research for approximately a year with Dr. Shoup and Dr. Herb Hayre from the University of Texas. Together, we audiotaped people representing the distinct groups I was identifying, and to our delight we began to see distinctions in the voice patterns on voice spectrographs. However, I became concerned about the consequences of achieving a breakthrough in identifying these distinctions in voice patterns, and publishing the research, before I fully understood the significance of the discovery and its practical applications. So I chose to discontinue this line of investigation until I was clearer about its implications. Now that we know so much more about the meaning and value of what we are uncovering, we would like to resume research to show that the personality dynamic of any individual is encoded in the voice.

Despite postponing this particular line of research, the interest of the academic world, combined with the enthusiasm of the people attending the classes, further encouraged our investigations. Although it continued to be clear that every individual is different, distinct patterns of functioning became consistently evident. We identified three major themes, which we eventually termed "mentally centered," "emotionally centered," and "physically centered." (Later, we distinguished three variations on each of these themes, making the nine personality dynamics, as described in Chapter 3, "Basic Principles: A New Paradigm.") The people who attended the classes were clearly riveted by the emergence of these new understandings and none was more astounded than myself. The sessions were alive with new discoveries that had immediate application to our understanding of ourselves, our families, and other people in general.

I conducted the classes for about a year, but while we discovered more about the distinct patterns of behavior, I was unable to teach others the fine discriminations in sound that I could hear. At some point in the year, one of our colleagues suggested that we videotape people from each personality dynamic group that we were distinguishing. So we invited people whose personality dynamics I had identified through their voices to potluck dinner parties on successive evenings, and we videotaped their spontaneous behavior and conversation.

As I watched the resulting ten hours of unedited tape, tears came to my eyes. I realized for the first time that the personality distinctions I was apprehending aurally could be identified through other more generally accessible cues—people's appearance and behavior, gestures and movements (or lack of them), ways of communicating and interacting with one another, and the topics they spoke about. I now knew we could use this medium as a tool for teaching people how to identify the personality dynamic groups. Sound discrimination turned out not to be the point. My sensitivity to the sounds of the voice was simply the key that led to the discoveries about the human "design" that are at the heart of this work.

We have come to realize that the distinct personality dynamic systems we have identified are holonomic, and can be discriminated in many ways. They are evident in the focus of a person's eyes, in gestures, in the rhythm and pacing of spoken language, in the preference for certain words, in the kind of memory a person has, in the responses to stress, the way he or she learns, even in the area of the body where the main focus of energy is naturally situated. We can now teach recognition of the different personality dynamics through many cues. We have hundreds of videotapes of infants, children, and adults from many cultures, which we use to demonstrate these distinctions. Certainly no extraordinary sensitivity to sound is now required to identify someone's personality dynamic or comprehend the Human Dynamics body of work.

Since the original group of investigators formed, we have conducted countless interviews and seminars, through which we have continually added to our understanding of these human systems.[2] At the same time, we have constantly sought ways to apply the knowledge practically by creating programs for personal and organizational development, teacher and parent training, health maintenance, and cross-cultural bridging.

It has been an inspiring journey! In recognizing these fundamental patterns in the human design, we share the awe felt by astronomers and physicists as they perceive in action the laws governing the structure and

---

[2] For more information about our research and database, please see Appendix A, p. 313.

dynamics of the universe, of naturalists as they observe the complex designs and systems of nature, and of anatomists and neurologists as they explore the workings of our bodies and the universes of our brains.

We share the awe felt by astronomers and physicists as they perceive in action the laws governing the structure and dynamics of the universe, of naturalists as they observe the complex designs and systems of nature, and of anatomists and neurologists as they explore the workings of our bodies and the universes of our brains.

The structures and qualities that we are describing are so fundamental that people have reported to us, over and over again, that once the light of these understandings was shared, they had the sense of recognizing something consciously that they already deeply *knew*. What at first seemed new to them was quickly experienced as having been *awakened*. We believe that this phenomenon reveals that while the distinctions in functioning that we have identified and to which we have given language are new to our collective consciousness, the *life behind* the work lies deep within the human soul.

Thus, this work lifts the human spirit. It reveals us to ourselves and shows us that we are more than we thought we were; it nurtures our finer sensibilities and illumines our paths of development; it encourages learning and inquiry; and it recognizes that diversity is the intended purpose of nature—to be respected, celebrated, and utilized.

It always comes back to this:
we cannot take the life of our times
further than we have taken ourselves.

—Laurens van der Post

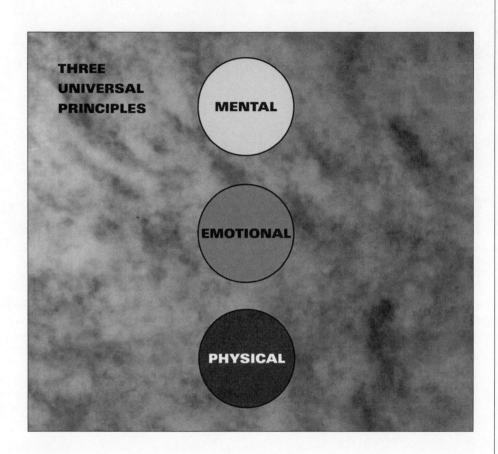

Basic Principles: A New Paradigm

As Chapter 2 indicated, our early investigations led to the understanding that the three frequencies detected in the voice relate to three primary aspects of human functioning—mental, emotional, and physical. All people have mental, emotional, and physical capacities; these are basic threads in the human system so fundamental and universal that we have termed them *principles*. However well or poorly expressed, we see the mental, emotional, and physical principles active in everyone.

Further, we have found that these three principles combine in highly specific ways in people to form distinct patterns of functioning, distinct "ways of being" that we have termed "personality dynamics." We have identified nine personality dynamics in all, but of these nine, four occur so rarely that the other five seem to make up over 99.9% of the population. Therefore, it is these five personality dynamics that will be the detailed focus of this book.

All people have mental, emotional, and physical capacities; these are basic threads in the human system so fundamental and universal that we have termed them *principles*.

It is important to re-emphasize the point made by Peter Senge in the foreword that identifying the different personality dynamics is not to "put people in boxes." In fact, participants in Human Dynamics seminars have consistently and gratefully reported that they feel released from the constrictions of people's interpretations of them. Instead, they feel "seen," understood, and appreciated, often for the first time, in the fullness of who they really are and how they really function. Old negative labels such as "slow," "aloof," "uncaring," "pushy," "oversensitive," "insensitive," and so on are dropped in favor of truer and more empathic understanding.

Moreover, each "way of being" is recognized as a dynamic system *with an infinite capacity for development*. Human Dynamics points out how human life seems to be organized, not for the sake of categorization, but to illuminate our different ways of functioning so we may make more efficient and enlightened use of ourselves. To draw an analogy, it is extremely useful to make the distinction between roses and daffodils. Both are flowers; both are beautiful in their respective ways. But by recognizing the differences, we are able to understand each plant's specific needs with respect to sunlight, soil, and water, and can consequently better foster their growth.

Through recognizing and understanding distinctions in the fundamental makeup of people, we are better able to appreciate people's specific ways of experiencing their environment; processing information; communicating; learning; problem-solving; relating to themselves and others; maintaining wellness; and developing, both personally and transpersonally. We can therefore work consciously to meet the needs of each personality dynamic group, helping them to grow and learn, communicate and cooperate, make use of their particular gifts, and avoid the misunderstandings that arise through not recognizing that the groups do indeed experience life very differently.

The Three Principles

Let us begin our exploration of the five personality dynamics by first describing the three principles that are common to all of them, and defining what we mean by "mental," "emotional," and "physical."

The Mental Principle

Emphases: concepts, structures, ideas

Process: linear, logical, sequential

Functions:
- thinking
- envisioning
- planning
- focusing
- directing
- creating structure
- seeing the overview
- establishing values, principles
- maintaining objectivity
- conceptualizing
- analyzing

Figure 3.1

The mental principle is associated with the activities of the mind. It is expressed in a person's capacities for logical thinking, objectivity, seeing the overview, strategic planning, establishing values and principles, maintaining focus, and setting structure. It provides the first step in any meaningful endeavor.

People with a well-developed mental principle direct their actions with detachment, perspective, clear vision, and well-defined values and principles, while focusing on the long term. People in whom the mental principle is relatively undeveloped act on the basis of thinking that is less clear, more irrational and unfocused, blind to principles of operation, and resting on a value system that may be narrow or confused.

The Emotional Principle

Emphases: relationships, organization

Process: lateral (by emotional association rather than logical connection)

Function:
- feeling
- connecting
- communicating
- relating
- personalizing
- empathizing
- organizing
- harmonizing
- processing
- imagining

Figure 3.2

The emotional principle is the principle of relationship and connection. It is that part of us that knows and values the world of feelings in ourselves and others. It is also the part that needs and offers communication and that knows how to collaborate and organize. The creative imagination, which accesses the inner life and connects things in new ways, is also an expression of the emotional principle.

As with the mental principle, the emotional principle can be expressed more or less maturely. Someone in whom the emotional principle is well developed is aware of his or her own feelings without being dominated by them, expresses those feelings appropriately, is communicative and empathic, and forms positive relationships with others. He or she is also self-aware, well organized, flexible, creative, and able to find the middle ground between enjoying the diversity of life and maintaining focus. People in whom the emotional principle is expressed less maturely tend to be either less aware of their feelings and lacking in personal expressiveness, or dominated by their feelings and characterized by behavior that is emotionally reactive rather than appropriately responsive. They may also exhibit judgmental attitudes, poor relationships, disorganization, and lack of specific focus.

The Physical Principle

Emphases: actions, operations

Process: systemic (by a comprehensive process of gathering, linking, and seeing the interconnections among relevant data)

Function:

- doing
- making
- producing
- concretizing
- detailing
- making operational

- utilizing
- ensuring practicality
- cooperating
- synthesizing
- systematizing

Figure 3.3

Whereas the mental principle is associated with the mind and thinking, and the emotional principle is associated with feelings and relating, the physical principle is associated with the body and the translation into action of what is thought and felt. This principle is the pragmatic part of people, expressed in making, doing, and actualizing. If a house is *designed* on the mental level, and its construction is *organized* on the emotional level, it is systematically *built* on the physical level.

People in whom the physical principle is well expressed have a strong affinity for group life and cooperative effort. They are reliable and produc-tive and either complete tasks competently or see that those tasks are well performed. In any project, they ensure that ideas are carried into effective action by creating systems for realizing the original objectives. They are also acutely attuned to their instincts and the sensory world, but are not dominated by them. Because they have an innate sense of the systemic nature of things, and experience that everything (including themselves) is at once whole and part of a larger whole, they commonly feel responsibility for the well-being of any system in which they are involved.

Those in whom the physical principle is less developed may appear "ungrounded." They perform tasks poorly, lack practicality and attention to detail, and may have difficulty bringing ideas to fruition. They may also have a tendency to be either dominated by the senses or disconnected from their physical selves, lacking sensory feedback and unaware of their own natural rhythms, processes, and instincts. They lack full appreciation of the systemic interconnectedness of things and events in both the natural and human worlds, and their approach to endeavors is not systematic.

Each of these three principles and their attributes are active in all people, but to varying degrees and in varying combinations. The major attributes of these three dimensions of the personality can be summarized in the following way:

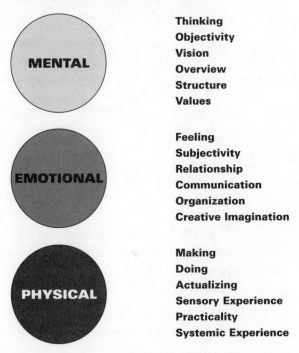

THE THREE UNIVERSAL PRINCIPLES

MENTAL

Thinking
Objectivity
Vision
Overview
Structure
Values

EMOTIONAL

Feeling
Subjectivity
Relationship
Communication
Organization
Creative Imagination

PHYSICAL

Making
Doing
Actualizing
Sensory Experience
Practicality
Systemic Experience

Figure 3.4

In general, when the mental, emotional, and physical principles are developed and integrated, individuals function well, with the ability to think clearly, relate empathically, and express their thinking and feeling in practical actions.

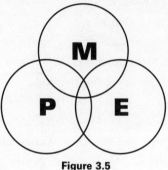

Figure 3.5

However, when one or more of the principles is undeveloped or unintegrated, the result is a functional imbalance, a lack of wholeness, and relative ineffectiveness in certain areas of the person's life.

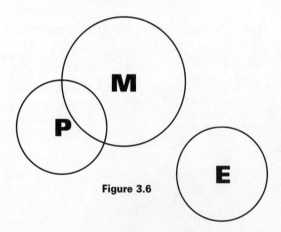

Figure 3.6

This imbalance is by no means uncommon. We are all likely to "favor" one or two of the principles at the expense of the other(s). And for all of us, personal and transpersonal growth usually requires conscious work in developing and integrating the "third" principle, as explained in Chapter 12, "The Developmental Continuum." In some cases, however, the disharmony can be extreme enough to render the person dysfunctional or even emotionally or physically ill. For example, someone might be quite brilliant, but if the mental principle is not sufficiently *integrated*, may be so unable to detach from the emotional stresses of the environment and other people's pain and needs that he or she may become dysfunctional, possibly sick.

It is encouraging to know, however, that because all three principles are in dynamic life in all of us, we can work consciously to further their development and integration and promote our own health, well-being, and effectiveness.

Are We Operating on All Cylinders?

Not only are the mental, emotional, and physical principles equal in value and all necessary for the well-being of individuals, but they need to be equally active and integrated in organizations, teams, families, and communities.

It is helpful to ask, for example, "Does an organization have the attributes of the mental principle—a clear vision, solid principles, capacity to plan, and so on? Does it include the attributes of the emotional principle—good communication and organization, caring for people, support for creativity and individual self-expression? And is it expressing the physical principle well—are its systems of operation in order, is it pragmatic, does it carry out its mandates effectively, and does it understand itself as a part of larger systems (for example, the community)?" The answers to these questions may indicate areas that need attention.

It is an equally salutary exercise to assess the functioning of a team or even the success of a single meeting in terms of these principles. We can ask of a meeting, for example, "Is each of the three principles being well-represented and actively taken into account?" Addressing this question helps ensure that both the process and the outcomes are as complete and qualitative as possible.

Mental, Emotional, and Physical Centering

We have found that while all of us have mental, emotional, and physical dimensions, we seem to be "organized" in such a way that one of these three principles predominates as central in our functioning. Some people are "centered" mentally (rationally), some emotionally (relationally), and some physically (practically).

We might try to illustrate how people are centered in the following way:

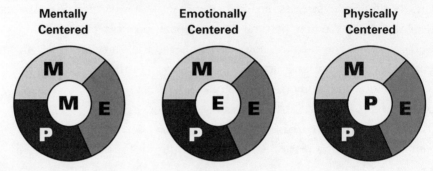

Mentally Centered   **Emotionally Centered**   **Physically Centered**

Figure 3.7

Of course, each of these systems is much more dynamic than the illustration is able to show, each being comprised of an interplay of mental, emotional, and physical energies, with a central processing element that is different in each case. The significance of the centering, and its relationship to the other aspects of the personality, will become clear as we explore the different personality dynamics (which constitute variations on these three major themes). At this point, let us just say that the principle at our core (our "center") determines *how* we typically process information. Generally, mentally centered people process information in a rational and linear way. Emotionally centered people process information in a lateral way—that is, more through unpredictable association (in which feelings play a part) than through a process of logical connection. Finally, physically centered people process information in a systemic way—they tend naturally to think in terms of the interconnections that make up whole systems of functioning, whether that whole system is on a large scale (like the interconnection of elements in our weather systems), or a relatively small scale (such as the systems involved in operating a restaurant, or the electrical and plumbing systems in a house).

Mentally centered, emotionally centered, and physically centered are strikingly different ways of being and functioning. However, it is most important to emphasize here that although these broad groups function very differently, they are *equal in value*. It is not "better" to be centered in one way than another. As we shall explore, representatives of each of these different "ways of being" tend to have characteristic qualities, gifts, and affinities for certain functions. But anyone in any of the groups will be more or less intelligent, more or less caring, and more or less effective in contributing to life, depending upon the degree of his or her development. In fact, not only are the different groups equal in value, but each can be said to "need" the complementary attributes of the others. The gifts of each complement those of the others, forming a more complete whole.

Nine Personality Dynamics

We have identified nine "personality dynamics," nine basic patterns of functioning, each a variation on one of the ways of being centered. As Figure 3.8 illustrates, there are three ways of being centered mentally, three

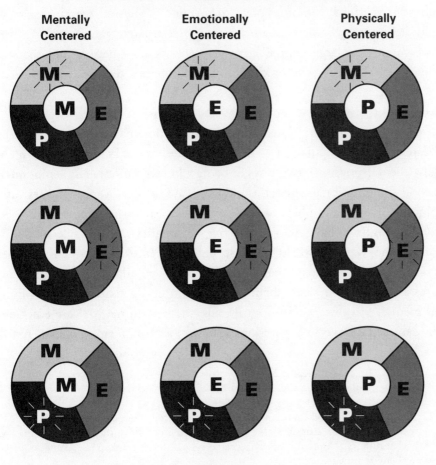

THE NINE PERSONALITY DYNAMICS

Figure 3.8

ways of being centered emotionally, and three ways of being centered physically, making nine personality dynamics in all.

Each personality dynamic system is distinguished from the others by its particular pattern of interaction between the central principle and the other dimensions of the personality. In Figure 3.8, one of the letters designating the mental, emotional, or physical aspects of each personality dynamic has radiating lines around it. These lines indicate that there is an especially significant connection between this aspect of the personality and the central principle. Because of this association, we term the first personality dynamic in the mentally centered column "mental-mental," the second "mental-emotional," and the third "mental-physical." Similarly, in the second column we have "emotional-mental," "emotional-emotional," "emotional-physical"; and in the third column "physical-mental," "physical-emotional," and "physical-physical." As we shall explore in detail later, the central principle determines to a large degree *how* one processes information, and the secondary principle drives *what* kind of information one tends to process.

Five Predominant Personality Dynamics

Of the nine personality dynamics, five constitute the vast majority of the Western world's population.[1] These five—one way of being centered mentally (mental-physical), two ways of being centered emotionally (emotional-mental and emotional-physical), and two ways of being centered physically (physical-mental and physical-emotional)—are the focus of this book.

Although we have found these five personality dynamics to predominate in the Western world, they do not seem to exist in equal numbers (Figure 3.9). We estimate that 5% or less of the population in Western cultures are mental-physical, about 15% are physically centered (10% physical-mental, 5% physical-emotional), and the remaining 80% are emotionally centered (about 55% emotional-physical and 25% emotional-mental).[2]

---

[1] We are essentially defining the "Western world" as non-Far Eastern.

[2] These figures are derived from our experiences with groups of people mostly in the context of large cities. It is possible that in other environments, the proportions may be somewhat different. More physically centered people, for example, may choose to live in rural environments.

THE FIVE PREDOMINANT PERSONALITY DYNAMICS

(with approximate proportions of populations in Western cultures)

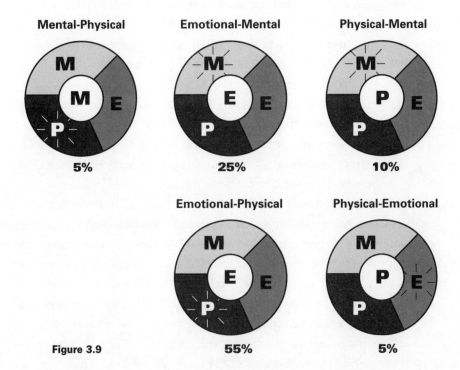

Mental-Physical
5%

Emotional-Mental
25%

Physical-Mental
10%

Emotional-Physical
55%

Physical-Emotional
5%

Figure 3.9

These approximate percentages have appeared consistently in our seminars at organizations in the United States, Canada, Europe, and Israel, and they match the proportions we have found to exist among the students in the classrooms and schools in which we have worked in these countries.

In our experience, therefore, the majority of Western populations appears to be emotionally centered—either emotional-mental or emotional-physical. This contrasts strikingly with the proportions that we have found in the Far East, where the vast majority of individuals seem to be physically centered. In fact, most of the people we have met of Japanese heritage, whether born and raised inside or outside Japan, have been physical-mental; while the majority of people we have met who were Chinese nationals or of Chinese heritage have been physical-emotional. This finding holds extraordinary significance. It suggests that some of the fundamental differences between East and West may derive more from differences in personality dynamics than from differences in culture. In fact, we have created successful programs for cross-cultural communication and collaboration between East and West that are based on understanding the contrasting processes and needs of those who are emotionally centered and those who are physically centered, rather than on the more superficial differences of particular cultural expressions (see Chapter 13, "Visions: Looking Ahead").

Central Processing and Secondary Linking
Emotional-Mental and Emotional-Physical Distinctions

As we noted earlier, the central process determines *how* a person processes information (linearly, laterally, systemically). The secondary principle is strongly related to *what* kind of information is processed.

Let us use the two emotionally centered groups to illustrate briefly how this interaction seems to work. For people in the emotional-*mental* group, the emotional system and the mind are closely linked. *How* emotional-mental people process is essentially emotional; *what* they process is primarily mental. They process ideas, but in a relatively nonlinear, free-flowing way. Emotional-mental people typically love the brainstorming process, in which new ideas are generated, one idea triggers another, and the participants follow enthusiastically where inspiration leads. The linking of emotions to the mind can also be seen in the intensity with which the members of this group typically express their ideas and the energy they show in translating those ideas into action.

For individuals in the emotional-*physical* group, the central emotional principle has close links with the *physical* principle. How these individuals process information is emotional; *what* they primarily process are experiences of the physical world. They have a great range of feelings about forms—people, in the first place, but also food, art, movies, clothes, appearances, and so on.

Emotional-physical people also experience a particularly close connection between their emotions and their physical bodies. Not only are they usually highly aware of their feelings, but they are also attuned to their bodies' reactions to their feelings. They can often explain precisely how they are feeling moment by moment, and also where in their bodies the feeling is registered or reflected. In addition, their emotional-physical systems are extremely sensitive to the feelings of others, so that if someone else is afraid, or sad, or uncomfortable (even without overtly expressing it), emotional-physical peo-ple will often know because they register the other person's feelings directly in their own bodies. They not only experience the other person's emotion, but also have a physical response, such as a tightening in the stomach, constric-tion in the throat, or a general feeling of physical discomfort. All of this is in contrast to the emotional-*mental* group, who are relatively unaware of the moment-by-moment condition or sensations of their physical bodies, and who usually do not register the feelings or physical condition of other people.

Alternative Terminology

Because the distinctions between the two emotionally centered groups are so pronounced and vivid, we have given them an alternative nomenclature that seems to capture the key differences between them. Because of the linking of the central emotional system to the objective mind in emotional-mental

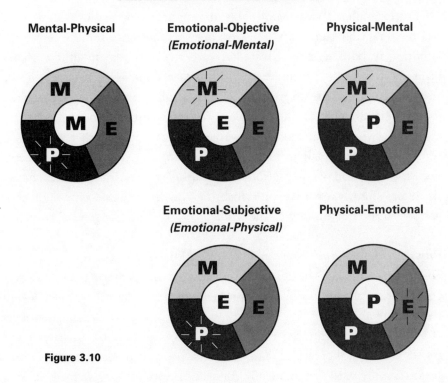

ALTERNATIVE TERMINOLOGY

Mental-Physical

Emotional-Objective
(Emotional-Mental)

Physical-Mental

Emotional-Subjective
(Emotional-Physical)

Physical-Emotional

Figure 3.10

people, we refer to this group as emotional-*objective*; and because of the sensitivity of the emotional-physical group to the personal inner life, we refer to them as emotional-*subjective*.

Again, we must emphasize that the terms "objective" and "subjective" have no judgmental connotations. Objectivity and subjectivity are complementary and equally important. In addition, distinguishing between the two emotionally centered groups by the use of these terms does not mean that emotional-objective people are incapable of subjective introspection or reflection, or that emotional-subjective people lack the capacity for objective reasoning. But it does point to a key distinction between the two groups—whereas emotional-*subjective* (emotional-physical) people respond with a wide range of feelings to their life experiences, moment by moment, and in a highly personal way, the feelings of emotional-*objective* (emotional-mental) people are linked more to their ideas, interests, and pursuits. The primary focus of emotional-objective people is thus external; that of emotional-subjective people more internal.

For example, if two people of equal maturity, one emotional-*objective* and one emotional-*subjective*, are working together on a project team, the attention of both will be directed toward the achievement of the team's goals and the quality of the interpersonal process. However, the focus of the emotional-objective team member will be slightly more weighted toward the explicit task, and on the quality of the interpersonal process in the second place, whereas the emotional-subjective participant will tend to give significance to the quality of relationship among the individual team members slightly ahead of completion of the explicit task. Although the emphasis differs slightly, each person will bring equally valuable gifts and inclinations to the functioning of the whole.

Physical-Mental and Physical-Emotional Distinctions

To illustrate further the relationship between the centering and the secondary principle, let us differentiate briefly between the two physically centered personality dynamics: physical-*mental* and physical-*emotional*. Members of both physically centered groups think systemically and pragmatically and collect a great deal of factual data. However, physical-mental people are concerned mainly with systematically connecting *ideas and principles* in order to create *logically connected structures* that will serve given *purposes* (facets of the mental principle). Physical-emotional people, by contrast, are concerned with processing the *dynamic interconnections* (emotional principle) among the various elements involved in any situation. Physical-mental people, being more detached from their data, create diagrams and models on their way to solutions; physical-emotional people tend to immerse themselves in their data until, through an often lengthy interior process, they evolve a comprehensive systemic understanding of a situation or solution to a problem.

Distinct Self-Organizing Systems

One of the most significant and distinctive contributions of Human Dynamics is the perception that *each of the personality dynamics constitutes a distinct self-organizing system.* That is, each personality dynamic is not a collection of randomly acquired traits, but rather a whole system of functioning that naturally expresses its particular underlying pattern of mental-emotional-physical "organization."

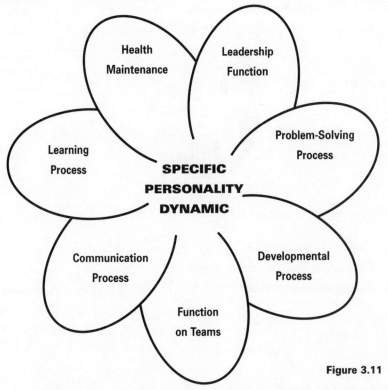

Figure 3.11

Therefore, to know someone's personality dynamic is to know a great deal about that person's fundamental processes and paths of growth. Figure 3.11 shows some of the expressions of self-organization for each personality dynamic that we have explored so far. This is by no means a complete picture. Human Dynamics will always be "work in progress," continually exploring new areas of functioning of each of these human systems.

Uniqueness

We must emphasize that everyone within every personality dynamic is unique. There are as many variations on these patterns of functioning as there are people in the world. The most important point to remember is that everyone is in a process of development along the continuum characteristic of his or her personality dynamic. This developmental aspect, which creates distinctions in each person's *quality* of expression, is explored at length in Chapter 12, "The Developmental Continuum."

Another distinguishing feature deserves mention. In Figures 3.7–3.10, we depicted the distribution of mental, emotional, and physical energies as being equal, as if they always constituted 33% of the whole, like this:

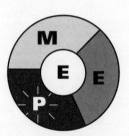

Figure 3.12

But this is never precisely the case. The distribution of energies is unique to each individual, so that three people of the same emotional-subjective (emotional-physical) personality dynamic might be represented more accurately like this:

EMOTIONAL-SUBJECTIVE
(Emotional-Physical)

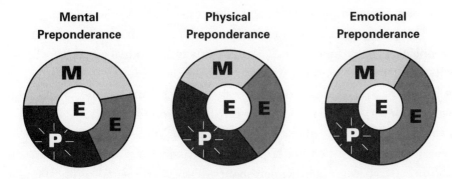

| Mental Preponderance | Physical Preponderance | Emotional Preponderance |

Figure 3.13

Each of the people represented in Figure 3.13 is emotional-subjective, but one person expresses a preponderance of mental energy, another of physical energy, and another of emotional energy. All three share the same fundamental emotional-subjective processes, with the same sensitivity to feelings and the same desire and ability to connect personally with others, but the individual with the preponderance of mental energy will move a little more quickly than the others, generate more ideas, and be somewhat more detached; the person with the preponderance of physical energy will move into action more deliberately and be somewhat more detail-oriented and pragmatic than the other two; and the person with the preponderance of emotional energy will be *extremely* sensitive to feelings and highly aware of nuances in people's communications. In spite of these differences, all three people are by nature kindred spirits because they share the same fundamental infrastructure. They would recognize in each other a great similarity in how they experience life, process information, and interact with others.

It is important to note that, as with the personality dynamics, none of these energy distributions is "better" than another. Each person will tend to show particular gifts and inclinations within the emotional-subjective theme, and each will face particular challenges in his or her developmental journey.

Continuity of Personality Dynamic
So far as we have been able to observe, this *quantitative* distribution of a person's mental, emotional, and physical energies changes little, if at all, over time, although the

principles can become more completely realized and integrated. While the quantitative distribution seems to be a consistent characteristic of a person's "instrument," every individual can learn to play his or her instrument more *qualitatively*.

While the quantitative distribution seems to be a consistent characteristic of a person's "instrument," every individual can learn to play his or her instrument more *qualitatively*.

The personality dynamic seems to represent such a fundamental pattern in any individual's makeup that it stays constant throughout the lifetime. To illustrate, we have recorded the development of a number of children on videotape since 1983, when they were less than a year old. In each case, the personality dynamic that we identified at the beginning has matured over time, but has not shifted to become another personality dynamic. A mental-physical infant becomes a mental-physical 12-year-old and, we believe, will be a mental-physical 70-year-old.

The change that does take place with age is a developmental unfolding of the particular personality dynamic. For example, a physical-mental eight-year-old will tend to work methodically, think systemically, and be factual, deliberate, and pragmatic in communication. At the age of 28, he or she will exhibit the same characteristics, but may exercise a typical physical-mental capacity for detailed strategic planning that would probably not have been evident at the younger age. Ten years later, the same person will have retained these characteristics, but as a result of greater integration of the emotional principle, may have more emotional awareness and capacity for personal connection with others. The individual may have changed qualitatively and become more skilled, but the underlying physical-mental process will have remained the same.

Environmental Influences

Does this mean that the environment exerts no influence on the child's (or adult's) behavior or development? Not at all. It simply means that environmental circumstances do not *determine* the personality dynamic, but act *upon* it for better or worse, supporting or hindering the individual's particular system of functioning. For example, it would help a young physical-mental person, such as the one described above, to be given sufficient time to work methodically and carefully, so that his or her inherent capacities for systemic planning and detailed construction can bloom. Likewise, he or she would be hindered if pressured to make instant responses or switch quickly from one task to another, and further harmed if then judged negatively as being "slow" and unable to complete tasks.

We might illustrate the situation broadly as follows:

ENVIRONMENTAL INFLUENCES

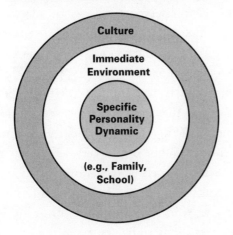

Figure 3.14

At the center of these spheres of influence is someone, say a child, of a particular personality dynamic. Influencing the child most strongly are elements within the immediate environment, particularly the family. Further affecting the child are the influences of the surrounding culture. To some degree, the impact of external influences will be determined *by* the personality dynamic. What is beneficial for one personality dynamic may be frustrating or even harmful for another. For example, it may be extremely positive for an emotional-subjective child to be asked to make an imaginative or dramatic presentation. But a physically centered child could easily experience this well-meant intervention as disturbing or even as an invitation to failure. He or she would feel much more at ease and competent providing a straightforward, factual presentation. For such reasons, parents and teachers need to know and understand the personality dynamics of their children and students. They can then modify their approaches to best connect with the individual child and meet his or her specific learning and developmental needs. The same considerations apply no less to adults in the workplace.

We are often asked, "Does all of this mean that while there is environmental influence, the personality dynamic itself is genetically determined?"

Our observations lead us to believe so, although it will require scientific research to determine this for certain. For example, in our experience, a person of a particular personality dynamic usually has at least one parent of the same personality dynamic; in cases where this has not been true, a grandparent has been of that personality dynamic.

Additionally, we have observed a number of infants adopted soon after birth by families in which both parents' personality dynamics were different from that of the infant. In these cases, the child's fundamental "way of being" has remained the same over time, despite the different family "culture," an observation which also suggests that the personality dynamic results from nature rather than nurture. However, the influence of nurture may be seen in some nuancing of the personality dynamic. For example, if a physical-mental child is adopted at a very young age by a family whose members are all emotionally centered, he or she may become more apt to express personal feelings than physical-mental children whose parents are physically centered and who therefore grow up in an environment where personal feelings are less likely to be expressed.

In the same way, environmental influences—life experiences, professional demands, the corporate culture, and so forth—may modify an adult's *behavior* to some degree, but they will not change his or her fundamental inherent *processes*.

In the next chapter and in Part II, we explore in detail the functioning and typical characteristics of each of the five personality dynamics—and their interactions with one another.

We must emphasize that everyone within every personality dynamic is unique. There are as many variations on these patterns of functioning as there are people in the world. The most important point to remember is that everyone is in a process of development along the continuum characteristic of his or her personality dynamic. This developmental aspect, along with the different distribution of mental, emotional, and physical energies, are what create distinctions in each person's *quality* of expression.

Five Brief Portraits

T he following five "portraits" summarize the major characteristics of the five personality dynamics most frequently encountered in the Western world. The portraits are expressed in the first person to provide a sense of the "voice" of each group, and to capture some of the experience of living each personality dynamic.

The purpose of these brief portraits is to convey an overall impression of each of the five personality dynamics and to allow you to make immediate general comparisons among them. Chapters 5–9 then provide fuller accounts of each personality dynamic.

Some readers may be able to identify their personality dynamic accurately from these portraits alone. However, we encourage everyone to read the longer descriptions in chapters 5–9 to help ensure accurate self-identification, and to gain the deepest possible understanding of each personality dynamic, the distinctions among them, and the roles they play in organizations. It is this in-depth understanding that enables us to fully and consciously empathize and work with all the groups.[1]

While reading these "short stories," remember that no story completely describes each member of a personality dynamic group. Every individual embodies his or her own variation on a personality dynamic theme. Moreover, as we noted in Chapter 3, everyone is in a process of development. Therefore, though we have tried to emphasize the most fundamental

---

[1] Conveying the living quality of the different personality dynamics through the medium of the printed page has been a major challenge. Words and still pictures can only go so far! Therefore, we have made available videotapes showing families whose members represent different personality dynamics. Interested readers can also explore the CD-ROM "The Ultimate Journey," which also includes videotape segments of adults and children. Further information can be found at the back of the book.

and unchanging characteristics in the stories, every word in any one story may not totally represent any individual. However, if about 80% of a story does ring true for you, it is probably describing your personality dynamic. Certainly, reading the stories can narrow the choice to perhaps two or three groups for some readers, who might then choose to explore these personality dynamics first in reading chapters 5–9.

The Mental-Physical Personality Dynamic

General

I am most attuned to the world of thoughts, vision, concepts, and overviews. I am easily able to maintain focus and can inspire that gift in others. I often bring structure, objectivity, and precision to projects and interactions. Because my mind is more central to my personality than my emotions, my mood is generally stable. I am not given to emotional or impulsive display.

Most central to my personality is a value system through which I structure my life. The values I uphold do not change easily. Therefore, if you want to know more about me, ask me what I value. One of my major concerns is that people more often hold values theoretically than maintain them at the practical level of daily living. I "live" my values consistently and carefully select the relationships and endeavors to which I commit.

I have a natural affinity for solitude, which facilitates my capacity for careful thinking and meticulous, precise work. It also helps me to become conscious of my feelings and values. I am most comfortable working alone.

Body

Although I am centered in the mind, I am well aware of my physical body and its needs and sensations. I experience keenly the subtle nuances of the sensory world. But because I tend to take in information selectively, I am not easily overwhelmed by either the sensory or the emotional worlds. I tend to maintain an even, steady rhythm in whatever I do.

Communication

My communications are generally thoughtful, purposeful, objective, and logically connected. Because clarity and precision are important to me, I am usually meticulous in my choice of words. For this reason, written communication may have a particular appeal for me. I am comfortable with silence and do not feel a need to speak if others are saying what needs to be said.

When I do speak, the content of my communication is more likely to be conceptual, factual, and informational than expressive of my inner world. The degree to which my communication is personally expressive and concerned with feelings depends upon the breadth of my values and the level of personal consciousness I have cultivated.

I am rarely fully at ease in primarily social situations. I am most comfortable in gatherings with a purpose that I value. Because I carefully select those with whom I am willing to open myself emotionally, people may not always be aware of how I am feeling, or that I can be compassionately aware of others' feelings. Sometimes others mistakenly interpret my natural reserve and capacity for detachment as meaning that I am aloof or uncaring.

Function

It is natural for me to see through long-range "lenses" and to plan long term. I do not easily lose sight of the overview or of the ultimate purpose of any endeavor. It is important to me to help establish, articulate, and maintain the guiding vision, values, and principles in relationships, groups, or organizations. I also contribute structure to the endeavors in which I become involved.

Because I have an affinity for precision, focus, and careful discrimination, I welcome highly detailed work, provided that I value its purpose.

I can be relied upon for my objectivity, constancy, and ability to perceive and articulate essential factors and principles in any situation.

Developmental Direction

One of my deep purposes is to encompass all factions and help bring unity to a divided world. Out of compassionate concern, I seek to articulate overarching principles and values to which all can subscribe.

Emotional-Objective

The Emotional-Objective Personality Dynamic

General

I am a problem-solver with an affinity for generating new ideas and promoting innovation. I relish change and challenge and am alert for windows of opportunity. One of my major functions is to light the fires of new endeavors and initiate the process of movement into unknown territory.

My attention is focused on the immediate future, and thus I feel a sense of urgency in relationship to time. My inner clock tells me that tomorrow will bring new challenges and opportunities. Therefore, I prefer to clear each day's agenda so as to avoid leaving "unfinished business." This need may make it difficult for me to strike a comfortable balance between the demands of my family and of my work.

My mind is usually focused, but may pursue several ideas and alternatives to each idea at once. Because my emotional and mental systems are closely linked, it is hard to tell whether I "think my feelings" or "feel my thoughts." I identify with what I do rather than with who I am.

Body

My body functions as a quiet "support" for my personality; I usually do not pick up many signals from my body, nor am I aware of absorbing emotions from those around me. My physical energy, therefore, is usually stable, and I can work long hours without conscious fatigue. I am often identified as a "workaholic" and may need to be made aware of my body's need for rest and care.

Communication

My communication reflects my orientation toward the movement of work and events rather than toward subjective experience. I am less likely to engage in self-disclosure than to process new ideas with others. I enjoy a brainstorming mode of communication, in which I often express my ideas intensely and enthusiastically. Others can sometimes judge this behavior as over-assertive, though I am really seeking a creative exchange. I like communication to be purposeful and direct and to convey a general picture rather than much detail.

Although my communication is generally work or project oriented, I am willing to engage in extensive personal communication with my family and the few others who play a "personal" role in my life. This communication is often directed toward facilitating cooperative effort or individual forward movement.

Function

I am a natural innovator, interested in generating and articulating new ideas and moving events forward. I like to create essential models and structures to facilitate solving problems and getting work done. These traits give me a natural entrepreneurial capability, though I am very aware of the need to work with groups.

I often prefer to leave details to others while I move on to new initiatives. The new and unknown is far more interesting to me than the tried and true. Because of my emphasis on movement and new ideas, and my desire to link goals and purposes with people, I often play a visible leadership role.

Developmental Direction

One of my deep purposes is to create innovative methods for making ideas or principles that serve humanity practically effective. I also try to empower others, individually and collectively. Recognizing that manifesting any vision requires group effort, I engage in continuous work with groups, striving to cultivate group synergy for the purpose of building something new and enduring that will benefit humankind.

The Emotional-Subjective Personality Dynamic

General

All of my experiences are personalized. I have personal responses to everything, and want to connect personally with everything and everyone. I have a wide range of feelings and am sensitive to and interested in the feelings of others. Relationships with others are most important to me. Maintaining harmony between myself and others, and among those around me, is a constant concern.

I am highly intuitive but sometimes lack the confidence to act on my intuition. I am learning that when my thoughts and feelings contradict my intuition, it is my intuition that is my most reliable signal.

I have an affinity for diversity and am attracted to a myriad of activities and interests, including a deep interest in people. I am also attracted to the many forms in which objects are created; I appreciate their aesthetic content, the values they represent, the skill that went into their construction, and their effect upon those who use them. I often find that, given the availability of materials and time, I am stimulated to creative activity.

My attraction to diversity is reinforced by my ability to be involved in many things simultaneously and to keep track of them all. However, at times I become over-stressed or scattered when I participate in too much. Part of my life's work is to learn to value the "middle way"—to balance the extremes within myself and in my commitments. When I do so, I stay focused and clear. I am helped by having time alone, which balances the intensity of my involvement with others and allows me to find my own center.

Body

Because my emotional and physical systems are closely linked, my body is usually extremely responsive to my feelings. How I feel emotionally is reflected in my physical condition, and vice versa. My body tends to hold emotional trauma from the past, and if the issues are not made conscious and resolved, this buildup can deplete my energy and lead to physical distress.

My body is a messenger, constantly picking up from the environment subtle signals which often include the emotional and physical condition of others. Thus I sometimes find it difficult to distinguish between my own emotions and physical sensations and those of other people. With this discernment, I can function optimally; without it, I can lose my sense of self.

Because I am sensitive to the shifting world of emotions, I find that my energy is often uneven and that I experience a wide range of moods. To maintain stability, I need to select carefully the people to whom I relate and the environments in which I place myself. As I understand myself and my needs more, I become increasingly conscious and precise in my choices.

Regular physical exercise and time alone are essential to my well-being, because they enable me to release accumulated tension resulting from emotional or physical stress.

Communication

Through communication, I strive to establish genuine personal connection with others, in which feelings as well as information are exchanged. Indeed, it is crucial that I process both my feelings and my thoughts with selected people, for it is through such dialogue that I clarify my thinking, identify my feelings precisely, and understand the meaning of my subjective experiences. When I come to clarity through such dialogue, I often feel a sense of completion and release within my body and am able to take appropriate actions. I am able to help others gain insight, understanding, and release through the same process. I can also achieve clarity about my experiences through inner dialogue in the silence of my own contemplation.

Function

I am a natural connector. One of my functions is to understand the nature of people and to use this understanding to enhance communication and promote harmony. I am a good organizer. My affinity for seeing and making new connections may find creative expression in the form of scientific insights, artistic expression, or innovative business methods, as well as in relation to people.

If I am true to my natural gift, I ensure that the world of feelings is understood, valued, and taken into account.

Developmental Direction

One of my deep purposes is to shed the light of understanding on the human condition. Through taking my personal experiences seriously, I learn to understand them deeply and to find the larger meanings behind them. In the silence of my own contemplation, I come to understand my experiences, so that I can offer insights or take purposeful actions that are of service to others.

I have a visionary capacity, which can enable me to be an inspirational communicator and an effective long-range "seer."

The Physical-Emotional Personality Dynamic

General

I am a natural systems thinker interested in concrete work. I want to translate thoughts and ideas into practical results that satisfy a need or solve a problem. I especially excel in the tactical implementation of work. Details are important to me, and I will perform repetitive tasks if that is what is required to complete the job.

I have an innate sense of continuity and a respect for the past—historical context is essential to me. I think naturally in terms of whole systems and all the interconnections within them. I experience life organically and am highly attuned to all the people, things, and situations that compose any environment. Because I tend to think in terms of connected systems, group life affects me deeply. Community is an important value to me. I understand the purpose of teams and work well in them. I am not the point—the point is the whole.

In any situation, I take in a great deal of the information around me, including the physical details of the environment and the people present. I take in every word that is said, including any ambiguity and paradox. I absorb all this information without preselecting or sorting it. I am like a giant data bank, assimilating and storing information. My factual memory is usually excellent, although it may sometimes take me time to retrieve what I have absorbed.

Because of this organic and comprehensive kind of information processing, it may take me considerable time to learn something new. But given this time, I master the new information in a detailed and connected way. Once I have learned something, I rarely forget it.

Body

My body rhythm is generally even and steady. I am often unaware of signals from my body, but as I become conscious of them I appreciate the accurate information they bring about me and my environment. Because of my group orientation, I sometimes lose touch with my own needs and goals. When I am aware of these, my flow of energy is much greater.

Because my body absorbs and records so much data, I need considerable time alone to process all the information I have collected, to attune to my own emotional responses, and to release any negative input. It is important for me to reconnect regularly with the natural environment and to resynchronize myself with nature's slower rhythms in order to stay balanced and healthy.

Because I tend to just accept and endure any ailments, others may not know when I am sick or in pain.

Communication

My verbal responses may tend to come slowly because I have so much data to distill. I am often unaware of "personal processing." I like to talk about what I am doing, not about who I am. In fact, rather than discuss my activities, I prefer to just do them! My natural tendency is to accept "what is" and to move on to action.

A challenge for me is to become more conscious of myself as an individual, to emerge from the "collective" and establish my own identity. I therefore need to separate myself from people sometimes and listen, alone, for my own clear voice. It sometimes takes courage for me to speak with that voice when I am with others.

Function

My function is to respect the "whole" in my thinking and my actions. In any undertaking, I absorb and synthesize large amounts of data in order to construct comprehensive systemic plans. In this way, I ensure that work proceeds in accordance with the initial vision and that all the details necessary for implementing the plans are in place. It is important that I am given the time this inclusive process requires.

I am orderly in my working habits, which makes me reliable to myself and others. I generally follow this sequence: (1) Obtain consensus on the project to be implemented; (2) immerse myself in data; (3) make detailed tactical plans; (4) put the plans into action.

I do what is needed.

Developmental Direction

One of my deep purposes is to ensure that visions serving the collective are realized through detailed systemic planning and practical concrete action. Another deep purpose is to create unity out of diversity by maintaining bonds among all group members in the spirit of community.

The Physical-Mental Personality Dynamic
General

I am practical, detailed, thorough, and precise. I am also a natural strategic planner and systems thinker. I have a strategy for almost everything I do. I tend to assemble and reassemble data until interconnected patterns or systems emerge.

At the outset of any undertaking, I need to understand clearly the purpose and the essential context—where we want to go and why, where we are now, and where we have come from (future, present, past). This understanding lays the foundation for future planning. As I proceed, I create diagrams, models, maps, charts, and graphs, which I use as tools for creating structures and facilitating my own thinking, learning, and communicating with others.

I am deeply interested in how things work, both mechanically and systemically, and in making things work well. I like my efforts to result in systems of operation that are efficient and can be applied to other situations. Logical thinking and spatial intelligence are key strengths.

I am orderly in my work habits, a trait that makes me reliable to myself and others. I generally follow this sequence: (1) Obtain consensus on the purpose to be achieved; (2) gather and assimilate relevant data; (3) make detailed strategic and tactical plans; (4) put these plans into action in order to fulfill the original purpose. This process is quite similar to that of physical-emotional people, but is more structured, based on more selective data, and less detailed.

Body

I experience two inner rhythms, a fast rhythm in my head and a slower rhythm in my body. Conflicts between these rhythms can be a problem for me. Because my mind tends to move at top speed when I am interacting with others, I rarely find opportunities to move into my deeper, slower rhythm. This imbalance can cause me stress. Regular physical activity, relaxation exercises, and time alone for contemplation help me reconnect with my deeper rhythm. I also benefit from spending time in nature to resynchronize myself with its calmer, organic rhythms. Regaining my deeper rhythm enables me to process the considerable amount of data that I assimilate, to become aware of my emotional state, to release any stored negative input, and to register signals of stress from my body that may not be apparent to me in my "fast" mode.

Because I usually focus on what I am doing rather than on how my body is feeling, I am regarded as having a high tolerance for pain and discomfort.

Communication

Because I am always focused on the action to be taken, I want to establish the purpose of any communication at the beginning. Being group-oriented as well as pragmatic, I usually ask, "What needs to be done? Who is this for? What plans can we make? How do we take action?"

The amount of data I need depends on the significance of the communication. If I judge the purpose of the communication important, I am willing to receive a great deal of information and spend the time to process it. This processing helps me see both the micro and macro levels in any situation and understand the relationships among the parts. However, because my mind thinks and remembers in terms of key points, I appreciate structured and succinct communication, provided it includes sufficient relevant details.

Written communication appeals to me because it seems to offer reliability, precision, and structure, and it allows me time to assimilate the message fully before making a response.

Function

My function is to ensure that the agreed-upon vision and purposes are fulfilled. I serve this function by making and enacting systemic strategic plans with enough detail to ensure effective, practical, concrete action. One of my inherent needs and capacities is to make plans that are comprehensive enough to take into account all of the relevant data and possible outcomes; another is to achieve maximum effectiveness and efficiency.

My methodical and inclusive process may take time. This fact needs to be respected if I am to make my fullest contribution.

I do what is needed.

Developmental Direction

One of my deep purposes is to formulate and implement plans and activities that reflect a compassionate concern for the welfare of people and that answer a collective need. Another is to promote and maintain qualitative relationships as tasks are performed.

*The pursuit of self-knowledge is the mark
of a developed personality and a characteristic
of an enlightened leader. Self-understanding
is the most secure bedrock on which to shape
one's life.*

*Nothing is more important in conditions of
turbulence and change than a secure sense of
self. Self-understanding also provides a basis
for understanding others—it is difficult to be
conscious of another's needs, motivations, and
processes without first having awareness of
one's own.*

Part II:
The Five Personality Dynamics

The following five chapters elaborate basic themes that are intrinsic to each of the five personality dynamics. We begin each chapter with a personal story to illustrate how the basic gifts of someone of that personality dynamic found expression in the context of his or her organizational work.

Each chapter then presents a metatheme, or core function, for the personality dynamic. A metatheme is like the center of a spoked wheel—a theme that connects with every aspect of a person's basic functioning. The text then explores each "spoke," subthemes in that personality dynamic's story. Some subthemes, under headings such as communication, memory, the physical body, change, relationship to time, conditions for learning, and "When Something Goes Wrong," are common to all of the personality dynamic chapters (although each personality dynamic expresses them very differently). Others are idiosyncratic to a particular personality dynamic—for example, the subtheme of "Two Different Rhythms" is characteristic only of the physical-mental personality dynamic.

Each personality dynamic chapter is introduced by an illustration of a fractal. The fractal symbolizes the fact that each personality dynamic is a self-organizing system with its own pattern integrity. The specific fractal in each case suggests qualities of the personality dynamic it illustrates. For example, the mental-physical fractal is symmetrical and structured, while the emotional-objective fractal suggests movement.

Below each fractal is a list of capacities that typify the personality dynamic. The last line, in italics, indicates the group's distinguishing capacity when personal and transpersonal integration is achieved (see Chapter 12, "The Developmental Continuum").

A fractal object repeats a similar pattern or design of ever-smaller levels of scale. No matter where you look, the same pattern will be evident. In any fractal object, we are viewing a simple organizing structure that creates unending complexity.

—Margaret J. Wheatley

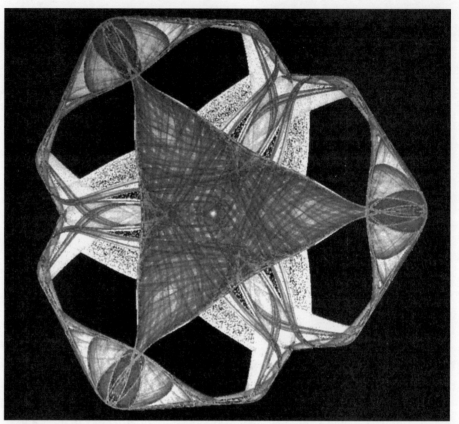

Capacities
Mental-Physical

- To determine and maintain long-range vision for self, others, and groups.
- To perceive and articulate guiding values and principles.
- To create structures.
- To listen carefully to diverse points of view and find the common points of agreement.
- To be objective and detached while maintaining qualitative relationships with others.
- To adopt and express unconditional love as *the* highest value.

- *To be teachers of both objectivity and compassion, by example.*

The Mental-Physical Personality Dynamic: Seeing from the Mountaintop

How do you see where you're going without a vision? How can you answer questions like: What strategies are needed? Who should serve on the board of directors? If you don't have the vision, you don't know what fits and what doesn't. You don't have guidelines and you can't see where you are going. The vision is everything. If you don't start there, everything is haphazard.

For seven years, I served as president and CEO of a medical center foundation in Los Angeles. The corporate mission was to make healthcare services available to everyone in the community regardless of the patient's ability to pay. I saw that to realize this mission we needed a new vision for the foundation—that of a *community* of people committed to actively supporting the medical center's mission.

To create that community, we had to find ways to connect diverse groups: all the people who provided services at the medical center; the medical center's management; the foundation's board of directors, who were pillars of the community; prospective donors; the patients we served; people who lived in the community whose awareness needed to be heightened about who we were and what we did; and key local agencies, foundations, and corporations that we wanted to educate and possibly apply to for grants.

Over time I built a staff to support the programs that I instituted for realizing the vision. In the beginning, I asked many questions of the people around me; and I listened. The vision needed consensus. With consensus, people become motivated. They can embrace the vision and participate in realizing it. And with a shared vision, managing doesn't become such a big issue. The vision is your guide. If it's a sound vision, well articulated, and implemented on a daily basis, it becomes alive!

You maintain the vision by constantly inviting input and, above all, by constantly communicating and living the vision. You also regularly tweak the process of realizing the vision. It's a living process and, as such, is constantly evolving.

My most important contribution was to articulate the vision constantly, as well as lead its implementation. Our efforts together were so successful that we received national recognition.

—MARGYE S. BAUMGARDNER, CFRE, FORMER PRESIDENT AND CEO,
SANTA MONICA HOSPITAL MEDICAL CENTER FOUNDATION

Vision and Perspective: A Metatheme for Mental-Physical People

Being centered in the mind, mental-physical people naturally see things as they would from the top of a mountain. From this elevated perspective, they typically regard events with a high degree of objectivity and detachment, and with a long-term focus. The natural gifts of mental-physical people for seeing the overview and for logical, analytical, long-range thinking often make them effective strategic planners. A phrase frequently used by many mental-physical people in any endeavor is, "Let's work backwards." By this they mean, "First, let's clearly define our guiding vision and ultimate purpose; then we can create the essential steps and structures that will lead to achieving our goal." They take great pains to ensure that the vision, values, and purposes have been clearly articulated before proceeding further, because they know that everything else must flow from and be guided by them. Often they relentlessly ask questions, beginning with, "Why?"—essential questions that lead to examining fundamental motives, goals, and purposes. Once these are established, mental-physical people usually play the role of "keepers of the flame"; they continue to articulate the vision and essential guiding principles, and sense when decisions or actions might lead to deviation from them.

Although they *may* not be as highly creative as others in generating ideas for realizing a vision, mental-physical people are likely to stay steadfast in ensuring its accomplishment. Their eyes usually stay riveted on the end point, which may be quite distant.

A mental-physical human resources manager writes,

My mind is usually anchored well into the future—six months to two years out. For one project, I formulated a ten-year plan. I am now in the seventh year. Although details have changed in the unfolding of the plan, the basic structure remains the same. Most importantly, the beneficial effects of the program have been as I foresaw. I took a personal risk in initiating the project seven years ago, because no one else saw the outcomes quite as I did.

Another mental-physical individual, who had chosen to work with children in an innovative setting involving both research and education, made his choice objectively based on a remarkably long-range vision. He said,

I have always seen my life in the perspective of the future beyond my own life span. I chose this work because I thought it would contribute to an eternal human process of gaining enlightenment and trying to create a better world. Though I did find satisfaction in the personal relationships that the work entailed and in the immediate effects on people's lives, this wouldn't have been sufficient to motivate me without the framework of the larger perspective.

Vistas

Many mental-physical people have described how their affinity for perspective extends concretely to their topographical preferences. One of them puts it this way,

"If I'm hiking, and I come to a hill or rise, I have a profound urge to get to the top of it. I enjoy vistas and the exhilaration of being on the edge of space, looking out to the distance. When flying, I book a window seat so I can feel part of the endless space outside and observe the changing patterns on the ground below. When driving, I pull into scenic overlooks. In cities, I ascend observation towers. My preferred locations in nature are in the mountains or on the seashore. In theaters, I prefer the circle to the stalls; in classrooms, the back of the room. I enjoy maps; they also give me perspective. These are not so much preferences as inner compulsions."

Perspective is a word often used by mental-physical people. They will say, "This is my perspective . . ." or "There are a number of perspectives on this issue," which they will then articulate. One consequence of their capacity for perspective is that they typically see many sides of any question. This tendency may sometimes dismay colleagues, friends, or family members who might be expecting automatic support for their point of view. Sometimes the aptitude of mental-physical people for seeing all around an issue can make decision-making difficult for them, especially as they like to be clear about consequences before making decisions. However, their detached perspective helps them come to balanced decisions that are based on long-term, rather than short-term, considerations, and to articulate over-arching principles that accommodate diverse points of view.

Objectivity and Detachment

Experiencing life primarily through the medium of the mind, rather than the emotions, mental-physical people consistently view events—including the events of their own lives—with a high degree of detachment and objectivity. This capacity enables them to make valuable contributions to understanding situations, clarifying issues, and solving problems, even in emotionally charged situations. Their inherent detachment permits them to remain unaffected by the swirl of feelings around them. In fact, they commonly respond to times of crisis or high emotion by becoming even *more* objective as they focus on understanding and clarifying the issues.

Although their natural objectivity is clearly valuable, it can sometimes be frustrating or puzzling for others who are seeking or expecting a more emotional or a more personal response. In fact, mental-physical people can be perceived by others as being aloof, cold, uncaring, even unfeeling. This is usually far from the truth—a misinterpretation that mental-physical people, when they become aware of it, find exceedingly painful.

The misinterpretation arises because they express their caring through an "instrument" that is not naturally emotionally expressive. As one mental-physical person has put it,

> I have an absolutely consistent feeling of general goodwill toward people. I know myself to be exceedingly reliable in my caring. I simply do not experience

many fluctuations of feeling moment by moment as others seem to, so I am not outwardly demonstrative. Even when I am making a point that I feel strongly about, I am sometimes not heard because I do not express it in an emotional way.

In fact, the emotional life of mental-physical people is usually extremely stable with few changes in mood. This is partly because they do not readily register the emotional climate around them and partly because, in their experience, the movement from feeling to objectivity is swift. As one mental-physical person has put it,

> I will experience something as touching or moving or sorrowful or frightening, but the feeling is assimilated so quickly that my response is objective. An observer may not be aware that I had a subjective experience at all. I may not even be well aware of it myself.

Mental-physical people generally report that they rarely become angry ("I become mildly irritated maybe twice a month!"), and they certainly rarely express angry feelings. Indeed, they are likely to be reticent even in expressing *positive* feelings. They usually find it easier to show their love or caring through the quiet actions they take to meet needs, the reliability of their presence, and their thoughtful attention to matters of concern, rather than through direct communication of personal feeling.

As a very small minority in a largely emotionally centered world, many mental-physical people have had an uncomfortable sense of being somehow different from other people in a way difficult for them to identify. One young college student, however, was clear about the reason for this difference:

> I've realized that what separates me from most people is that before I let an emotion grab hold of me, I pass it through a filter. This filter is logical, rational thought.

Then he went on to say something of great significance in understanding mental-physical people:

> The things that *do* cause an emotional response in me are those that are really important to me, those that touch upon my values.

Beneath the objectivity and relative impersonality of the mental-physical personality dynamic lie depths of sensitivity and emotion closely related to the individual's value system.

The Primacy of Values

Values are a central motivating force and point of reference for mental-physical individuals. Although *everyone* has values that influence their decisions and actions, mental-physical people as a group tend to consciously structure their lives around a well-defined value system. They learn best what they value, remember best what they value, usually live by what they value, and probably know that they *value* values. They are likely to explain who they are in terms of the values they hold.

Mental-physical people therefore feel uncomfortable if values have not been clearly established in any endeavor; and if values *have* been established, they are sensitive to any deviation from them. A natural role for mental-physical people, therefore, is to raise issues concerning values for any group in which they participate. John is a mental-physical executive, aware of playing this function:

> My big issue is honesty, and I often find myself in the position of being one of the few people who are willing to point out that the emperor is naked. . . . I usually find myself taking responsibility for the integrity of the organization, which in a large organization is often hard work. Learning how to do this without becoming overly judgmental has been a continuing struggle.

The major life choices of mental-physical people are usually consciously dictated by their value system, as the following typical statement from a mental-physical person suggests,

> My values had a great influence on my choice of employers. When I was a young man I received a very attractive offer to manage a business. But I couldn't seriously consider the offer, because I didn't value the kind of business. I joined my present company, instead, because of its reputation for integrity and my belief in the social value of its products.

Because their relationships are usually based on shared values, mental-physical people tend to be highly selective in choosing friends. Although they may have many acquaintances, they usually have few close friends; but because they choose carefully, their friendships tend to endure. Their sense of shared values is also likely to play a decisive role when it comes to marriage or forming deeper relationships. As one mental-physical man put it,

> I did not marry until I was fifty-two. This wasn't because I did not wish to be married and raise a family, but because those alliances I formed previously seemed to always have something essential missing. I thought for a while that perhaps there was something lacking in me—that I was unable to commit to a relationship—but when I met the person who became my wife, there was no hesitation. There was a sense of spiritual connection that I had not experienced before. This made all the difference.

It seems that the emotions of mental-physical people are very much tied to their values. They are most likely to feel and show emotion when a deep value has been either touched or violated.

A Deep Chord Touched

"Recently I saw a television interview with Reginald Denny, the truck driver who was almost beaten to death during the 1992 Los Angeles riots. Although still suffering the effects of his beating, he spoke about the necessity for forgiveness because without forgiveness there is no end to the cycles of violence and revenge—they just keep repeating themselves. I was moved to hear this simple man speaking ultimate wisdom from his heart. When I tried later to describe the interview to my wife, I could not complete the account because emotion choked my words, no matter how hard I tried to keep my composure. His words had touched a deep chord, and my habitual calm was shaken."

As a mental-physical manager at a major healthcare facility has described,

I don't usually get upset, but if I do, it's because a principle has been violated. On one occasion, the top executive team wanted to introduce a no-smoking policy in the hospital. We were told that we should ask potential employees if they smoked, and then not hire them if they did. Although this issue was being approached as a health issue, to me it was a bigger issue of discrimination and people's rights. I felt so strongly that when I was given the opportunity to express my views in front of the decision-makers, I found myself raising my voice, telling them in passionate detail how I felt, and even pounding on the table to make my point. Everyone, including myself, was astonished. I'm still famous for that speech.

On another occasion, the same manager expressed her commitment to her sense of values with the kind of reticence more typical of mental-physical people. Her organization was to be drastically restructured in ways that would require her to impose changes that would aggravate her staff's stress and, in some cases, even result in loss of jobs. Recognizing that she herself would be relatively unaffected by the new policies, she privately refused to accept her annual pay raise so that she would not feel unfairly favored. It is worth noting that before a Human Dynamics course changed their perception, staff members had evaluated this same manager as "uncaring," a judgment based on her relatively impersonal way of communicating and interacting.

The obverse side of mental-physical people's depth of feeling around values is that they can sometimes be uncompromising in relation to others. If they feel that a deep value has been transgressed, it may not be easy for them to come to forgiveness. For example, one mental-physical manager tells the following story:

My former boss, who was head of the Human Resources department, was instrumental in firing several employees who had been caught stealing. When he left the company to become self-employed, however, I discovered that he had copied many of the company's PC software programs for his personal use as a consultant. This so transgressed my sense of values that I have since been unable to force myself to do business with him in his new role. I can barely be civil with him. I am sure this baffles him, as we worked closely together and our relationship was very amicable.

Even with family members, if a mental-physical person has experienced a value conflict, he or she may keep the relationship distant or indeed sever it forever.

Because mental-physical people *are* centered in the mind rather than in the emotions and are naturally given to detachment, it may be relatively easy for them to "solve" deep relational issues by simply cutting themselves off.

> Much to my detriment, I'm sure I have completely cut off relationships—entirely. They're done, finished, there's no more discussion. Now I've become more aware of this tendency and its limitations, and I'm trying to work with it.

As they mature, mental-physical people may come to adopt a broader value system that leaves the door open for reconciliation and forgiveness. When they can develop an inclusive value system and personal empathy, and integrate these with their typical gifts of detachment and perspective, they commonly prove to be extraordinarily patient, objective, and nonjudgmental—though not necessarily personally demonstrative—colleagues and counselors.

Solitude and Space

If the emotional principle is the principle of connection and the physical principle that of systemic relationships, the mental principle seems to be the principle of oneness. Most mental-physical people assert that they feel extremely comfortable with solitude, and many describe a sense of being "at home" when they are alone. Though their efforts may have a collective purpose, they usually prefer to think, learn, and work alone rather than in interaction with others.

Mental-physical people typically don't feel lonely or disconnected in solitude, nor do they need a great deal of personal interaction with others in order to feel fulfilled. As one mental-physical person has said,

> When I was a youngster, I used to enjoy taking long bicycle rides out into the countryside by myself. I felt connected to everything about me—the air, the sky, the fields, and the sun. As an adult, I often hike by myself, camp by myself, study and work by myself, go to concerts by myself, and wander

There is a tremendous statement, you get it in Dante, you get it in Jung, when they discover that love ultimately is the overriding law of the universe.

This love gives us the freedom to choose between truth and error, and make our stand in truth.

—Laurens van der Post

streets by myself in a strange city, with pleasure. This is not to say that I would not be happy to share my delights with a kindred soul, or even souls. But in their absence, I can be content. I certainly prefer solitude to company that is not highly compatible.

As we have said, mental-physical people typically enjoy vistas—they seem to feel a connection with the element of space itself. Most mental-physical people say that when they are in nature, it is the *space* of nature they enjoy most. Although mental-physical people are relatively few in number, we find that a comparatively high proportion work in (or have a keen interest in) the fields of aerospace and astronomy. This affinity for space seems to extend to respect for the physical and psychological "space" of others, as well as maintenance of their own space. This should not be taken to mean that they are uncaring or antisocial—many mental-physical people have explained that, in fact, they *feel connected* with others "in space."

One of our videotapes of children gives a touching demonstration of this separate-but-connected phenomenon. The video shows in turn five groups of three nine-year-old children, each group representing one of the five personality dynamics. Each group was given the identical task: to create on a table-top from a variety of materials their ideal park or recreation area. That was their only instruction—they weren't told whether they should work alone or collaborate on the task. Each group's process proved entirely different. In the mental-physical group, each youngster worked silently and meticulously alone to create his own park. Each occupied almost precisely one-third of the table, and each took care not to intrude on another's space. At one point in the video, we see how one child has difficulty keeping a fence that he has constructed upright on the tabletop. It repeatedly collapses. Each time he patiently and impassively replaces it. When the fence falls yet again, one of the other children moves quietly over, stands it up securely, and then returns wordlessly to his own task. Though they worked independently, they remained aware of and concerned for one another.

This preference for working alone characterizes most mental-physical adults as well as children. In part, it stems from their logical way of thinking, which can be disrupted by a highly interactive group process (see "The Challenge of Teamwork," pp. 77–79).

Time: Connecting with the Eternal

The affinity that mental-physical people typically feel for space, perspective, and long-range thinking seems to include a dimension related to time. Many mental-physical people speak of having a strong sense of timelessness, of dwelling in eternal time, even as they grapple with the practical moment-by-moment timelines imposed by the demands of their work and daily lives. Everyone lives with this paradox, but mental-physical people, as a whole, seem most aware of the context of eternal time. One of their deep joys while being in nature is their sense of reconnection with the eternal—with temporal as well as physical space.

This sense differs from the feeling of connection to the continuity of time that the two physically centered groups, especially the physical-emotional, often describe. Physically centered people typically refer to *historical* continuity—to time measured in terms of human events and experiences, in terms of the evolution of the universe, or as perceived in the enduring manifestations of nature and its recurring organic cycles. Mental-physical people seem to be attuned not so much to these more substantive phenomena as to the fact or condition of timelessness itself.

One mental-physical manager has described in quite extreme terms how this connection affects her thinking and behavior:

> Everything's eternal to me. Everything. Every issue, every person. And when I make a decision or look at an issue or tackle a problem, it's as though I want to be sure that this will prove to be the right decision ten years from now, twenty years from now, and even in the context of eternity. When I'm long gone, will this decision I'm making right now still have been the right one?

For some mental-physical people (not all), this sense of connection to timelessness, combined with their desire to produce meticulous work, can sometimes cause difficulty in circumstances demanding quick action. However, their long perspective and the eternal values they often articulate constitute a healthy counter-balance to short-range thinking and to decision-making geared to passing circumstances and momentary advantage.

Memory: Retaining the Essentials

As a whole, mental-physical people seem not to have extensive, detailed memories, but rather to remember essentials and general impressions. One reason for this may be that they tend to transcribe experience into lessons, principles, or essences and remember these, rather than the details of the events.

Unlike emotional-subjective people, those who are mental-physical do not carry an abundance of memories related to feelings, nor do they have the capacity to relive incidents from the past as if they were taking place in the present. One mental-physical individual described his astonishment at hearing his mother, who is emotional-subjective, describe a week-long trip they had taken together the year before. "She could recall the entire sequence of events with all the nuances of conversations and interactions, details of people's appearances, the furnishings in rooms, etc., and her feelings in response to every incident. I had thoroughly enjoyed the trip, but I was left with mostly general impressions."

Mental-physical people often confess to having a poor memory for people's names and appearances, unless they have trained themselves in this skill. Instead, they tend to register and remember people's essential qualities. In general, the events they remember most vividly and consistently are those that are value-related—occasions on which a personal value of theirs was expressed, violated, challenged, changed, or formed. Around such occasions, they may remember not only factual details but also their feelings. They may also retain what they have deliberately set out to learn because they value the subject matter.

Most mental-physical people take notes as an aid to memory, usually in the form of essential points. The mental/physical act of writing itself seems to aid memorization, whether or not the notes are ever consulted.

Perhaps because of their connection with the physical principle and their liking for maps, mental-physical people usually have a good memory for routes and the locations of places. Of the places themselves, however, they may be more likely to remember essential qualities and atmospheres, rather than an abundance of specific details.

> "I have always loved to read—all kinds of literature—but I could tell you very little in detail of what I have read. I derive *meaning* from whatever I read, and I believe the reading has an *effect*, but I don't remember much of the contents unless I make a special effort to do so. For example, I can recite certain poems or passages from Shakespeare, because I was delighted by them and made the effort to learn them; but the process of memorization was not easy and required much repetition."

Change: Will It Be of Value?

Because they hold consistent values, look far ahead, and discriminate carefully, mental-physical people do not change direction often or heedlessly. For example, they may be content staying with the same job for many years, as long as it matches their value system and capabilities. They may only leave a position if either their values change or they perceive their work situation to be no longer congruent with their values. This consistency of outlook shows up even in inconsequential day-to-day choices—for example, many mental-physical people eat the same meal or wear the same kinds of clothes day after day because, having found what suits them, they see no good reason to make changes.

This does not mean, however, that mental-physical people are necessarily resistant and unadaptable to change. But because of their long-term perspective and precise way of thinking, they typically need time to evaluate proposed changes with care and be assured that the changes make rational sense, would indeed serve long-term purposes, and align with values they can comfortably uphold. Once they are satisfied on these points, they can change direction swiftly and with total commitment. In fact, the more important the issue, the more readily they may embrace change, provided that they clearly see the value of the consequences. By the same token, mental-physical people can prove equally adamant in resisting change if they conclude that it will not enhance value or align with their value system. As one manager said,

> Our whole leadership team went to a seminar that emphasized the need to help employees understand that major change was going to be a constant in our field for years to come. Everyone became extremely enthusiastic about the whole concept of change—"We have to move with the times, etc." I found myself becoming uneasy. I have initiated many changes in my work environment, but I found myself pulling back. I realized the reason was that I placed no value on change just for the sake of change. Some things have such value that they should never change—respect for craftsmanship and quality, for example, like Amish quilts versus mass-produced quilts. So we must use our best judgment and carefully consider what shouldn't be changed as well as change what we must and should.

A mental-physical person's acceptance or initiation of change is likely to be expressed more by actions taken than enthusiastic verbal pronouncements. This relative lack of outward enthusiasm should not be interpreted as lack of commitment or support.

Quality and Meticulousness

Quality, whether of performance, character, product, thought, or expression, is one of the most important values for mental-physical people. Everyone values quality, of course, according to their own criteria, but mental-physical people consistently think in terms of quality and consciously apply standards to ensure it. This appreciation of quality is commonly evident in how mental-physical people conduct their lives and the choices they make. They typically spend considerable time planning and investigating various options before buying something, because they want the highest and most enduring quality they can afford. The same careful concern for quality is expressed in their workplace decisions and practices.

Because of the internal interplay between the mental valuing of quality and the physical concern for detail, mental-physical people have a strong affinity for meticulous and precise work. They want to ensure that everything they do, say, or write is logically connected, and that each detail accurately reflects or fulfills the particular vision or purpose. Mental-physical people typically rework or rewrite something time and again to ensure that their intention is perfectly achieved, even if no one else but themselves would ever be aware of the difference:

> I love to put things in writing. People bring issues to me and say, "Can you write a letter about this for me? Can you finish this? Can you write to the president of this company?" and I love doing that. Writing permits me to go back and rewrite, pick the perfect words, really clarify the issue. This allows me to be very precise. Sometimes I write it over and over, pick different words and put them in to see how the sentence sounds. And if when I'm done, it's to the point, says exactly what needs to be said, and has the right mix of feelings, issues, reality, and futuristic thinking—then it's perfect.

> ### *Elegant Precision*
> Both Bertrand Russell, the eminent English philosopher and mathematician, and Fred Astaire, the famous American dancer and actor, were mental-physical. Both sought the clearest possible articulation of their thinking and vision, one in words, the other in movement. Bertrand Russell was renowned for his ability to convey abstruse thinking in extraordinarily clear and elegant prose in pursuit of his goal of making philosophy generally accessible. And Fred Astaire would repeatedly rehearse and shoot scenes, even to the point that his partner's feet would bleed, in his determination to achieve the perfect expression of his cinematic vision.

Sometimes their meticulousness can get mental-physical people into trouble. Others may perceive them as taking longer than necessary to complete a task, as being obsessively overscrupulous, and, if they extend the same standards to others, as overcritical. With maturity, and given the practical limitations of deadlines, they learn to accept the necessity of compromising occasionally in their relentless pursuit of perfection.

The Physical Body: Finely Tuned

Because of the close relationship of the mental and physical principles in mental-physical people, members of this group are usually sensitive to their bodies. They *know* when they are hungry, tired, in pain, in need of exercise, or not feeling well. They seem to be finely tuned sensory recorders who register, for example, subtle changes in temperature or atmosphere. They are aware of and relish the wide world of sights, scents, sounds, and physical sensations, but because they often do not outwardly express this sensitivity, others might not be aware of it.

Most—not all—mental-physical people seem to be leanly built, and most seem to be able to eat quite heartily without accumulating weight. There is some evidence that their metabolism may be faster than the average. Their weight seems to remain stable over many years—consistency seems to be their trademark in this respect as well as in others.

Mental-physical people are characterized by a steady, even pace in all that they do, and tend to persist in pursuing their goals over an extended period of time. These traits even seem to characterize the athletic activities in which they excel.

> I've always enjoyed running. When I was competing in cross-country events in school, I would simply wear down most, if not all, of the opposition by setting quite a fast pace and just keeping going. I never had much of a sense of running *against* anybody—I was simply enjoying the activity itself and the experience of being more or less alone in the countryside. The same is true of other physical activities, such as swimming or walking. I keep a steady, even pace, and can continue for a long time, sometimes surprising myself by the distance I have covered.

Roger Bannister, the first person to break the 4-minute mile barrier, is mental-physical—as is Swedish athlete Anders Gärderud, who won an Olympic gold medal in the steeplechase. And 16-year-old Andrew, a mental-physical boy from Canada who has had the ambition to be an Olympic swimmer since he was eight, now competes in the longer distances at the provincial level. When mental-physical people are athletically inclined, it seems that they excel more in events requiring a steady pace over time rather than sudden bursts of energy—a characteristic which marks their lives as a whole. Something in their basic "construction" lends itself to steady long-distance achievement.

Communication: Verbal Precision

Mental-physical people tend to use words carefully. The rhythm of their speech is usually quite deliberate, and they typically prefer to pursue one idea or topic at a time and complete it before moving to another. They like communication to be clear, concise, objective, and logically connected. If they are receiving communication that is not of this nature, they try to clarify it internally or by asking such questions as, "What do you mean by . . . ?" They try to ensure that they and the person with whom they are talking share common definitions of words and attach the same meaning to what is being said.

This kind of process can be extremely helpful in gaining clarity in conversations and discussions. Other people, however, especially those who are

On a sensory level, the visual is probably their most significant modality. Many mental-physical people say they enjoy simply observing— people, places, nature, sometimes art. They seem to learn mostly through visual means— especially reading. Most describe themselves as life-long avid readers.

emotionally centered, may sometimes find that it interferes with the natural flow of their speaking, thinking, or feeling. They may especially feel this way if they are not necessarily seeking immediate precision but are more intent upon simply getting something expressed.

Difficulties can also arise because in their quest for precision, mental-physical people usually give considered responses in the course of conversation or discussion and state the conclusions of their thinking rather than thinking aloud. They prefer a measured kind of discussion to a brainstorming kind of exchange. They also do not readily express their personal feelings, even positive feelings of affection or respect, but usually prefer to show how they feel by the actions they take. These traits can make mental-physical people hard to "read" and may lead to misinterpretation. If someone wishes to know what a mental-physical person is really thinking or feeling, it is best simply to ask him or her, rather than infer. Usually mental-physical people appreciate being asked questions. It facilitates communication for them, and permits them to make their communication agreeably precise because they know exactly what the other person wants from them. Their responses may not be immediate, however—they may need time for reflection.

"When an emotional-objective colleague of mine and I first had to work together, she found my process of discourse frustrating. She experienced it as nit-picking and an interruption of her flow of ideas and movement toward action. Now she values it, and when she wants to clarify her thinking, allows me to sort it out with her in this way. Even so, I know that the process requires a stretch of her patience. I, for my part, have had to learn to recognize when this process is appropriate and when it is not."

Mental-physical people are usually comfortable with abstract thinking and discussion, but being mental-*physical*, they also have an affinity for the concrete. In their quest for clarity, they like to illustrate generalizations or abstract propositions with concrete examples; and they like that kind of communication in return.

The best way to connect with a mental-physical person may be to frame the communication in terms of values or, more personally, to enter into a discussion about whatever he or she specifically values. When confronting a mental-physical person, or even discussing a highly emotional situation, it is usually not necessary to make an emotional presentation in order to be heard. The more objectively the issues and the values involved are presented, the more responsive the mental-physical person can be.

Generally, mental-physical people do not enjoy "making small talk." They don't feel facile with it. In situations where they are expected to make casual conversation with strangers, as at a cocktail party, they tend to find one or two individuals with whom they can converse intently around some topic of common interest. Otherwise, they will probably be content to listen, to observe, and to leave as soon as the opportunity and good manners permit. They are usually more comfortable with groups that have a defined, rather than a merely social, purpose. They typically enjoy small gatherings of friends, but only with age and experience feel at ease in social situations with strangers.

> "I seem to come at things from a different angle than anyone else. At work, I often ask myself, 'What's wrong with these people that they can't see the bigger issue?' or 'What's wrong with me that I keep blowing things up into a bigger issue than the others see?' I realize now that it's because I tend to see and speak to the principles involved rather than the specific instance. This has sometimes caused a failure in communication."

Mental-physical people greatly appreciate written communication. Putting things in writing enables them to think things through carefully and to find the precise words to make themselves clear. Receiving written communication affords them time for reflection before making a response. For example, one mental-physical manager said,

I love to put things in writing. I like to get words clear. My staff know that, so sometimes they will bring a report or letter to me and say, "Help me make sure this sounds O.K. before I send it," thinking they can just stand at my desk and I'll do it. But I can't do it that way. I have to ask a lot of questions to be sure I completely understand the situation. And then I pull out the red pen and start going through it—"You might say this in a different way; you might use this word here; it would be a more logical flow if . . ." Sometimes all they wanted to know was, "Is the grammar O.K.?"

Words Used Frequently by Mental-Physical People

plan	precise	future	see
logical	value	assessment	objective (in both senses)
focus	principle	information	
structure	literal	point	vision
perspective	idea	definition	purpose
visual	decision	why	clear
example	mental	essential	

The Challenge of Teamwork

Because mental-physical people are so few in number, teams commonly have only one mental-physical representative or none at all. In the latter case, teams can benefit from either appointing an individual to compensate for the missing function, or alerting themselves as a group to do so.

Mental-physical people offer to teams their capacities for long-range planning, detached observation, and objective assessment. They also ensure that values, vision, and principles are clearly established in any endeavor and that these are kept at the surface as the group proceeds so that decisions accord with the group's larger purposes and values. Because of their affinity for structure, they can offer a logical plan for the team to follow, and they are usually adept at organizing the results of a team's interactions into a clarifying structure, either during the team process or at its end. They usually have a keen sense of what is essential.

Mental-physical people are sometimes very quiet in team or group situations. One reason for this is that they are usually not concerned with having their own voice heard, provided that the purpose of the meeting is being served. If they feel that what needs to be said is being said, they remain silent.

Sometimes mental-physical people are quiet because they are unaware of the contribution they can make:

> I used to think that what was clear to me was clear to everyone else, so I didn't say anything. When I eventually realized that this was not necessarily the case, I began to intervene more often. Now I try to ensure that everyone at the table is clear on points that are being made or issues that are emerging. I want to be sure that everyone shares the same understanding of words and phrases. And I'm more likely to say something if I feel that the discussion is going off track.

Another reason that mental-physical people may be quiet in group sessions is that they prefer to think through the issues carefully, and then speak deliberately in completed thoughts. This can make it difficult for them to find an opening in the flow of a lively discussion. By the time they are ready to make a comment and a space is open, the moment for intervention may have passed.

Most mental-physical people do not enjoy a brainstorming process unless it is conducted in a relatively methodical manner. And those who do can only participate with comfort if they know they will have time later to reflect on the outcomes and give further input before final conclusions are reached or irreversible decisions are made. Engaging in a more spontaneous process is a skill mental-physical people may need to develop over time. Other participants can help them by recognizing the possibility of this difficulty and consciously making space for their contribution.

While it may not be easy for mental-physical people to problem-solve in the context of a free-flowing discussion, they usually sense immediately if a point is not clear or if something is happening that is not in accord with the individual's or group's fundamental principles, guidelines, and values.

"I believe that when others see me as withdrawing, I'm actually listening hard to what's being said and trying to understand what I either agree or disagree with, or where I am on a particular issue, or what principle is involved. In reality, I'm very much with the issue."

They are also usually skilled clarifiers and summarizers of a group's *thinking*, but may not be so aware of the more subtle undercurrents of *feeling*. They are more likely to be attentive to the words themselves and their literal meaning than to the unexpressed feelings behind them. In situations of conflict, however, the relative detachment of mental-physical people can enable them to function as effective mediators who discriminate facts from feelings. They can also often articulate a principle or perspective that accommodates different points of view and establishes unity.

Because mental-physical people do not generally express personal feelings and may also be relatively quiet, others may perceive them as disconnected or uncaring. Emotionally centered people in particular need words to be assured of a connection. To avoid this misunderstanding and foster the comfort of the team, mental-physical people may need to make a conscious effort to share more of what they think and feel.

Equally, other group members can rest assured that when mental-physical people are silent, they are usually connecting mentally with the group process and *do* care about its members and its purposes. If others have any doubt, they should always ask. Because they feel in active participation while they are silent, mental-physical people might not be aware when others want them to communicate more.

Because they are comfortable thinking things through and working alone, many mental-physical people find that a useful strategy for working on a team is to bring the products of their solitary deliberations to the team for discussion, input, and possible amendment, and then work alone again to refine their thinking and pursue new lines of thought that may have opened.

Conditions for Learning

Mental-physical people learn most effectively under certain conditions. These conditions include:

- a clear, logical, structured presentation;
- an overview presented first, then the parts;
- key points articulated;
- the value of the learning and values inherent in the subject matter made clear;
- a visual emphasis (reading is an agreeable learning mode);
- opportunities for solitary work;
- opportunities to participate in dyads after working with the material long enough to feel ready to share and discuss;
- sufficient time available to complete tasks to the individual's satisfaction.

When Something Goes Wrong

A meeting didn't go as well as expected.
A communication was seriously misunderstood.
Plans were changed without everyone being informed.
A project or some part of it fails.

How do mental-physical people respond to such situations? They usually begin with Step 1 of the following sequence and then proceed as far as the level of their development and self-understanding permits. However, individuals often stop at the earlier steps and rarely reach Step 4.

Step 1

When something goes wrong, mental-physical people first step back and look at the facts. They try to see the interaction of the different elements, the flaws in planning, and the "logic" in the sequence or interaction of elements that led to the unfortunate outcome. Are there principles to be discerned as guidelines for the future?

Often, analysis stops here.

Step 2

Next, they examine their own role closely. In their perfectionist way, they want to know what they might have done to bring about a more desirable result. They also want to discern any personal lessons in the incident. Are there principles to be derived as guidelines for their own future thinking and behavior?

Sometimes, analysis stops here.

Step 3

They apply the same scrutiny to the other parties involved and ask what *they* might do differently in the future to bring about a better result. Are there principles to be derived and communicated for others to follow in the future? *Analysis rarely continues to this point. But if it does, one more step remains if full understanding is to occur.*

Step 4

They look at the situation as a whole and try to see what steps, if any, should be taken to deal with the situation and continue moving toward long-term goals. What are the operational principles for future individual and collective functioning that will ensure better results? This reevaluation includes examining the self, others, and the situation.

It is rare for anyone to engage in the whole sequence consistently.

Mental-Physical Characteristics: A Summary

Qualities

- objective
- focused
- calm
- reliable
- precise
- consistent
- independent, while respecting the principle of unity

Basic Learning Process

- linear
- visual
- solitary
- interactive with subject
- selective: intake depends on values and purposes

Management Process

- directive
- work closely with one other person or with a small group
- delegate management of people and tasks, while maintaining overall direction
- sometimes unaware of the effect of decisions and timing upon others
- may need some help with "people issues," personal communication and flexibility

Values and Affinities

- objectivity
- clarity of vision
- long-range perspective
- quality
- logical thinking
- precision
- attention to detail

Function

- articulate values, vision, principles
- maintain overview, perspective
- ensure long-range strategic planning
- set structure
- set standards
- formulate precise, objective communication
- determine overarching values and common ground

Interpersonal Relationships

- reliable
- consistent
- rarely expressive of feelings
- feelings subordinate to tasks
- use words carefully
- may need help connecting with others personally

Factors Causing Stress
- insufficient time alone
- too many tasks at once
- insufficient time for careful consideration of issues and for task completion
- conflict with personal values

Body Movements
- restrained
- often in the vertical plane (up and down)
- upright posture

Eyes
- focused
- objective
- observing

Hands
- used with restraint
- used to make points

As we go further into space and look down onto the earth,
we see it whole, not fragmented as it appears from here . . .

This, I feel, in the end will contribute to a unified view
of human diversities designed not for conflict and
fragmentation on earth, but to enrich our meaning
in a common preparation for our journey to the stars.

—Laurens van der Post

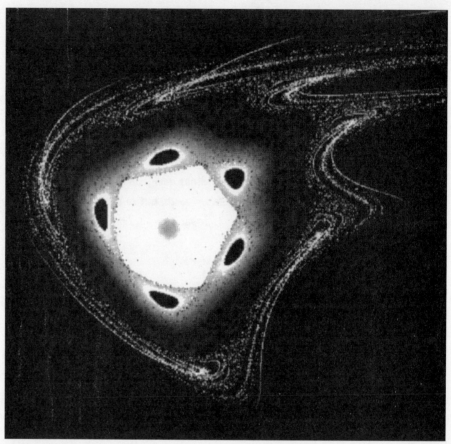

Capacities
Emotional-Objective

- To move events forward.
- To sense the emergent directions and new possibilities in events, individuals, and groups.
- To challenge inertia by breaking through old forms.
- To participate in helping build new forms with others.
- To deeply understand that nothing of real value can be created and sustained without collaborative effort.

- *To be teachers of both innovation and qualitative group life, by example.*

The Emotional-Objective Personality Dynamic: Movement Forward

CHAPTER

6

The following is a story about the capacity to initiate—to move something new forward. It's about the intuition to sense the need for change and the urge to begin the process—even without having all the necessary data or knowing completely how to do what is needed. And in the end, it's about how my "way of being" moves through change and how that change is sustained within a large organization.

The story begins in the spring of 1990. At that time, I had been designing and implementing new methods for Systems Engineering in the networking software segment of a large multinational corporation. This work of systems specification, design, development, and testing had been ongoing for about five years. New roles for people were also being designed—systems project leadership, systems technical leadership, and program management—in addition to the existing component product focused roles. That spring, a colleague sent me a copy of Peter Checkland's *Systems Thinking, Systems Practice*. I read the first twenty pages and knew that what we were really trying to create was a shift toward systems thinking!

In August the same year, a colleague urged me to read the newly published book *The Fifth Discipline*, by Peter Senge, and so I did. I couldn't put it down! I read it cover to cover in four days, bought several copies, and gave them away to key people I worked with all over the company. Now I was really convinced that systems thinking was what we were trying to do. I couldn't stop talking to people about Senge's work and soon began experimenting quite successfully with different ways of implementing some of the five disciplines for the specific needs of our business environment.

In the spring of 1991, a colleague gave me a copy of Chris Argyris' *Overcoming Organizational Defenses*. I began reading it one weekend and got about halfway through before I had to *do* something! The book named the "undiscussables" and explained how the key issues that people do not surface for fear of unpleasant consequences (real or imagined) often result in even worse unintended consequences for all.

For the rest of 1991, I was busy with a large-scale visioning process for the Networks group. But I continued to mull over how to begin the "undiscussables" work. Late that fall the opening came. While we were having some successes with improving quality and time-to-market, our VPs wanted more. So I went back and finished reading Argyris' book—in fact I reread the entire book and was able to design a simple, safe, and very effective process by which we were able to surface some of the key undiscussables in the group. We implemented this process over the next six months, involving over 200 people (at all levels and in all roles) in open dialogue with the management team.

In August of 1992, I decided to give a copy of Argyris' book to the group VP, timing the gift carefully for the day before he left on a week's vacation. He read the entire book and immediately saw its significance for our business. When he returned from his vacation, he spent an hour and a half at his next staff meeting talking about what he had learned. He was very eager for everyone in his group to share in this learning and asked me to prepare a seminar and to order copies of the book for everyone. This presented a dilemma: first because I had just participated in a five-day Human Dynamics seminar and now believed Human Dynamics to be foundational to addressing the "undiscussables"; and second because I still didn't know the Argyris material well, though everybody thought I did because I'd been talking about it for eighteen months!

I studied the book a third time, and prepared an introductory seminar. I called Chris Argyris—who willingly reviewed the presentation—and then I proceeded to deliver the seminar with good results. We also launched the foundational understandings of Human Dynamics. At the same time, I developed a working relationship with an experienced practitioner of Argyris' concepts. He himself participated in a Human Dynamics seminar in April 1994. Together we have noticed that perhaps half or more of the "undiscussables" are linked directly to unacknowledged distinctions in personality dynamics. I therefore have a deep need to connect these two important bodies of work. This is exciting, as it is a completely new and very challenging project with powerful ramifications that are as yet unknown.

I see that I sustain work of value to me through a constant alertness for windows of opportunity. I sustain the Human Dynamics work in the same way, but with the additional direct involvement of being a facilitator of workshops. I am now looking for an opportunity to initiate a pilot project with a team that already works with Human Dynamics and that wants to build the Argyris understandings on top of that. If this happens, we can take new, firmer, and more sustainable steps toward meeting our goals as a division and as a company.

—CHRIS STRUTT, CONSULTING ENGINEER,
DIGITAL EQUIPMENT CORPORATION

Movement Forward:
A Metatheme for Emotional-Objective People

Keeping events moving forward is a sacred trust for emotional-objective people—a theme played out in a multitude of forms, depending on the circumstances and the maturity of the individual. It may be expressed in an individual's constant inner imperative to set new goals and gather new experiences over the course of a lifetime, or it may show up in taking actions to move a meeting forward, initiate a brainstorming session, or generally "make things happen" in an organization.

One distinctive way in which emotional-objective people move events forward is by spontaneously helping people come together to share ideas or create effective alliances. They typically say such things as, "You could have a fruitful discussion with Jim Hathaway or Jane Fields about that issue," or "Diana Ferguson could help you with that," and immediately provide telephone numbers or suggestions for making the connection.

Because emotional-objective people focus on the *initiation* of new movement, beginnings are often easier for them than endings. Many emotional-objective people create wonderful launching pads for new projects, but once the project is under way may lose enthusiasm because they want to move on to the next new endeavor. Careful planning and attention to detail tend to test their patience. Emotional-objective people who take projects from beginning to end are those who are mature in their development.

It is sometimes difficult for emotional-objective people *not* to be engaged in activity. Their natural tendency is to think and act quickly, so

> "Many people feel their intuitions as a kind of signal in space or in their gut. My intuition is in my feet! I experience it as a kind of inner-directed urge to move that I have learned to trust, although often I don't know consciously exactly where I'm going."

stopping to spend time in reflection, assessment, and silence may have little appeal for the "young" emotional-objective personality. For one thing, stopping to reflect may invite awareness of not only the *possibilities* that exist in any given moment, but also the *limitations*. Emotional-objective people are often so focused on the opportunities they perceive and on moving forward to realize them that they fail to recognize evidence of inherent problems. In this sense, they can be "blinded by the light." They may not even *want* to see limitations, because grappling with them stops their movement onward—their strongest instinct and greatest joy.

Recurrent Dream

Behind the movement that characterizes emotional-objective people is a deep impulse to advance life as a whole along the path of evolution. As they mature, they seek to initiate changes that have broader and deeper implications for the good of the whole. On an interpersonal level this may include helping others evolve through progressive states of awareness from unconsciousness to self-consciousness to self-empowerment. The following recurrent dream of an emotional-objective woman illustrates this desire to help others move along in their development.

"I am in a foreign land that looks and feels like a Third World country. An older woman is sitting on the ground, pounding corn. I am moved by the simplicity, grace, and timelessness of the movement. But I am also saddened by the fact that she has been sitting there for so many years, repeating the same thing.

"I say to her, 'You need to stand up!' and she replies that she cannot; she doesn't know how. I say again, in a stronger voice, 'Stand up,' and after a while, she does.

"Time passes. She is still standing. I say to her. 'Walk! You are to walk!' She tells me that she cannot walk. This time I almost command, 'Walk! You must walk now!' And she begins to walk.

"Then I say, 'Now it's time for you to fly. You can fly!' And again, she doesn't believe that she can do it. This time, my voice is gentle. I say to her, 'I know you can fly. Believe in yourself, and in what you need to do.' She looks at me and smiles. She shows a new strength and confidence. Though she does not actually fly, I know that she will continue to grow and to risk more."

Time: "Tomorrow Is Today"

Emotional-objective people experience time as clock time, ticking away moment by moment. They are continually aware that each day, with all its opportunities, will never come again. Whether consciously or not, they carry the sense that life on earth is finite, that they will live but a certain number of years, and that in that limited time there is much to achieve—for themselves, for their families, and, depending on their maturity, for the larger human community.

This sense of urgency concerning time in part accounts *for* their need to push events forward and in part results *from* their need to do so. It has advantages, driving them to achieve much, but sometimes at the expense of their own well-being, their patience with others, and their ability to relax. Because their inner clock tells them that tomorrow will bring new challenges, emotional-objective people feel compelled to clear each day's agenda, no matter what it takes, so that tomorrow will not be hindered by yesterday's "unfinished business." This compulsion can make it difficult for them to strike a comfortable balance between the demands of family and job, between work and play, between the achievement of goals and the *process* of living.

Paradoxically perhaps, emotional-objective people seem best able to escape the insistent pressure of clock time by deliberately adding further commitments to their agendas in the form of periods of time for contemplation, reflection, or meditation. When these periods are part of their schedule, they can relax sufficiently to move into a more timeless experience. They generally find it easier to be at one extreme or the other: intensely active or totally relaxed; intensely aware of the passage of time or completely absorbed in timelessness.

**I am being driven forward
Into an unknown land.
The pass grows steeper,
The air colder and sharper.
A wind from my unknown goal
Stirs the strings
Of expectation.**

**Still the question:
Shall I ever get there?
There where life resounds,
A clear pure note
In the silence.**

—Dag Hammarskjöld

Work First, Play Later!

"I've learned in giving workshops to structure things so that, rather than setting a particular time for a break, I allow a block of time that includes both a task and a break; people can take the break at whatever point they choose. This arrangement suits everybody. In my experience, when a group is working on a task, and I say, 'You've got to report out in forty-five minutes, and in that time you can take a

> break,' half the room empties out at once, and the other half stays. And you can guess which half stays. The emotional-objective people don't move. They don't even talk about whether they'll take a break. It's work first and play later!"

Change: "Let's Go!"

Emotional-objective people relish change, a corollary of forward movement. Indeed, they often *initiate* change—they light the fires of new endeavors and begin movement into unknown territory. Typically, they become bored by repetition. They discard the customary in favor of something innovative, or they at least find new ways of doing old things.

In their enthusiasm for change, emotional-objective people may unwittingly upset the members of other personality dynamic groups, who usually need more time before they are ready to institute change. Emotional-*subjective* people, for example, *feel* the impact of proposed change; they experience physical tension because of the uncertainties inherent in change and the possible effects on the people involved, including themselves. They need time to assess the new situation, process their feelings, and become comfortable before moving into action. Mental-physical people need time to evaluate carefully the nature of the proposed changes, to examine their consequences, and to reassure themselves that the results will serve long-term values and principles. And neither of the two physically centered groups will be ready to implement change until they understand its systemic ramifications and are assured of its benefits for the whole. They will want a detailed operational plan to be in place, so as to minimize subsequent adjustments because they know that change and subsequent adjustments always affect a system of interrelated parts.

In contrast, emotional-objective people prefer to move into action quickly, provoke new events, examine the results, and then make adjustments accordingly. They make their initial thrusts into the future with minimal data, gathering more along the way.

Each personality dynamic's approach to change has its advantages and liabilities. The following is an excerpt from an article written in *LA Times Magazine* about the first months in office of U.S. president Bill Clinton, a

We are now faced with the fact that tomorrow is today. We are confronted with the fierce urgency of now. In this unfolding conundrum of life and history there is such a thing as being too late.

—Martin Luther King, Jr.

leader we believe to be emotional-objective:

> In speaking about lessons learned from his first six months in office, the President claims a new appreciation of the importance of what he calls process. . . .
>
> To quote President Clinton directly: "I think that, if I can use a business analogy, my product jumped ahead of my process. That is, I think a lot of the mistakes I made early on in this office, which led to some not very favorable press, were legitimate mistakes, but they were more mistakes of process than product. I think if you started any vast enterprise like this and you really tried to push your 'product' to market in a hurry—your processes wouldn't be quite worked out. Particularly if you were new in town. . . .
>
> "I think I should have started a little more slowly and spent more time just in interpersonal relationships with people than I did. But I was in a hurry to get started." As one presidential scholar stated, "Clinton is a results guy who focuses on making things happen."

In this instance, an emotional-objective leader belatedly recognized the need to slow down and ensure that others involved were comfortably aboard before pushing ahead with his plans.

Windows of Opportunity

When an emotional-objective person sees a window of opportunity regarding something he or she cares about, movement is immediate, as the following story illustrates:

"A number of times in my career, I have leapt first and picked up the pieces later. I don't leap without any consideration at all—it is a kind of cerebral leap. I will mentally scan the landscape and make sure that I feel comfortable getting from here to there, and then I jump. But I still leave some people scratching their heads. Why would I give up 'security' to risk something new? For me, something new is always what I'm looking for. I've always needed to have a new job every year and a half. If I didn't, I'd be bored.

"When an opportunity that is close to my heart presents itself and comes from a credible source, I may not collect all the details. I feel the calling to move. I had the opportunity recently to play a major community development role in a large city in the United States. I asked only a few questions before taking the job. I didn't know fully what would be required of me, or even how many hours a week would be involved. But because I know that timing is everything, I wasn't going to let this opportunity slide by, even if I didn't have all the facts. I'd rather cut back on my time later than let a window of opportunity go by that's linked to something I'm passionate about. I would rather say, 'Yes, I can do that!'"

Challenge: "We Can Do It!"

Clearly, emotional-objective people are natural "movers and shakers." The new is far more interesting to them than the known. Challenge and risk excite them.

Emotional-objective people respond to challenge with relative ease because they solve problems conceptually, as if they were seeing them from some distance. They therefore feel less personal risk or vulnerability than others might. For this reason, and because they tend to see possibilities rather than liabilities, their self-confidence usually runs high, and they have little doubt they can meet their commitments. The following excerpt from an interview with two emotional-objective people illustrates this point, among others:

"It is thrilling to feel oneself always on the edge of a moving line. The movement to purposeful activity is where my spirit lies."

John: Where does my confidence come from? I'm not sure if I have confidence in *myself* in particular or if it's confidence in the fact that *anyone* can do anything that they decide to do. I can't separate it out.

Jane: I don't really think that it's personal confidence. It's a kind of intuitive certainty reinforced by experience that hard work will move almost anything forward.

John: I find that I sense the appropriate direction and pace for projects. Some things need to be done immediately and then they are finished, so to speak. Other projects need to be carried on for years.

Jane: Yes. I feel as if my body carries a sense for the short-term future. I sometimes "know" that I have to finish something *now* because ten things are going to happen tomorrow, and I have to create the space for them. Or I'll have a sense that I can linger a bit longer. It's totally intuitive.

John: I know when I feel that urgency to move something, it's usually very accurate.

Jane: When I know that something needs to be done, I feel tension building in my body. Once the work is completed, the tension dissipates completely.

Welcoming challenge can lead to problems for emotional-objective people. They may respond to its siren call without sufficiently considering an endeavor's value, consequences, or likelihood of success. They may even consciously or unconsciously create crises to have a challenge to meet.

Emotional-objective people's need for challenge may be met in a variety of ways ranging from competition with others, to expanding their skills, to exploring the unknown. In their maturity they assume the challenge of serving for the common good.

The Catalina Challenge

One emotional-objective person, Richard, decided to get back into shape by swimming in a neighborhood pool. At first he could hardly swim 100 yards, but he challenged himself to swim just a little farther each day. Two months after he began training, he overcame his lifelong fears of drowning and swam three miles in the ocean. Later he swam 10 miles. Then he set the goal of swimming across the 30-mile channel that separates the coast of southern California from Catalina Island.

"My experiences up to this point had supported my belief that human capacity is almost limitless. I saw that if I set myself a challenge and worked toward it in a disciplined way, I could keep expanding my capacities. I have never been exceptionally athletic, but I can succeed athletically if I commit to a goal and time line.

"On August 31, 1981, I purchased a one-way ticket on the big ferry to Catalina. I would swim back the next day in a race between myself and one other person. The weather was turbulent and threatened to be the same that night and the following day.

"We left Catalina at 2:00 A.M. It was dark and cold. I asked myself if I wasn't completely crazy to even consider swimming thirty miles in the ocean at night in poor weather—a swim that would take eleven and a half hours. Who does anything strenuous consistently for eleven and a half hours? But off we went. I observed my mind at work questioning my capacity to accomplish this goal. But then I fell into the rhythm of one stroke at a time, one mantra, one song, one thought. The experience was a kind of meditation—a breathing meditation. The simplicity of focusing completely on one event, one process, is quite extraordinary!

"I could have won the race, but I lost by less than a minute because my focus was not on winning, but on completing the race. I am still learning that if you do not approach life to win—meaning, to give it your very best—then you are approaching it to lose. This has been one of the most important lessons of my life. It's not that I want to 'beat' the other person, but I need to know I have done *all* I could to move ahead. If I give *everything* I can, whether in work, a physical endeavor, or a relationship, I feel that I have won a victory—a victory in not holding back. Then I have no regrets."

Risk: The Love of Adventure

Challenge is one thing; risk is another. Most emotional-objective people have a relationship to both. Their love of adventure often drives them to take risks, sometimes involving physical danger. James, a 40-year-old emotional-objective university professor, describes his relationship to risk:

I have become much more aware in the last couple of years of how crazy I can be in taking risks! At one time, I didn't even know the meaning of risk. What risk? For example, years ago, I was cross-country skiing around an alpine lake in the Austrian mountains. I really wanted to ski around the back side of this lake. It was probably only five miles in distance, but there was no road around the lake, and the mountainsides were very steep—literally diving right down to the lake shore. My wife and a friend of hers were with me. After about fifteen or twenty minutes of skiing, the ground got steeper and steeper, and my wife and her friend went back. They thought it was crazy to go further.

By this time, I was probably two or three hundred feet above the surface of the water. I had to dig the edges of my skis hard into the slope to keep moving. Finally, it got so steep that I started sliding, out of control. I managed to catch myself in a tree, and as I hung there with my skis dangling, I suddenly realized that I was in big trouble. I was looking almost straight down between my feet onto the rocky shoreline way below!

Finally, while dangling in this tree, I very carefully took off my skis and dug them into the snow. Then I made footholds with my ski poles so I could climb out. It took me about an hour and a half to get out of the tree. And then I had to go about ten more feet to reach a slope where I wouldn't slide anymore. It was a classic example of my being incredibly out of touch. I hate to say this, but I've operated like this for many years!

An apt description of emotional-objective people is that they "follow the wind." Though the wind may blow them into uncharted waters or close to dangerous rocks, they are still compelled to follow. Many emotional-objective people possess only a tiny "seed" of caution, which they bring to flower through their lifetime experiences.

For without belittling the courage with which men have died, we should not forget those acts of courage with which men have lived. . . . A man does what he must—in spite of personal consequences, in spite of obstacles and dangers and pressures, and that is the basis of all human morality.

—John F. Kennedy

Patterns and Rules: Guiding Structures

Rules, whether unwritten, such as those that govern personal relationships, or more formal, such as those of a game, provide structures that enable individuals and groups to function more efficiently, fairly, and harmoniously. They impose order on what might otherwise be chaotic. Perhaps *because* emotional-objective people are so open to challenge and change, they appreciate having a guiding structure of patterns and rules. Whether at home or at work, they usually conduct their lives according to a simple set of rules.

It's really important for me to have a few principles, along with a few rules, that totally ground my world. For example, I don't change things around in my home very often, because I feel I'm embroiled in change so much in the outside world. There are rules about where you put your scissors—you put them back in the same place all the time, and you ask others to do the same. There are rules for where things belong, and there are principles of comportment in your relationships with other people. And, there are rules and principles guiding how you and others collaborate in order to work effectively, efficiently, and joyfully. They provide a grounding pattern that is reliable and helps stabilize my movement into change.

Emotional-objective people share an intrinsic capacity to create simple designs through which to establish order. They do this in part because they see basic patterns easily. They use their imaginations to create simple and useful models that serve the needs of the moment, but that may be reworked later. They tend to value simplicity, and simplify where they can.

To emotional-objective people, the architectural structure of a home, for example, is often more important than the diversity of its furnishings. They tend to favor simple, clean designs that afford both space and light, and they typically prefer a minimum of decoration and memorabilia. They often structure their lives around a few basic routines. For example, they usually don't seek variety in food or clothing and they typically apply the same simplicity of design to their own lives. This frees them to concentrate on their endeavors.

As agents of change, however, emotional-objective people seek to break patterns and modify rules that they feel no longer serve the needs of the present or the future.

Brainstorming and Experimentation

Emotional-objective people gain great pleasure from involving themselves with others in an active exchange of ideas. They find the process of brainstorming particularly exciting. As one idea stimulates another, they discover new dimensions of thought that may not have occurred to them before and new possibilities for active experimentation. They typically gravitate toward flip charts, in part because these tools serve as memory containers and organizers for the abundance of ideas that brainstorming sessions produce.

Brainstorming can be seen as a form of verbal experimentation. Emotional-objective people love to experiment: indeed, they need to experiment in order to learn, develop, and feel alive. Whether in the context of their organizations or in their personal lives, emotional-objective people need to try out new ideas to see what happens, or move toward desired results by trying out new ideas. This process simultaneously energizes them and provides outlets for their energy. While the other personality dynamics usually take action only after they see clearly what needs to be done, emotional-objective people need to *act first* in order to see what is needed. Often they like to do their experimenting with a group. Especially as they mature, they recognize that effective action usually requires collaborative effort. The group also acts as a mirror, reflecting back to them the advantages and limitations of their plans and ideas.

Experimentation leads to changed situations, which lead to new ideas and the creation of new models and new experiments, which lead to further change, and so on. From this cyclical process of trial and adjustment, emotional-objective people gradually shape a consistent direction and form structures and procedures for pursuing goals most effectively. When this process has yielded a sufficiently satisfying end result, they typically move on to new endeavors, sometimes delegating more detailed implementation to others.

Model-Making: Simplifying Ideas

Emotional-objective people often find themselves creating models as personal tools that help them simplify the complexity of their ideas, concretize the abstract, form new ideas, and plan their experiments. Models also constitute aids to learning, teaching, and communicating. They are usually not very detailed, unless they are to become the basis for putting ideas into action, in which case emotional-objective people are likely to add more detail until eventually the model acquires the substance of an action plan.

Before settling on a final model, emotional-objective people create many little forms: "Let's do it this way; let's try it that way and see how it works." If part of the model works and part of it doesn't, they reshape it, knowing all the while that any form is going to change. In short, they constantly try to find the form that works best for that moment, knowing that the future's requirements and characteristics cannot be fully anticipated. Therefore, even the form of a "final" model is likely to be regarded as fluid and open to change.

Sometimes emotional-objective people are surprised to find that others

The country needs, and unless I mistake its temper, the country demands bold, persistent experimentation. It is common sense to take a method and try it. If it fails, admit it frankly, and try another. But above all, try something.

—*Franklin D. Roosevelt*

may not appreciate their models because, being designed to indicate general movements rather than detailed systems of operation, the models are too abstract and require considerable explanation. They may also not be appreciated for another reason. Emotional-objective people sometimes feel they have actually solved a problem or taken action simply by creating their model because the process has felt so satisfying. For example, one 50-year-old emotional-objective man described how he had been unable to understand the marriage problems that were tearing his wife and him apart. So one night he stayed up late and created a diagram that represented the interplay of all the major themes and subthemes of their relationship.

> I then identified the various possible outcomes depending upon the path of action taken. It took me all night. I felt a hundred percent better. The problems were clarified, and I felt almost as though they had been solved.
>
> In the morning I showed the model to my wife. I guess she doesn't learn the way I do, because she was furious! First of all, she couldn't understand the model. And second, she was upset because in my naiveté I felt that some of the issues between us had been simplified. In fact, it was only my *understanding* of them that was simplified. The issues between us remained the same.

Teamwork: Valuing Collaboration

Emotional-objective people's gifts for seizing the moment and for innovative thinking lend themselves to entrepreneurship, and many emotional-objective people enjoy the freedom of working independently. As they mature, however, they come to understand the value of teamwork. They recognize that endeavors of any consequence require both the labor and the creative synergy of a group. This realization comes from a deep conviction that nothing of *real* value can be created and sustained without collaboration.

For example, Penny is an emotional-objective consultant in the health-care field who was originally trained as a nurse. Working in a hospital early in her career, Penny had the opportunity to participate in creating a city-wide plan for responding to disasters. Her group put together a comprehensive trauma-response procedure, complete with an emergency triage team. Some months after they had completed their planning, an aluminum company exploded a few blocks from the hospital. The explosion was so massive, it could be heard 50 miles away.

> We quickly mobilized our triage team, activated our call system, and went out to the site. Our plan worked perfectly! With five physicians and five nurses, we got everybody organized, took them back to the hospital, and triaged the injured. Within the hospital, other teams were at work. One group sent some patients directly into surgery, while others were sent to the intensive care unit. Another team identified those who were emotionally but not physically traumatized and referred them to social workers.
>
> While I don't usually remember details, I remember that day vividly. The most memorable part for me was not so much the disaster itself as the experience of great teamwork. I have even had recurring dreams about this event. In the dreams, I am creating better ways to mobilize and empower larger working teams.

For the mature emotional-objective personality, *empowering* teams is even more satisfying than working *with* teams. Of course, this impulse is not the exclusive property of those who are emotional-objective. Any mature person will always want to empower others. But a passion for and enjoyment of this process seems to be a particular mark of mature emotional-objective people:

> I don't catch fish . . . I spend some of my time showing people how to catch fish with the tools they have and the rest of my time designing better fishing rods for them. But even those two things aren't the most important things I do. The best leverage for the group comes from my spending time helping people figure out whether they should be fishing in the first place—or whether they should be out hunting bear instead!

Because the ability to work successfully with teams is a complex skill that can be developed only through experience, emotional-objective people need to take every opportunity to practice it. Through sensitive participation in teams, they will learn that people's feelings play as important a role in teamwork as their ideas, and that they must therefore cultivate their awareness of the feelings and emotional needs of others, enhance their patience to allow feelings to be expressed, and open themselves to sensing feelings that may lie unspoken behind the words—train their "intuitive ears" to hear *intent* as well as *content* in communication.

Emotional-objective people naturally bring to teams their gifts for innovative thinking, problem-solving, risk-taking, and moving events forward. In working *with* and learning to empower teams, they must develop an appreciation for the contribution of personality dynamics different from their own, for those who may have a keener intuitive awareness of "people issues" than they do, and those who may work more carefully and systematically. As emotional-objective people grow in these ways, they are not compromising their capacity for moving things forward. On the contrary, they are ensuring that the team functions with maximum efficiency as a unit, that decisions are qualitative because of diverse input, and that the decisions will be effectively carried out because all of the members have been fully involved in their formulation.

With maturity, emotional-objective people grow increasingly sensitive to the next steps needed for the personal development of other people. Their capacity to move events forward develops into a deep inner drive to help others realize their potential more fully. In doing so, they more fully realize their own.

Communication: The Dance of Ideas

Because emotional-objective people are inherently relational, they prefer face-to-face communication to writing. They like the immediacy of response and opportunity to engage in spontaneous discussion that personal encounters afford. Since their communication tends to jump from idea to idea, person-to-person exchanges offer them the opportunity to elaborate their statements and fill in "gaps" in light of the responses and questions they receive. Face-to-face exchange with others also facilitates their flow of ideas—many emotional-objective people have commented on their astonishment at hearing themselves articulate ideas in the heat of discussion that they had never expressed or even consciously considered before, almost as if they were listening to someone else talking.

For the same reasons, emotional-objective people prefer discussion to making formal one-way speeches or presentations. They like communication that has the high energy and back-and-forth quality of a ping-pong game or tennis match—not necessarily interpersonal and sharing feelings, as emotional-subjective people prefer, but interactive in enthusiastically exchanging ideas.

Emotional-objective people usually like communication to be handled in a straightforward, direct, and objective manner. They typically do not hesitate to give directives and usually receive them without resentment, as long as there is a sense of mutually contributing to moving events forward. While subjective reflection is not absent, the focus of their attention is on outer problem-solving, on establishing the direction and the movement needed to reach a goal.

Because emotional-objective people tend to direct all their energy at one or two points and express their ideas with great enthusiasm, their communication tends to be intense. Others can experience this intensity as meaning that emotional-objective people believe only *their* ideas to be valid, and that they are not open to discussion. In fact, emotional-objective people are usually putting their ideas out as an offering to evoke discussion. They can be as enthusiastic about someone else's ideas as their own. They generally enjoy debate and challenge, provided they feel that others are sincere in their arguments and genuinely interested in finding the best solutions to problems.

Learning to Listen

"I learned the value of listening from an experience I had when I was a teenager. I served on a community hotline, and one time somebody called up and threatened suicide. At one point in the conversation, I started talking, probably for a couple of minutes, about how to solve her problem. At the end of my statement, there was complete silence. I was scared—had she killed herself?

"Finally she said, 'You know, you haven't listened to me. You haven't really *heard* what I'm saying.' When I got off the phone, I was really down because I couldn't figure out how she could say that to me. It finally struck me that she didn't want me to solve her problem. She just wanted me to hear and connect with her, not put my own little spin on her particular situation. Since then, I've tried to be a better listener."

> ### *Tunnel Vision*
>
> **Jane:** This tunnel vision thing is very interesting. When I focus on something, everything else disappears. All my energy is intensely focused on that one project. I can lose my peripheral vision.
>
> **John:** One time, we were meeting some friends for brunch at a hotel. We walked up to them, and I asked, "Where are the children?" And they were standing at the feet of their father, right in front of me! They were small, but they were right there—two of them, standing at his side, and I had not seen them!
>
> **Jane:** It has to do with intensity of focus.
>
> **John:** And people can interpret that as being rude.
>
> **Jane:** Right. I may not detach from a conversation to acknowledge somebody who's just walked in.
>
> **John:** I've learned how to do it better, because people get hurt, and that doesn't feel good to me or to them.
>
> **Jane:** It's a way of functioning. It's full engagement, moment by moment, with the feeling inside of wanting to complete something so that we can move on.
>
> **John:** And if you're stopped in the middle, it doesn't feel comfortable.

Their appreciation of direct, even challenging, communication may be illustrated by the following anecdote, supplied by an emotional-subjective manager who had identified his immediate boss as emotional-objective:

As a result of the Human Dynamics seminar, I began speaking to my boss in a slightly different manner. I term it a more "heroic" language. In trying to convince him of my point of view, I remember saying to him, "I would *stake my career* on the fact that systems thinking is foundational to building a learning organization!" I deliberately used that phrase, *"I would stake my career,"* as I saw that he was pleased with the challenge I proposed. In fact, it was true that I would stake my career, but I ordinarily don't speak in that manner. I felt that I was practicing a new language.

Since my initial language adjustment clearly gained his attention, I concluded our talk by saying that he could measure my success through the outcomes produced by the groups I was working with. I have continued to use language that is positive, direct, honest, and, when necessary, challenging.

As I look back over our relationship, I can see that the messages I now deliver to him are not new. However, the presentation of my messages is new. It has really helped in creating better communication between us.

The impression of an irresistible force that emotional-objective people sometimes give in their communication is heightened by their inclination to paint their verbal pictures in broad strokes, omitting all but the most essential details. Often they attempt to deliver their message through an image or symbol that, for them, conveys the whole story. Emotional-objective people usually understand and enjoy this kind of shorthand communication, though others may judge it insubstantial, insufficiently "grounded," and moving too quickly to conclusions. As they participate in an exchange, they tend to tune in less to the literal meaning of words than to signals regarding new possibilities. These signals may lie unspoken behind the words and may not be evident even to the speaker.

To make a musical analogy, any note produced by a musical instrument is accompanied by a number of "overtones," which only people with trained ears may detect. One could say that each personality dynamic seems to be sensitive to the "overtones" in communication in a unique way. Emotional-*subjective* people, for example, often register unspoken feelings vibrating behind spoken words. Emotional-*objective* people are attuned to overtones that suggest new possibilities and opportunities. To give a simple example, Bob is listening to a subordinate, Dan, who is complaining about a problem he is having with a colleague. On one level, Bob is considering how to respond in a way that would help Dan and his colleague relate better together.

But on another level, he senses the real issue: Dan is not working at an appropriate level in the organization. The problem Dan is articulating is merely a symptom of that deeper issue. Bob sees the opportunity to encourage Dan to seek promotion to a more responsible position, where he would be collaborating with peers, and his gifts would be more fully utilized.

The same phenomenon often comes into play when emotional-objective people are speaking. Though they may not be fully conscious of it, they are often trying to convey two sets of messages in a single strand of communication. For example, on a literal level an emotional-objective person may be discussing a news item that caught her attention, but on another level, she may be hinting at new possibilities suggested by the news item, "overtones" that caught her attention but whose significance she cannot yet clearly articulate.

Each personality dynamic is also sensitive to certain words. A word that has particular resonance for emotional-objective people is *fairness*. Anyone listening carefully to the language of emotional-objective people is likely to hear this word or its equivalent frequently. Its significance is related to their need to establish clear rules and behavioral guidelines, which must be fair. Mutual fairness in establishing and honoring agreements is a key principle for emotional-objective people, opening the door to true collaboration. Therefore, framing issues in terms of fairness uses a language that engages their full attention and interest (as framing issues in terms of values does with the mental-physical, for example). Because everyone can define "fair" differently, both parties need to agree what the term means to them in the context of their situation.

Respect is another concept and term to which emotional-objective people are both sensitive and responsive. In communicating with emotional-objective people, it is important to understand that they are actually more vulnerable than their intensity and drive may cause them to appear. So, although they appreciate direct communication, they can be hurt by what they might experience as an attack on themselves, their work, or their ideas. In fact, because they so identify themselves with their work, to demean an emotional-objective person's work is to demean him or her. Respect is therefore crucial. Emotional-objective people make a clear distinction between opposition that presents different points of view, yet is respectful of them and their efforts, and communication that has a disrespectful, dismissive, or personally hostile quality.

In fact, emotional-objective people may find it harder than emotional-subjective people to cope with a confrontation that is emotionally charged and may be experienced as an attack. Though emotionally centered, they lack the sophisticated emotional circuitry for handling emotions that emotional-subjective people naturally possess. The result can be a kind of paralysis, in which they don't know how to respond.

Blown Circuits

Jane: It is difficult for me to handle things like emotional attack. If somebody comes at me angrily about something I've done wrong, I can freeze up inside because I don't know how to deal with it.

John: Right. It feels to me that it blows my circuits and then all I have is the feeling of blown circuits and not understanding. . . .

Jane: I feel as if I lose my mind.

John: Yes. In order to go on I have to come to some kind of cognitive understanding. I do this through an intense process of inquiry.

Jane: I know that if I talk my heart out to somebody about a misunderstanding, I can walk away feeling better. But if I notice that there is still an "echo" of the incident, I know it's not finished in me, and I will need to discuss it more.

Words Used Frequently by Emotional-Objective People			
new	emergent	risk	model
idea	impatient	interact	rules
brainstorm	begin	independent	fair
innovate	possibilities	enthusiasm	respect
experiment	push forward	intense	let's go!
try	change	direct	great!
unknown	challenge	structure	

Feelings: "Growing" to Know the Subjective World

The feelings and thoughts of emotional-objective people tend to be intertwined. Indeed, it is difficult for emotional-objective people to separate their feelings from their thoughts. What they feel is what they think, and vice versa. In fact, many of their deep feelings are in their ideas!

Because their feelings are directly linked to their ideas, they are usually intensely involved in what they do; they tend to be either fully engaged in a relationship, project, or task, or not engaged at all. Moderation is not particularly their gift. Because, as we have said, their intensity is usually focused outward on problem-solving in the external world, the inner world of personal feelings may be comparatively unknown to them, and substantially undervalued. For example, during a recent Human Dynamics seminar, a young emotional-objective manager, Jim, asked to speak to us privately. He was about 35 years old, modest, vigorous, and engaging. He told us that he was successful in his work, generally well liked, and had numerous friends. He had felt that all was well with his life until about six months ago, when he returned home from work one evening to find that his wife had left him. Because he had been unaware of any significant difficulty between them, he was shocked. Half a year later, he was still in shock and unable to fathom what had gone wrong.

It was evident from our conversation that Jim's essential focus was his work and that he was relatively unconscious of the inner dynamics of human interaction. His world was the objective world "out there." Although he loved his wife deeply, he had clearly failed to connect with her emotionally in a way that she found satisfying. We don't know whether she had tried to explain the problem to him, but if she did, her communication must have been too subtle, for he had clearly not received her messages.

Many other emotional-objective people have described to us the shock of moving confidently into the future and suddenly running into a wall or finding that situations were not as they had supposed. It seems that their single-minded focus, combined with their lack of experience of the subjective world, can foster a naiveté or blindness, of which they are unaware until disaster strikes.

Painful as such experiences may be, emotional-objective people can benefit if they recognize them as a new kind of opportunity—the opportunity to slow down, reflect, and "go inside" to explore the subjective world. It is crucial on such occasions that they do not "recover" too quickly, as they are apt to do, and hurry on. They must find space for reflection, for getting in touch with their own subtle feelings, and for trying to tune into those of others. As they move on with the insights they gain, they will be better able to develop a more personalized mode of communication, and to create relationships with others that take into account feelings as well as results. They may also learn to be less intensely single-focused, and to temper over-optimism with a sufficient degree of caution. These are directions of growth. If they "heal" too quickly, they may fail to learn from the experience, and history will inevitably repeat itself.

Betrayal: The Other Side of Commitment

Emotional-objective people have a deep need and capacity for personal commitment. They put all their energies into their commitments, whether to a value, a principle, an idea, a project, a group, or an individual. If they do not honor their commitments, they feel that they have betrayed themselves. If they believe that others are not equally committed, or that someone has failed to honor a commitment to them, they can feel betrayed. Betrayal is the obverse face of commitment for the emotional-objective. For them, commitment tends to have the binding force of a legal contract, so that no matter how significant or insignificant the circumstances, they may respond to a perceived violation with an extreme sense of betrayal.

When they feel betrayed, emotional-objective people might do well to ask themselves certain questions:

- Have I *really* been betrayed, or am I misinterpreting the situation?
- Did the other person or people really set out to deceive me?
- Did I assume that we had a common understanding when in fact we did not?
- Am I projecting onto another person feelings of disappointment because a cherished project did not work out?
- If another person had some responsibility for a failure, did this really amount to betrayal on their part?
- If I was betrayed, do I have some responsibility for this outcome? For example:

  —Did I allow enough time to get to know this person?

  —Did I choose to ignore warning signs?

  —Did I take the time to find out the other's feelings about the process of our relationship as we moved toward our goals?

  —Did I let my optimism cloud my judgment?

  —Do I customarily disregard the shadow side of human nature?

If the experience of betrayal, whether real or imagined, leads to this kind of self-inquiry, it can serve to enhance subjective awareness and lead to greater understanding of human nature. Seen in this light, the experience of betrayal can be redemptive.

The Physical Body: Along for the Ride

Emotional-objective people do not easily register emotional or physical signals in the body. The body is essentially a quiet support, of which they are usually not particularly conscious. When their attention is focused on an activity or project, they may not notice fatigue or even hunger—they are commonly able to miss meals without discomfort. Their bodies are also relatively insensitive to pain (they would say that they have a high pain tolerance), so they may dismiss significant pain signals as slight and unimportant.

With their combination of intense focus—sometimes amounting to tunnel vision—and relative detachment from physical need, emotional-objective people can typically work long hours over extended periods with a zeal and energy that others can only envy. They then typically "collapse," going to the opposite extreme, either doing little or sleeping until they feel restored. Although they can maintain high energy over time, emotional-objective people tend to expend the most energy at the *beginning* of a new experience, the *beginning* of the day, the *beginning* of a project. It is as if they are designed to break through the constraints of established patterns and inertia, like a spaceship using the explosive power of booster rockets to overcome gravity before it can move freely toward its goal.

Emotional-objective people's ability to ignore their bodies' needs and stretch their endurance provides an advantage in the short run, but can create physical difficulties over time. Members of this group typically accumulate tension without knowing it, and their aptitude for forging ahead at full speed sometimes leads to burnout. They accumulate tension unconsciously as they struggle with inertia in themselves and others in breaking old patterns and initiating change. They may not be aware that they also accumulate stress from constantly sensing the immediate future in their bodies. They are in a permanent state of tension from living simultaneously in the present and the anticipated future.

For all of these reasons, stress can build up within emotional-objective bodies, surfacing after many years (sometimes catastrophically) to remind the person that the physical being, not only the mind and the emotions, has been fully involved in their living journey. Emotional-objective people will benefit if they become aware of their tendency to stress themselves, and learn to practice moderation. If they are expending the absolute limit of their energies, then they are probably not working at their best or getting the most out of their creative power. The messages they need to heed are, "Do less," "Don't try so hard," and "Stop more often to enjoy the process, smell the roses, and take the time to *really* experience subtleties and nuances." They must also create a balance in the attention they pay to home, work, friends, recreation, community, and so on. This is a lifelong and crucial task.

Many emotional-objective people like to work off accumulated tension through physical activity and competitive sports. But because they typically regard these activities as challenges and approach them with their usual

> "I wrote my dissertation after 11:00 P.M. every night after my family had gone to sleep. I worked during the day, so I would go to sleep typically at about 4:30 or 5:00 A.M. and get up at 7:00 or 7:30 A.M. On many occasions I would not go to bed until 6:00 A.M., and one morning I didn't make it to bed until 7:15 A.M. I remember that my first thought upon awakening at 7:30 was, 'This is not enough sleep!' I kept this up for six months, and it actually wasn't that hard. About once a week, I would sleep for five or six hours."

intensity, the relief they gain is likely to be incomplete and temporary.

Emotional-objective people in particular benefit from regularly practicing relaxation techniques. At the least, we suggest that they continually work to allow themselves to register and attend to some basic needs. Their emotional-objective bodies would be most appreciative if they would

• eat at least three balanced meals daily;
• allow themselves adequate rest, recreation, and sleep;
• balance their lives with regular pauses and times for reflection;
• slow down; and
• breathe!

Memory: Evanescence

There are always exceptions, of course, but emotional-objective people as a whole remember little of the past. This relative freedom from the weight of memory enables them to move quickly. Each day they feel born anew and eager to initiate new projects, unburdened by recollections of past difficulties or failures (though with maturity they learn to carry with them at least the essential lessons from the past).

"My experience, including memory, is evanescent. It dissipates like a vapor trail, where the beginning is always more pronounced than the tail, but soon vanishes with the rest. This is my experience, except for some moments of high drama that make a lasting impression. Not everything is lost."

Emotional-objective people do have an excellent memory in one respect: the short-term memory needed to accomplish the next steps as they move into the *immediate future*. For example, they can remember—sometimes compulsively—the organizational details required to move a project forward. But once the need for using the information is satisfied, they are likely to let it go.

They do not retain a multitude of factual and sensory details, as do the physically centered groups; nor do they vividly relive the emotional events of the past as if they were happening now, with all the associated feelings, as emotional-subjective people do. The recollections that do persist for them tend to take the form of general impressions, often characterized by certain themes: events in which they took responsibility or felt useful; events in which they advanced dramatically toward their goals or were brought to a painful halt; instances of broken commitments (betrayal); and moments of adventure, challenge, and inspiration.

This relative innocence from detailed memory can be misinterpreted by others as evidence of not caring (especially in the context of personal relationships) or of irresponsibility or lack of groundedness. However, it more accurately reflects their role as shapers of the future rather than guardians of the past.

Conditions for Learning

Emotional-objective individuals learn most effectively under certain conditions. These conditions include:

- a structured, though not extremely detailed, presentation that is brisk, enthusiastic, and inspirational;
- diagrams and models, rather than elaborate verbal explanation;
- movement forward—little repetition;
- purpose of the learning made clear;
- auditory emphasis (opportunities for discussion and debate);
- opportunities for independent and small-group work, followed by sharing the results with the group;
- opportunities for active experimentation;
- connection with the instructor through exchange of ideas and mutual respect;
- open-ended problem-solving.

When Something Goes Wrong

A meeting didn't go as well as expected.

A communication was seriously misunderstood.

Plans were changed without everyone being informed.

A project or some part of it fails.

How do emotional-objective people respond to such situations? They usually begin with Step 1 of the following sequence, then proceed as far as the level of their development and self-understanding permits. However, individuals often stop at the earlier steps and rarely reach Step 4.

Step 1

Their first impulse is to examine the circumstances of the event or situation for the causes of the problem. They ask themselves such questions as, "Was the room too crowded? Did the team have insufficient information? Was too little time available? Did something cause the market to change?"
Often, analysis stops here.

Step 2

They also consider the parts played by the other participants in the drama. They might think, "He talked too much. She strayed from the agenda. Their planning was extremely poor. She was not feeling well."
Sometimes, analysis stops here.

Step 3

They reflect on *their own* contribution to the situation. They begin an inner process. For example, they ask themselves, "Could I have facilitated the process better? Did I make clear what I wanted? Did I allow sufficient time for good planning? Are my priorities valid? Did I try to understand how he or she felt? Did I make my full contribution?" This step of entering into the realm of subjective reality marks a turning point in the growth of emotional-objective people. It is at this point that their consciousness takes a quantum leap.
Analysis rarely continues to this point. But if it does, one more step remains for full understanding to occur.

Step 4

They take the time to examine the situation fully from a perspective gained by undertaking steps 1–3. They thus grasp the whole story, and real learning takes place. Now it is up to them to act upon their new insights.
It is rare for anyone to engage in the whole sequence consistently.

The sequence from steps 1–3 is exactly the opposite of that typically undertaken by emotional-*subjective* people, whose first impulse is to look in the mirror and take the entire responsibility upon themselves (see pp. 148–149).

Emotional-Objective Characteristics: A Summary

Qualities
- animated
- individualistic
- communicative
- intense
- creative (ideas, models)
- relational (ideas, problems, work, activities)
- enthusiastic

Basic Learning Process
- lateral
- dialogue
- interaction with others
- exchange of ideas
- open-ended problem-solving
- experimentation

Management Process
- participative
- collaborative
- communicative
- involved in many parts
- may have difficulty delegating
- quick decision-making

Values and Affinities
- innovation
- challenge, risk
- forward movement
- structure and timelines
- regular, significant communication
- connection with people
- organization (connection of people with functions)

Function
- create new ideas
- move work forward
- communicate
- see emergent possibilities
- motivate

Interpersonal Relationships
- relational
- verbally expressive
- not too aware of own feelings; relatively aware of others' feelings
- relatively objective
- focused on ideas

Factors Causing Stress
- unawareness or neglect of physical needs
- repetitive activities
- lack of forward movement

Body Movements
- often in the horizontal plane (side-to-side)
- relative variety of movements and postures
- staccato quality to movements

Eyes
- intense
- penetrating
- focused outward

Hands
- many gestures, often conveying intensity about ideas

Forward! Thy orders are given in secret. May I always hear them and obey.
Forward! Whatever distance I have covered, it does not give me the right to halt.
Forward! It is the attention given to the last steps before the summit which decides the value of all that went before.

—Dag Hammarskjöld

Capacities

Emotional-Subjective

- To create and maintain harmonious connections (relationships) with others.
- To intuitively understand others' specific needs.
- To personally feel the joy and pain of others.
- To work through one's personal history and come to forgiveness of self and others.
- To live the full range from personal empathy to detachment.

- *To be teachers of both personal empathy and detachment, by example.*

The Emotional-Subjective Personality Dynamic: Connecting with Everything

In my ten-year history at IBM, I always exceeded the financial goals that were set for me and my unit. But, although I met IBM's bottom line, I usually did it in what company executives considered an unorthodox fashion. I was viewed as a "wild duck"—I used creativity, intuition, and quality relationships to be successful.

Some people told me that I was "too close" to my customers and therefore would not be able to be objective about our business deals and activities. I disagreed, and I used a great deal of my personal time to connect with my customers and establish mutual respect, trust, and appreciation. We had lunch and dinner, played golf on weekends, went to baseball and basketball games; sometimes I even attended their special family events.

I always became friends with my key customers, who were strong clients for IBM. Through our relationships, I created an extraordinary and invaluable bond of trust which enabled us to work collaboratively to the benefit of both organizations.

It has always been extremely important to me that everyone involved in a business deal or project is "on board"—the feelings and thoughts of others matter a lot to me. Perhaps the fundamental distinction in my management "style" is my objective to listen to and value the input of all the "players" involved. I also tried to make them feel comfortable about our ability to implement their project successfully. I chose business prospects very selectively—customers had to represent high revenue and profit potential for IBM. But I was more inclined to get heavily involved in a business project or marketing activity if I liked and respected my customers both professionally and personally.

Some managers expressed concern that I might be unable to give harsh criticism to my team members because I was too close to them on a personal level. In fact, the opposite was true. I only care about giving criticism to people when they mean a lot to me and I want them to do well. I am very capable of giving criticism—provided that it's constructive. I can even give extremely tough criticism if it supports someone's growth.

These strong relationships, coupled with my intuition and creativity, enabled me to be successful—even within a company as structured as IBM. But at first, there were many doubters. For example, the company's financial people often struggled with my revenue and profit forecasts—they would want line-item transaction details to support a $100 million forecast I had made. But I feel that such detailed processes do not reflect how business really works: some transactions fall by the wayside while others go through; and it is often necessary to redirect resources and efforts according to ongoing feedback from customers and the market. So, while I would normally track $50 million of my forecast, the other half was difficult to pinpoint. I used my gut feeling about the industry, the quality of my unit, and the current and projected business climates to comfortably forecast that an additional $50 million would come in.

Over time, the company's financial community and business executives began to value and trust my intuitive forecasting because it was consistently accurate. They also knew I would not move forward with a particular client or project if my experience and intuition told me that it would not pan out profitably or would eventually be discontinued because it lacked executive buy-in.

—JOHN BLASIG, FORMER EXECUTIVE IN MARKETING, IBM

Connecting with Everything:
A Metatheme for Emotional-Subjective People

For emotional-subjective people, making connections is a fundamental drive and primary satisfaction—connections with *people*, above all, but also connections with things, ideas, and events. Emotional-subjective people arrive at connection through a simultaneous orientation to both their inner and outer worlds. They constantly monitor cues from both realms in an inner/outer process that is at play whether they are creating relationships with individuals or groups, organizing, exploring new experiences, or connecting materials in new ways that feel satisfying.

Underlying their capacity to make connections with others is the fundamental impulse to create harmony in relationships. For example, when change is needed within a relationship, they will go to great lengths to make their presentation in such a way that a harmonious relationship will be maintained.

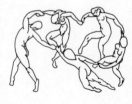

The emotional-subjective sensitivity to both inner feelings and outer circumstances determines how they express their feelings, thoughts, and actions moment by moment. It enables them to meet the needs of many parties.

On a deeper level, connecting their feeling responses to the outer world over time helps them to define and clarify their own personal identity.

The Keyboard

As a whole, emotional-subjective people have the capacity to experience and express the greatest range of emotion and finest nuances of feeling of all the personality dynamic groups. They are the great explorers of the emotional world who teach us about its extraordinary richness, diversity, complexity, and value. If we use the analogy of a grand piano, emotional-subjective people have access to all 88 keys, with all of their possibilities for chords and combinations of notes, while the other personality dynamic groups are usually restricted to a certain part of the keyboard.

Not that every emotional-subjective person plays all of the notes with equal facility or frequency. Some seem to be born emphasizing the extremes of high and low, and may in time add more of the notes in the middle. Others play a broad range around middle C, expanding outward as time moves on. In either case, they are sensitive emotional receivers, with the *capacity* to respond with appropriate emotional nuancing to any situation. The emotional life is central to their way of being.

Using the Keyboard

For emotional-subjective people, communication, learning, and problem-solving initially involve internal considerations. Let's say that an emotional-subjective man has just been assigned a new task. He will probably begin by assessing his feelings in relation to the task. He may ask himself such questions as, "How do I feel about my communication with the person setting the task? Do I feel respected . . . patronized . . . trusted? How do I feel about undertaking the task? . . . anxious . . . uneasy . . . eager . . . confident? Whom will this endeavor affect, and how will they feel about it?" Only after he has examined his feelings and arrived at a point of clarity can he put his full energy into accomplishing the task itself.

Whether young or old, male or female, emotional-subjective people create a rich inner world from their feeling-imbued experience of life—a world that is precious to them, invisible to others, and unique. They create this world from a lifetime of interpretations and reinterpretations of emotionally significant events. This inner world changes moment by moment as they respond to each new experience and interpret it in light of the past. Their sensitivity to the inner world is crucial to the development of their personal boundaries and their sense of self.

It is fascinating to watch how emotional-subjective infants constantly track people around them with their eyes. They clearly need to feel connected—especially, of course, with their parents—and often show distress if they sense that the connection is even momentarily broken (see "The Fear of Abandonment," p. 143).

Out of their capacities for both inner and outer connection, emotional-subjective people are able to bring to others the gift of empathy and their great skills in the arts of communication and creating relationships. In one-on-one or group interactions, they perform an intricate balancing act, in which they monitor the subtleties of their own inner experiences and those of others simultaneously, and shape their words and behavior accordingly so as to keep connection and maintain harmony. As they mature, they become masters of interpersonal communication.

Sometimes their need and capacity to maintain connection with others can work to their detriment, however. They can have difficulty establishing boundaries between themselves and others, which can jeopardize their sense of personal identity. And sometimes they will persist in trying to create or maintain a relationship when it is evident that the other person is unwilling to respond, or unable to relate harmoniously. As emotional-subjective people mature and integrate greater detachment, they become more selective in creating relationships and better able to let go of inharmonious relationships that are not amenable to change.

While connections among people are their primary focus, emotional-subjective people are also adept at connecting ideas to gain new understanding, or seeing connections among colors, shapes, sounds, or materials of various kinds to create new forms, which often have aesthetic as well as utilitarian appeal. Their rich inner lives may find artistic expression through the connective medium of the creative imagination. The majority of great actors and actresses, those with the widest emotional range and the capacity to fully "become" another person, are emotional-subjective. But emotional-subjective people may also use their ability to see and create new connections for scientific or corporate innovation.

A Bridging Role in Contract Negotiations

"I'd like to tell you about certain contract negotiations, during which I began to recognize the contributions of the emotional-subjective personality dynamic. Here's the situation: I was one of several management representatives from a multi-employer group that would collectively negotiate a contract with a nursing association representing about seven thousand nurses. The two groups had an almost fifty-year relationship of positional bargaining that tended to pull people apart rather than move them closer together.

"Before beginning this negotiation, the two sides had agreed that they needed to improve the quality of their relationship and their work together. As we bargained, I began to appreciate the pivotal role my personality dynamic played in sensing the subtle differences at the table and fostering connections among the people. For example, the intuitive recognition that some people were uncomfortable (even when they spoke words of agreement) helped us to delve deeper into issues. I was also able to experience the unspoken feelings in the room and verbalize them—which prompted further dialogue. Other emotional-subjective people from both parties contributed by voicing feelings and ideas that were deeply meaningful to people and translating them for both groups.

"In this role, I was able to see connections and bring covert processes forward. The ability to respond to those subtleties in an empathic way helped build relationships and connections over time. The role of the emotional-subjective people was that of translators, which I think was crucial to the development of common understanding. People of other personality dynamics played this bridging role too, but the function was fulfilled almost effortlessly by the emotional-subjective participants.

"I am clear that the ability to bridge was less about me as an individual, and more about my personality dynamic. The emotional-subjective instrument connected people and helped to create an environment in which the negotiations could advance."

Intuitive Sensibility: "I Just *Know!*"

Every person has some degree of intuition, but the form it takes for each personality dynamic group seems distinct. The intuitive faculty seems to be most consciously known and accepted by emotional-subjective people because they experience intuitive signals extraordinarily strongly and often even register them as physical sensations.

When the participants in our seminars divide into their personality dynamic groups to discuss their commonalities, the emotional-subjective people always emphasize their gift of intuition. At the same time, they almost always make the point that although they may eventually learn from experience to trust their intuition, they have often been dissuaded from acting upon it in the past, either by their own rational doubts or the skeptical responses of others. "What do you mean, you *feel* that this won't work? . . . You *sense* that this is the right course to follow? . . . You have a bad *feeling* about this person?" Of course, it is impossible to respond convincingly in the moment, because they can't back up their feeling with objective reasons and facts. They may find the words to lend credence to their feeling later, but not at first. So they go along with "logic" or "common sense," a decision they often later regret when their intuition proves accurate. With enough such experiences, emotional-subjective people may come to trust this gift more, but will probably still find it difficult to persuade others to share their faith.

The intuitive gift of emotional-subjective people seems to take two forms. The first is in relation to people: they sense when unspoken thoughts or feelings lie behind the words in a communication. They may register the signal so strongly that they feel it physically—perhaps literally as a "gut reaction." They may also sense *what* is unspoken, but here they need to be careful, for although they can trust the existence of the signal, they could interpret its meaning inaccurately. For example, a person who feels uneasy about hiring someone with outstanding credentials might ask himself or herself, "Do I feel uneasy because I sense that the person is dishonest, or because it might be difficult for us to work together cooperatively?" The implications of each interpretation would be very different. In the latter case, the problem and its solution might lie as much with the person having the feeling as with the job applicant. If the prospective employer were willing to make adjustments, perhaps the relationship could work out. In either case, the signal needs to be taken seriously, but the nature of the inquiry and subsequent actions would be different.

Accuracy in interpretation comes with practice and experience. In respecting their intuitive sense, emotional-subjective people increasingly make subtle distinctions in their perceptions and come to more and more reliable conclusions. Indeed, they may find that particular shades or varieties of sensing mean specific things. Because each person is unique, each will pick up signals and learn to interpret them accurately in his or her own way.

Emotional-subjective people often possess another remarkable intuitive skill: the ability to sense the future, to "see" ahead. For example, we have all heard of people who have changed travel plans because of a strong intuition of impending disaster—a feeling which later turned out to be justified. Of course circumstances like these are extreme, but we believe this kind of predictive ability operates all the time in all kinds of circumstances and is most strongly and consistently experienced by emotional-subjective people. Again, they may have to learn over time to sufficiently trust their intuition to act upon it. This gift can facilitate quick individual decision-making, but may extend the process in a group because it raises questions or proposes actions not previously considered. The result can be higher quality decisions, provided the group recognizes the validity of the intuition and is willing to take it into account. Most often they do not, and the following kind of situation occurs:

Alex is emotional-subjective and highly intuitive. He is attending a staff meeting where the leader is eager to persuade the group to invest heavily in a new advertising campaign. As the meeting proceeds, Alex becomes increasingly uncomfortable. He "knows" that the new positioning of their product in this campaign would be a mistake. However, when asked to explain, he cannot answer. His intuition at this point is an unformed "seeing/sensing," to which he cannot put words.

Alex may acquire the consciousness and the words in a few minutes, hours, or days—that's how intuition works—but at the moment he can only state his feeling. The rest of the group disregard him and make their own decision. His intuition turns out to be accurate, and the campaign falls flat several months later.

Perhaps if Alex had been with this group long enough to have established a record of accurate prediction, they would have been more willing to take his intuition into account. But the truth is that we tend to discount intuitive capacity in organizations. We require decisions to be made on the basis of concrete data and rational projections. Yet many of our most admired thinkers and practitioners in fields such as science, economics, philosophy, and psychology have acknowledged that it was often intuitive understanding or insight that catalyzed new achievement and discovery. The intuitive signal should therefore never be ignored, though its meaning may need time and conscious probing to become clear.

Multifocus: Diversity of Experience

Emotional-subjective people enjoy variety—variety of experiences, of people, of forms, of interests, and of activities. This appreciation of the diversity that life offers goes hand in hand with their gift of multifocus. Emotional-subjective people have a remarkable ability to track several communications and events simultaneously. At home, they may have no problem listening to music, cooking, talking to a friend on the telephone, and refereeing a fight between two children—all at the same time. In a restaurant, they may be able to follow many conversations flowing around them, even as they conduct their own. In organizations, emotional-subjective people are often identified as versatile and flexible—able to play many roles, participate in many projects simultaneously, and function capably even in the midst of chaos.

To be multifocused is by no means the same as being unfocused, although it may sometimes be mistaken as such. Because they do not share the same capacity for multitracking, people of other personality dynamics can sometimes perceive emotional-subjective people as being unfocused and their ways of communicating and carrying out tasks as confused. Nevertheless, all gifts have their liabilities. Emotional-subjective people risk becoming "scattered" if they open themselves to too many stimuli simultaneously or take on too many responsibilities or activities.

Attention-Deficit Disordered?

Our experience suggests that many children identified in schools as "attention-deficit disordered" are, in fact, emotional-subjective children whose natural gifts of emotional sensitivity and multifocus have become liabilities. Emotional-subjective children (or adults) can be susceptible to losing focus if they are subject to chaotic inner feelings resulting from past trauma, if they are picking up disturbing feelings from others, if the environment is disorganized or nonsupportive, or if any combination of these factors is present.

Rather than applying the label of "attention-deficit disordered," we could serve such children better by first regarding them as emotional-subjective children who need to: (1) be afforded frequent opportunities to move around and engage in physical activity, (2) have frequent opportunities to talk with others, (3) engage in activities in which they can externalize feelings appropriately (for example, through the arts), (4) acquire a precise language for their feelings, (5) have quiet periods with little or no stimuli, (6) practice focusing exercises, (7) receive frequent appropriate approval and feel that they are liked.

This is, in fact, a prescription for the well-being of any emotional-subjective person of any age.

To avoid overload, emotional-subjective people need to "stop the music" periodically and allow themselves quiet time alone in which to process and clarify their communications, experiences, and responses. In this way, they can regain equilibrium and become restored. They must also learn to be more selective in the activities and responsibilities they accept. This discipline does not come easily, because they enjoy variety and want to please others. In the end, however, neither their own well-being nor that of others will be served if they become overextended. So they must monitor their stress levels carefully and learn to say no at times—to others *and* to themselves.

Personalizing: On Guilt and Responsibility

Because they are subjectively oriented and highly self-aware, emotional-subjective people tend to personalize their experiences. They respond to life self-referentially. This is not to imply that they are more likely than anyone else to be self-centered, but merely that their first and most essential point of reference is their own feeling-based experience. In varying degrees, the members of the other personality dynamic groups have a more detached experience of life. In a sense, emotional-subjective people use themselves as "personal experiments," seeking truths about human experience that they can use and share with others for the common good. The obverse side of this gift is that sometimes emotional-subjective people can lose perspective and take things *too* personally.

For example, Janet is the emotional-subjective assistant to the chief executive officer of a large insurance company. She is highly skilled, very well organized, a good communicator, and valued greatly by the company. The CEO's work requires occasional absences on business trips. During one of these trips, a manager asked Janet for the CEO's itinerary in order to maintain contact with him. Janet replied that she did not know his full schedule. The manager did not say, feel, or think that Janet was responsible for lacking the information, but the following dialogue took place:

> **Manager:** I'm thinking it might be a good idea to create a new system so that the managers can keep track of his movements.
>
> **Janet:** I didn't have any way of letting you know, because he didn't inform me. I'm really sorry, but I didn't get that information. I will in the future.

> If you want to write the truth,
> you must write about yourself.
> I am the only real truth I know.
>
> **—Jean Rhys**

Manager: I know. That's why I think there should be a system.

Janet: If he had informed me, I would have distributed the information.

Manager: I'm not saying that you were responsible. I'm simply suggesting that we should create a new system.

Janet: Oh.

As this example illustrates, the personalizing tendency of emotional-subjective people can lead to exaggerated feelings of responsibility and even guilt. When something goes wrong, they typically look in the mirror and blame themselves. Even if they are outwardly pointing the finger of blame at someone else, inwardly they are sure that it is *they* who are in some way really responsible. As they mature and integrate greater detachment with their capacity for connection, they are able to view situations more objectively (see Chapter 12, "The Developmental Continuum"). Then they can see that responsibility for mishaps is nearly always shared, and recognize that, in any case, such occurrences are opportunities for everyone to learn, rather than triggers for blame or self-blame.

Where guilt or blame exist, however, the ultimate antidote is forgiveness—forgiveness of oneself and forgiveness of others. Because of their self-referential tendency, many emotional-subjective people find it easier to forgive others than to forgive themselves. A helpful affirmation for them to remember and repeat to themselves, especially when things go awry, might be, "I stand in the light of *shared* responsibility for the whole."

> **"On one occasion, my wife and I took a vacation with two of our friends, one of whom was extremely moody. Every time his mood changed, I would think, 'What am I doing to cause his mood swing?' Even though over the years of our friendship I have known him to be moody, I couldn't stop feeling that his behavior was due to something I was doing. It wasn't until I asked him directly if I was bothering him and we talked about it that I could let go of the feeling that I was responsible for his moods. This kind of thing happens to me a lot."**

Creative Expression: Play, Humor, and Levity

Emotional-subjective people are sensitive to and attracted by all the sights, sounds, and sensations of life and respond to them all with feeling. They notice and are affected by colors and smells, textures and tastes. They may select the clothing they wear on a particular day to reflect, or affect, their mood. They take an interest in the interplay of colors, shapes, and textures and usually enjoy creating environments that feel good to them and are aesthetically satisfying. They may choose to rearrange their workspace or their furnishings at home from time to time for no other reason than the pleasure of fitting things together in new ways for new effects. They are often creative in the kitchen, enjoying both the *process* of mixing ingredients to make new dishes and the *result* of offering to others something they have personally created.

**Rainbows!
Rainbows!
Rainbows!**

—Pablo Casals

Whether on a large or small scale, such efforts reflect the emotional-subjective delight in and need for creative expression. Creative talent is by no means restricted to emotional-subjective people, but this group shows the most drive to express themselves through "playing" with materials, whether to create a work of art, invent a recipe, design a room, or coordinate a brilliantly contrasting shirt and tie. Often these creative acts are responsive to the circumstances or the mood of the moment and are woven spontaneously into the ongoing experience of life, but they may also be the result of considered planning. For example, emotional-subjective people's creativity may manifest itself in finding new ways to mobilize people in a company, design sales presentations, or mount a new training program. They are very good at answering questions beginning with the word *how*— at finding new and ingenious ways of doing things.

One form of creative expression that emotional-subjective people value is play. Playing and having fun are attractive and important for everyone— but they are essential for the health and well-being of this group because they help modify and balance the emotional-subjective sensitivity to the pain in the world. Play brings respite and the transformative power of joy.

Emotional-subjective people characteristically delight in humor and often demonstrate an impressive capacity for telling jokes and stories, enhanced by their facility in playing roles and their ability to connect emotionally with an audience. They may use this gift spontaneously to embellish or enhance the moment, or more purposefully as a social tool for easing tension, facilitating communication, and promoting a harmonious atmosphere.

However, in order to be themselves and use their creative capacities most fully, emotional-subjective people need to feel safe. When they feel they have "permission," their capacities for fun, play, humor, and creative expression flower; in an atmosphere of expressed or implicit threat or disapproval, they wither. This benefits neither them nor any organization of which they are a part.

Yet unless the "raison d'être" of an organization is specifically related to creative expression—as in a design or film studio, arts center, or advertising agency—the creative resource of emotional-subjective employees is usually barely tapped. This is a sad thought when we consider that, except in the Far East, emotional-subjective people usually constitute the majority.

Invariably, in our seminars in organizations, under conditions of safety and comfort, emotional-subjective participants demonstrate their extraordinary creative abilities. A seminar for trainers from the Swedish Total Defense provides an apt example. The Swedish military had become interested in Human Dynamics in 1990, when a retired general attended a presentation given by one of our Swedish facilitators. The general was especially intrigued by the idea that leadership could take many forms and be differently developed, depending on the personality dynamic.

In the course of the seminar, 12 of the officers identified themselves as emotional-subjective. As each day passed, they became more comfortable and less formal. On the fourth day of the training, we asked each of the five personality dynamic groups to go off on their own for two hours and return with a 10-minute presentation on the topic of the environment. The assignment was deliberately open-ended and had a two-fold purpose: (1) to demonstrate the distinct problem-solving processes of each personality dynamic group, and (2) to prepare the whole group for the following day's assignment in which they would be working in teams of *mixed* personality dynamics on an actual organizational issue.

A variety of materials was available for the groups to use, if they wished, in preparing their presentations—not only the usual flip charts and overhead transparencies, but also colored paper and pens, tape, glue, scissors, clay, balls, colored ribbons, and even some items of clothing, including hats, gloves, scarves, ties, and so on. As always, in our experience, the emotional-subjective group was the most eager to examine the materials *before* they left

"Unless I feel safe, my creativity and humor shut down. That's how it is in our corporate environment. In most meetings, I have at least two or three laughs—but to myself, rarely outwardly. Occasionally I will write a note and pass it to the person sitting next to me so he or she can share the humor with me.

"When I had my own team, I got the group to a point where we could laugh freely. Our meetings became really enjoyable because people could be themselves, and I could be myself. It took me about a year and a half to create that, a place where people actually felt comfortable and safe."

to work on their assignment. (The other personality dynamic groups usually select materials, if at all, *after* they have worked out their presentation.)

When the groups returned two hours later, the emotional-subjective group asked to make their presentation last. When their turn came, we were summoned to a room that they had prepared. All the lights were off—it was pitch black. We had to stumble around in the dark to find our chairs, which had been organized in a large circle. When everyone was finally seated, the room fell quiet, and we waited in the darkness.

Suddenly, a flashlight shone. It was held by a "BBC correspondent," and it illuminated a high-ranking officer from the Swedish Total Defense who was crouched under an upturned chair, smoking a cigarette, and dressed as a rat with whiskers, pink ears, and a long pink tail. Indeed, they were all rats, all crouched under chairs with the exception of one who was curled up in the fireplace. As each was interviewed in turn by the BBC correspondent, we learned that they were refugee rats who had taken up residence in the sewers of Stockholm, because the pollution in the city above was so severe that it was impossible for even rats to live there.

Nobody, on the first day of that seminar, would have believed that the riotous, unbuttoned performance of the fourth day could be possible. But afterward, there was a touch of melancholy because, as many of the officers remarked, they realized that they had neither had so much fun, nor felt so free and energized, since they were children.

So why have we inhibited these wonderful creative gifts? Our answer is that the *function* of emotional-subjective people is not sufficiently valued in corporate cultures. Corporate cultures as a whole are uncomfortable with the world of emotions, intuition, artistic expression, fun, and lateral thinking. Rather, they tend to value and reward conformity, objectivity, and staid seriousness—in fact, an almost military image. Even corporate suits are suggestive of uniforms. As a result, many emotional-subjective men, in particular, come to repress or deny their emotional-subjectivity and try to behave as if they were emotional-*objective*.

In not valuing emotional-subjectivity, we stifle creativity and repress feelings. This suppression leads to tension, undercurrents of unexpressed emotion, and people trying to live as if they were someone else—all with the attendant problems of stress, lack of energy, and even sickness.

The Body as Messenger

Because the emotional and physical principles are so directly linked in emotional-subjective people, whatever they feel emotionally they also experience physically, and vice versa. Physical health or discomfort are reflected in emotional well-being or emotional distress, respectively; and emotional well-being is reflected in physical well-being, and emotional distress in either a generalized physical discomfort or specific symptoms such as a headache, chest pain, restricted breathing, or tightness in the stomach.

The body is, therefore, a messenger to emotional-subjective people. It responds positively to emotions such as joy and laughter, and negatively—with discomfort and pain—to such emotions as sadness, anxiety, anger, or fear. From their physical cues, emotional-subjective people are given vital information, not only about themselves and their own emotional condition, but also about other individuals and the general emotional condition of an environment. For example, if an emotional-subjective person meets someone who is feeling sad, depressed, or angry, but who is not expressing the feeling openly (and, in fact, may not even be aware of having the feeling), the emotional-subjective person is likely to experience a physical reaction that indicates that something is amiss, or sometimes even directly experience the other person's emotion. Similarly, if emotional tension is rising in a group, emotional-subjective people will almost certainly register physical discomfort.

> "My body is strongly affected by environments that are stressful or unhealthy. I get sick, and I'm stopped dead in my tracks if I don't pay attention to my body."

Physical signals are one of the most important ways in which emotional-subjective people gain feedback from the environment. They must check, however, to ensure that they *interpret* their signals correctly; and they must identify whether the signal is reflecting someone else's condition, or their own.

An area of the body that is often extremely sensitive in emotional-subjective people is the solar plexus. Approximately 95 percent of the thousands of emotional-subjective people we have seen from many cultures have identified this area as a frequent source of pain and discomfort. Consistent feedback from emotional-subjective people suggests that this is a place where they store tension from emotional trauma and unresolved painful memories.

Emotional-subjective people can ease this physical distress by tracing the links between their current reaction and related past events. Let's say that, over the course of years, an individual has had the experience many times of feeling rejected. The person may or may not have actually been rejected, but if he or she *interprets* an event as a rejection, it can cause tension in the solar plexus. If the situation is not dealt with and resolved, the experience or its effect becomes unconsciously "stored." Each new event interpreted as a rejection will trigger pain that is directly linked to the experiences of rejection from the past. As these experiences accumulate, the pain can become increasingly recurrent or even chronic.

Pain in the area of the solar plexus may not be a symptom of a physical disorder, therefore, but might more accurately be regarded as a call for emotional and spiritual healing. The signal offers the person the opportunity to examine the event and gain awareness of the connection between the present incident and past experiences. Then he or she can consciously work through the unresolved issues related to feeling rejected. This process involves tracking the chain of memories of rejection, including those from earliest childhood, and attempting to understand them clearly and objectively. It involves distinguishing between actual, intentional rejection and one's *assumptions* that rejection was intended; and it involves seeing as clearly as possible the roles and motivations of the participants in the situations, including the part played by oneself. Finally, it involves forgiveness—forgiveness of oneself and others for intended or unintended transgressions. Through such a process, the stored feelings and the physical pain triggered by them can be released.

The Need for Processing

"Processing" refers to engaging in an inner dialogue, a dialogue with someone else, or, often, a combination of both, in order to clarify confusing or undefined feelings, gain objective understanding of the situation that gave rise to the feelings, and take appropriate action. Processing was involved in the above example of tracking experiences of rejection to gain clarity about them and resolve the situation through forgiveness. The individual could go through this process alone, but would be greatly helped by undertaking it with a trusted friend. The role of a partner in this process is not to offer opinions or solutions (unless they are specifically sought), but rather to listen empathically and aid clarification by occasionally repeating what he or she understood the speaker to have said.

Emotional-subjective people in particular need to process because of their emotional sensitivity. Emotions are meant to move and flow; processing helps ensure that they do. If feelings are unacknowledged or held back—especially negative feelings such as shame, anger, or guilt—the feelings accumulate in the body, resulting in pain, discomfort, and sometimes emotional or physical illness. At the very least, stored, unresolved feelings drain energy and inhibit productivity.

Successful processing involves four steps:

Step 1   *Acknowledge* feelings.
Step 2   Find a *specific language* for those feelings (which promotes relaxation of the body).
Step 3   Gain *understanding* of and *perspective* on the feelings and their link to earlier events.
Step 4   Take appropriate *action* based on the new understandings.

Step 1: Acknowledge Feelings

The first commandment for emotional-subjective people, then, is *honor your feelings!* Because feelings are central to their existence, emotional-subjective people should never undervalue or deny them. They need to be aware that they respond with emotion to any situation. They may register the emotion physically—as pain, laughter, tension, a change in body temperature, or restlessness, for example—but at the root of the physical response lie feelings.

Step 2: Find a Language for Feelings

Expressing feelings appropriately requires identifying them precisely—bringing them to full consciousness and attaching specific words to them. *Finding a language for feelings* is a process in itself. It requires dialogue, either with oneself or with others. The stronger the individual's emotion, the less clear his or her immediate interpretation of it may be, and the more protracted the dialogue may need to be before the person can articulate the feeling clearly. The person may need to delve into ever deeper layers and discover even more painful feelings to acquire this language. Sometimes the feelings they eventually identify are very different from those they felt initially. For example, someone may initially feel extremely angry, but come to understand that underlying this feeling are others, such as sorrow or deep love. Emotional-subjective people know when they have found the right words to express their feelings—they feel a flood of relief, and their bodies relax.

Step 3: Understand the Feelings

The next stage is *gaining understanding of the feelings*. In this step, emotional-subjective people should strive to see the link between the triggering event and their past experience, view the triggering event with objectivity and compassion, and identify the learning to be gained.

Again, exploring these connections with someone who is patient, interested, objective, and supportive can be most helpful. Saying the words while connected with someone else makes feelings and intuitions conscious and clear. Because of the complexity of feelings and the richness of their associations, the conversation may shift and turn and take a convoluted path, but it will follow an inner logic of emotional connection, and the end result—perspective and objective understanding—will be well worth the effort.

This processing will be brief or lengthy, and more or less profound, depending on how much the triggering event touches such central emotional issues of the person's life as, for example, those related to parents. Experiences with parents are so varied, numerous, and personal that it can take a lifetime of effort to understand their legacy. People usually achieve this only piece by piece, as opportunities arise. By continually analyzing personal relationships, particularly family relationships, emotional-subjective people can free themselves of any unresolved issues, feelings, attitudes, and behaviors that are unproductive. In the process, they heal themselves and their important relationships with others.

Step 4: Take Appropriate Action

Ideally, this process of tracing connections ends in a fourth step, *taking appropriate action* based on the understanding gained in the earlier steps. Omitting this final step keeps energy bound up in old issues and unproductive behavior patterns. Appropriate actions might include making a

**A word is dead
When it is said,
Some say.**

**I say it just
Begins to live
That day.**

**—Emily
Dickinson**

better connection with people involved in the triggering event or past events; explaining to someone, with compassion, that their behavior was unwittingly hurtful; writing a letter; having a conversation; or making a considered decision that the best action would be no action at all.

For emotional-subjective people, words are *felt* experiences, which may at any time trigger strong feelings and associated memories or fantasies. Emotional-subjective people must process and assimilate these inner feelings before they can again focus outward on the speaker and his or her message. Because the inner life is idiosyncratic, someone speaking to an emotional-subjective person cannot always predict the reactions his or her words might provoke.

Therefore, to maintain a free flow of energy, it is best to "process" negative emotions as they happen. This processing could be initiated by the person having the negative feelings, or by someone else, as in the following example.

On one occasion, during a Human Dynamics seminar, it was apparent that a participant, Don, had turned his attention inward, and from the look on his face, we could see that his feelings were not positive. During the next break, we asked him if something was troubling him. He replied, "I'm really angry, but I don't know why."

As we talked about his feeling, the underlying issues became clear. He had grown up in a large family, and establishing a sense of his own identity had posed a lifelong challenge for him. Our identification of an emotional-subjective *pattern* had triggered old feelings associated with being "just one of the crowd." He understood intellectually that we were describing common *processes*, not identities, and that we were emphasizing, rather than denying, individuality, but his emotional sensitivity to the issue had caused him to relive some of the events and feelings from his childhood. The more we talked together, and the more he was able to locate the source of his discomfort and put words to his feelings, the calmer he became. By the end of the conversation, his sense of relief was evident. Through "processing" his feeling, he had successfully harmonized the new information with his hard-won sense of self. Having rebalanced his inner world, he could once more open himself to new learning.

Sometimes it is impossible to resolve a difficult personal issue directly with someone. For example, Jack has moved out of the country to a new job, and he no longer works for the man with whom he'd had a very difficult 10-year relationship. But he hears that his former boss has suddenly become critically ill. Although Jack feels concern, he still carries unresolved negative feelings about him. Though Jack cannot process his feelings with his former boss directly, he can still take action. He can conduct an honest *inner* dialogue with his boss, write him a forthright letter that he never mails, or share his feelings fully and deeply with a trusted friend. Again, the most positive position to reach is that of forgiveness: forgiveness of oneself and forgiveness of others for any past hurts. Only with forgiveness can painful feelings or memories be released and relationships move forward.

Finally, we want to emphasize the importance of this kind of processing for emotional-subjective children. One of the greatest services that parents and other significant adults can provide for children is to help them follow the preceding four steps: acknowledge and identify their feelings, express their emotions through language, objectively interpret the situation that gave rise to the feelings, and take appropriate action. In so doing, parents can help young ones stay emotionally as well as physically healthy, and stave off the stomachaches and headaches that so often burden children.

This may sound like a tall order—as if we are asking parents to be professional therapists—but, in fact, many parents provide this kind of support without knowing it. We are simply identifying the steps of a natural process and bringing it to a conscious level to emphasize its importance and ensure that it is available as a tool for everyone. Apart from the benefits for children that we have mentioned, there are also benefits for parents. Through engaging in this process, parents strengthen their relationship with their children; build closeness and trust; and ensure that emotions rooted in the family relationships are openly acknowledged and discussed as they arise—a wise investment in the quality of family life.

Resolving Painful Feelings

The following is a moving example of how one emotional-subjective mother helped her emotional-subjective seven-year-old, Barbara, to process and resolve some painful and confusing feelings. The story also illustrates how unresolved feelings can interfere with a child's ability to accomplish schoolwork—just as they can hinder an adult's efficiency.

Barbara's older sister, Lauren, who had spent several years in boarding school, had recently returned home for a short period and then moved away again. Barbara painfully missed her big sister. She began to resist leaving her mother at the school gate, she had difficulty concentrating on her schoolwork and homework, and she cried at night. Her mother helped her talk about her sad feelings regarding her sister. Then, as her mother relates,

About two weeks ago Barbara said, "Something's wrong. I don't know what it is. I think I did something wrong when I was very little." (She was only two-and-a-half when her sister first left home under difficult circumstances.) I asked, "Do you know what it was?" She said, "No," and I said, "Do you know where you were when it happened?" And she said, "No, but you were there." I asked, "Do you have any pictures in your mind?" and she said, "No." Then she cried a lot and was really sad.

She went on for a long time about how something bad was going to happen to somebody close, and she didn't know what it was, and it hurt so much that she could hardly stand it.

And then she said, "No, I don't think that's what's wrong. Remember a while ago I told you I had done something wrong when I was a baby?" I said, "Yes," and she said, "I'm remembering something, I'm having a memory, and it's so scary." I asked, "What's the memory?" She said, "Well, remember when Lauren was home and she went away again?" I said, "You mean when she came home from school for a while about a year ago, then went back to school?" She said, "Yes. You didn't tell me she was going. It was awful and scary, and I didn't want Lauren to go. It hurt so much."

She cried a lot, and I told her again that having the feeling come out was really painful, but it was something that would help her feel better. Then she finished crying and was pretty much OK, although she said, "I'm afraid more memories are going to come." I said, "If that happens, and it probably will, I will help you." Then she wrote a letter to Lauren about how much she loved and missed her.

The mother goes on to tell how Barbara did come crying to her again, saying that the memory of her sister's original departure was coming back to her. This time, as she talked, Barbara remembered that she had been taken to say good-bye to her sister, but Lauren was talking to a friend on the telephone at the time and hardly paid Barbara any attention. With her mother's help, Barbara was able to put words to her feelings of rejection. She could not yet acknowledge her anger at her sister's behavior, however, so this is not the end of the story. Nevertheless, as this process has continued, Barbara has complained less of physical pains and has been able to function much better in school than before. There is no doubt that she will feel even better when she is able to acknowledge her anger and write a letter to her sister in which she puts words to *all* her feelings, including the angry ones.

Even at so young an age, the help of a sensitive parent allowed Barbara to engage in the healthy process of moving from being overwhelmed by feelings, to finding a language for her feelings, to understanding and clarifying her interpretations, to taking an appropriate action (communicating with her sister). As the process continues, her understanding will become even more complete, and her actions even more appropriate. Above all, she will not carry this particularly painful experience of separation and rejection in her body. She will have only a conscious memory with which she has come to terms.

Setting Boundaries

Emotional-subjective people often have difficulty setting boundaries between themselves and others. It is as if only a thin, permeable membrane separates them from the complexity of life, especially of emotional life, around them. The pain of others can become their pain; the joy of others, their joy. This trait makes possible a remarkable natural capacity for empathy with others. The ability of emotional-subjective people to "tune in" to another's feelings and concerns almost as if they were their own enables them to help others feel understood and supported. It can also contribute to artistic expression. The capacity for identification with others enhances the ability of every artist—whether poet, novelist, playwright, singer, painter, or dancer—to communicate the range and complexity of inner human experience.

The obverse side of this gift, however, is that emotional-subjective people may have difficulty distinguishing their own feelings from the feelings of those around them. This tendency may make developing an individual

Five Living Systems

We have identified the personality dynamics of the eminent individuals whose photographs and words appear on the following pages through studying videotaped or filmed interviews.

The personality dynamics of three of the artists whose work is represented here were identified in the same way. The other two are known to us personally.

My being alone
like this has given
me something
tremendous, and it's
just what I need . . .
My mind is so
serene, but
concentrated and
I am watching it like
a cat a mouse.
—*J. Krishnamurti*

MENTAL-PHYSICAL

Perspective
Objectivity
Detachment
Values
Vision
Precision
Order

What one sees from the air is so simple and so beautiful I cannot help feeling that it would do something wonderful for the human race—rid it of such smallness and pettiness, if more people flew. —*Georgia O'Keeffe*

Katharine Hepburn

Is there a way of living that is noble, in what does it consist and how shall we achieve it? —*Bertrand Russell*

Man often becomes what he believes himself to be. If I keep on saying to myself that I cannot do a certain thing, it is possible that I may end by really becoming incapable of doing it. On the contrary, if I have the belief that I can do it, I shall surely acquire the capacity to do it even if I may not have it at the beginning.

—*Gandhi*

Ingrid Bergman

Kay Anderson

Forward movement
Challenge
Risk
Experiment-
ation
Innovation
The time
is now!

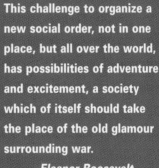

This challenge to organize a new social order, not in one place, but all over the world, has possibilities of adventure and excitement, a society which of itself should take the place of the old glamour surrounding war.
—*Eleanor Roosevelt*

We may cry out desperately for time to pause in her passages, but time is deaf to every plea and rushes on. Over the bleached bones and jumbled residues of numerous civilizations are written the pathetic words: "Too Late!"
—*Martin Luther King, Jr.*

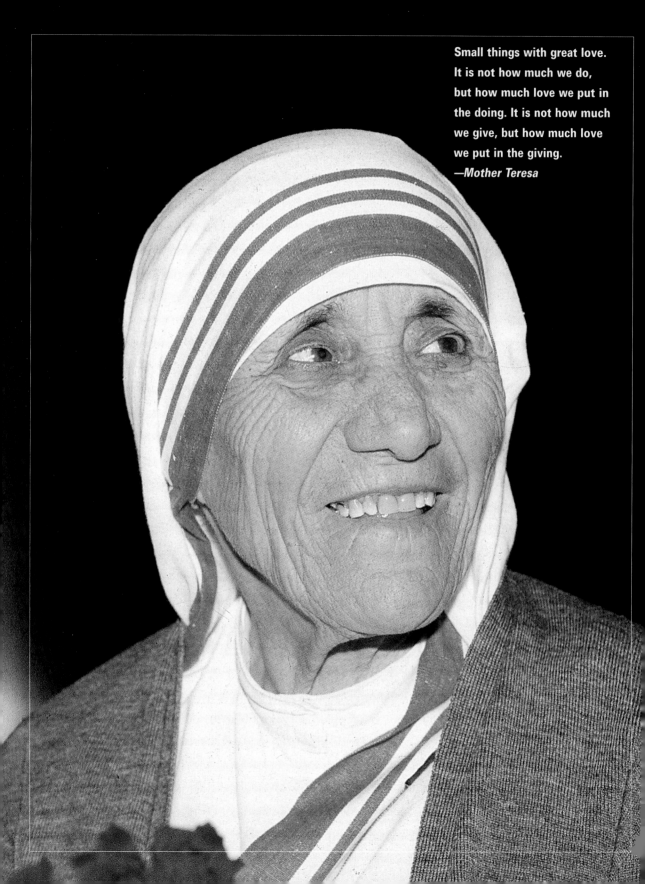

Small things with great love. It is not how much we do, but how much love we put in the doing. It is not how much we give, but how much love we put in the giving.
—*Mother Teresa*

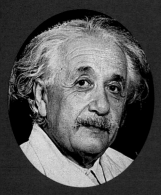

Concern for man himself and his fate must always form the chief interest of all technical endeavors . . . in order that the creations of our mind shall be a blessing and not a curse to mankind. Never forget this in the midst of your diagrams and equations.
—*Albert Einstein*

Judy Walker

Connections
Relationships
Personal
  empathy
Intuitive
  sensibility
Personalization
Subjective
  expression

Every time you take up the instrument you are making a statement, your statement! And it must be a statement of faith that this is the way you want to speak!
—*Isaac Stern*

Meryl Streep

In the past we have had a light which flickered,
in the present we have a light which flames, and
in the future there will be a light which shines
over all the land and sea.
—*Winston Churchill*

*Immersion
in the
environment*

*Systemic
thinking*

Organic time

Practicality

*Group
orientation*

Continuity

Nature

Tom Burgas

Always fall in with what
you're asked to accept. Take
what is given, and make it
over your way. My aim in life
has always been to hold my
own with whatever's going.
Not against: with!

—*Robert Frost*

I have tried to describe the kinds of experiences
that might become part of a way of bringing up
children and of seeing the world that includes
the past and the future as aspects of the
present—the present of any generation.

—*Margaret Mead*

Everyone has the responsibility to try to shape the future of humanity. So let us try to contribute as much as we can.
—*Dalai Lama*

M. C. Escher

Systemic thinking
Practicality
Model-making
Nature
Essentiality
Order
Purpose

Future generations are unlikely to condone our lack of prudent concern for the integrity of the natural world that supports all life. This is an era of specialists, each of whom sees his own problem and is unaware of or intolerant of the larger frame into which it fits.

—*Rachel Carson*

Clint Eastwood

Let there be justice for all. Let there be peace for all. Let there be work, bread, water, and salt for all. . . .

The time for the healing of the wounds has come. The moment to bridge the chasms that divide us has come. The time to build is upon us. . . .

—*Nelson Mandela*

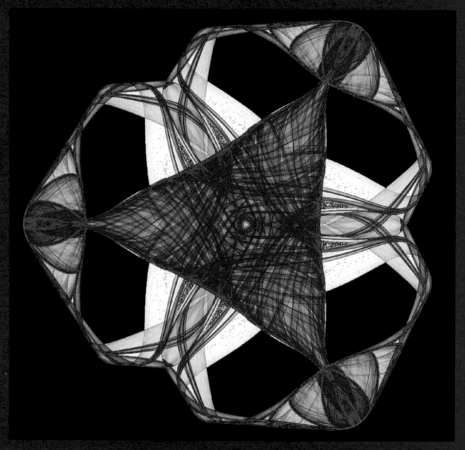

Capacities

Mental-Physical

- To determine and maintain long-range vision for self, others, and groups.
- To perceive and articulate guiding values and principles.
- To create structures.
- To listen carefully to diverse points of view and find the common points of agreement.
- To be objective and detached while maintaining qualitative relationships with others.
- To adopt and express unconditional love as *the* highest value.

- *To be teachers of both objectivity and compassion, by example.*

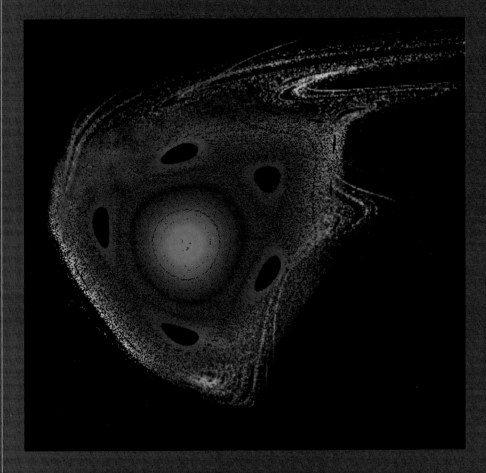

Emotional-Objective

- To move events forward.
- To sense the emergent directions and new possibilities in events, individuals, and groups.
- To challenge inertia by breaking through old forms.
- To participate in helping build new forms with others.
- To deeply understand that nothing of real value can be created and sustained without collaborative effort.

- *To be teachers of both innovation and qualitative group life, by example.*

Capacities
Emotional-Subjective

- To create and maintain harmonious connections (relationships) with others.
- To intuitively understand others' specific needs.
- To personally feel the joy and pain of others.
- To work through one's personal history and come to forgiveness of self and others.
- To live the full range from personal empathy to detachment.

- *To be teachers of both personal empathy and detachment, by example.*

Physical-Emotional *Capacities*

- To experience that everything is at once a part-within-a-whole and also itself a whole.
- To respect, understand, and utilize the laws of nature.
- To be fully immersed in the detailed world of matter.
- For systemic thinking and implementation.
- To detach from the material world and gain perspective on one's collected data. This perspective results in the creation of a realizable vision.

- *To be teachers of both detailed systemic thinking (or planning) and the formulation of vision, by example.*

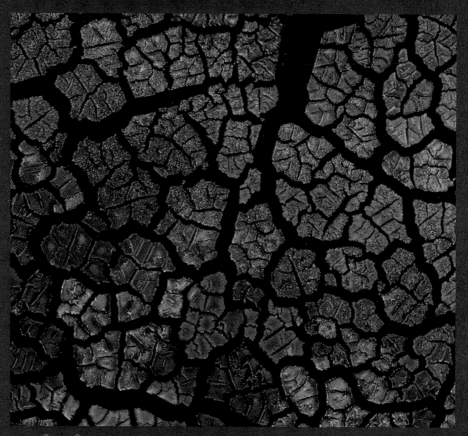

Capacities

Physical-Mental

- To perceive patterns in the complex interplay of events.
- To create and implement strategic, systemic models.
- For order, efficiency, and simplicity of form.
- To link the objective data of things with the subjective data of people.
- To value love as the highest law in the universe.

- *To be teachers of strategic, systemic thinking and compassion,
  by example.*

identity difficult. Without a measure of detachment, they can be at the mercy of whatever is happening around them. This vulnerability to outside influences can have relatively trivial consequences, such as feeling overwhelmed by scenes in movies; but it can also lead to more serious problems, such as inexplicable changes in mood, a sense of being out of control, and uncertainty of identity. As one emotional-subjective person has said,

> Sometimes I can be feeling wonderful, then suddenly I am feeling terrible. And then I change again. What has happened to me? . . . Am I experiencing my own pain, or have I picked up someone else's? . . . I don't know . . . Sometimes I feel I am going crazy.

Their sensitivity to others can sometimes make it difficult in the corporate world for emotional-subjective people to cope with situations when clients or members of a business unit are having problems. But as the following story illustrates, as they mature and set boundaries they can use their identification with others to be of compassionate service while maintaining their objectivity and sense of self.

> I can recall a number of circumstances where very loyal customers with whom I had developed a close relationship would lose their power within their organizations or even get fired. I felt horrible about the impact this unfortunate situation would have on them and their families. During my early years in corporate America, I would have a tough time trying to remain objective about the situation; I could actually get to the point of feeling sick. I also felt negative about the client's organization and senior executives.
>
> As I matured, I began to focus on the aspects of these situations that I could influence. I knew I had to start from scratch to build quality business relationships with my new clients. However, I would often do whatever I could to help the people who had been dismissed. I would maintain contact with them, try to buoy their spirits by working with them on their resumes, and hook them up with other organizations who were looking for business and information systems executives.
>
> The key thing for me to understand was that I couldn't personally prevent the negative situation from occurring. Those were the cards that were dealt. I

I celebrate myself and sing myself And what I assume, you shall assume, For every atom belonging to me as good Belongs to you.

—Walt Whitman

could only do my very best to improve everyone's current position, and that's what I focused on. This position helped me cope with the pain of the situation.

Jacob

One remarkable example of the emotional-subjective need to set boundaries is the story of Jacob, a four-and-a-half-year-old emotional-subjective boy. This story is also an example of a parent helping a child to "process" his life experiences.

Jacob complained frequently of headaches and stomachaches, which his parents came to suspect were physical responses to emotional tension. Because they were avid videotapers of their family, they were able to record his experiences. In the first videotape, Jacob is refusing to go to nursery school. He has a stomachache. His mother, a good student of Human Dynamics and an emotional-subjective person herself, asks him, "Jacob, is this your stomachache or somebody else's?"

Jacob: (after a few moments of thought) It's not mine!

Mother: Then what shall we do about it?

Jacob: (pointing to his stomach) Let's pretend this is a birthday cake with candles in it. One, two, three, we blow out the candles and it's all gone!

Jacob's stomachache did indeed vanish, and off he went to school! The second video records a scene that occurred one morning two weeks later. Jacob is irritable and complaining of a headache.

Mother: Jacob, something has upset you to cause your headache. Did something happen at school yesterday?

Jacob: No!

Mother: Did something happen this morning that is bothering you?

> **Jacob:** I *don't* want to talk!
>
> **Mother:** Jacob, something is bothering you to have caused your headache, and I'm going to sit here with you until we figure it out.
>
> **Jacob:** (begins to talk—goes round and round in circles for about 15 minutes and finally says) A new boy came to class and he said hello to everyone except me.
>
> **Mother:** So you felt left out, didn't you?
>
> **Jacob:** Yes. (pointing to his head) I feel as if something is coming right out of my head!
>
> And the headache disappeared.

Change: Light *and* Shadows

Emotional-subjective people are accustomed to experiencing change in the form of many shifts in moods and feelings and in the variety of experience to which they are attracted. However, they may be reluctant to embark on a new venture or change of course if it involves rearranging established relationships, whether with people, environments, prized possessions, or even ideas. Even as they move into the future, emotional-subjective people try to maintain valued connections. For example, they typically stay in communication with friends long after they have moved on to new environments, and their homes may overflow with memorabilia that they find impossible to relinquish. Often they do not embrace change until they have had time to get comfortable with its implications for their present relationships.

Emotional-subjective people have another important reason to approach change with caution; they are sensitive not only to the advantages, but also the possible problems inherent in the new. Unlike emotional-objective people, they usually see the shadows as well as the light. In fact, they more than *see*—they often *feel* what might go wrong. Therefore, they usually avoid precipitously jumping to something new. As a result, they may sometimes "miss the boat"—but their decisions may also be the wiser for their having waited.

As emotional-subjective people weigh decisions, they must analyze whether their concerns about change stem from their own fears and insecurities, with no basis in current actuality, or from real danger—or from a mixture of both.

The Need for Affirmation

Everyone appreciates genuine approval, recognition, and affirmation; but for emotional-subjective people, whatever their age or gender, giving and receiving approval is a real need. This does not indicate self-centeredness or weakness, but rather reflects their deep understanding, in a world that is too often mechanistic, of the general human need for positive connection. They are the guardians of the human touch. In both giving and receiving approval genuinely, they foster caring and appreciation among people.

Emotional-subjective people welcome acknowledgment for other reasons. It helps strengthen their sense of identity and, since they are the most self-critical group, bolsters their sometimes fragile sense of self-worth. Also, every day, whether speaking with people, reading a book or newspaper, listening to the radio, or watching a movie or television, emotional-subjective people register vividly not only the good in the world but also the harmful. Unless they have cultivated a capacity for detachment, they not only feel the world's sadness or pain, they may also feel *responsible* for it. Therefore, given that so much in the world is *not* okay, it is particularly important for them to receive reassurance from others that *they* are okay. Approval reminds them that the world has light as well as darkness, joy as well as sorrow, and demonstrates that people care enough about one another to reach out in appreciation.

Managers, teachers, and parents alike can reassure, energize, and motivate our substantial emotional-subjective population by frequently offering words of genuine appreciation, recognizing not only the gifts in performance and achievement that they share with others, but also their special skills and sensitivities in matters of relationship. For emotional-subjective people, just a few words of sincere recognition can make a significant positive difference. (And, of course, they do no harm to anyone!)

The Fear of Abandonment

Years ago, when Sandra worked as a therapist, she was surprised to hear many of her clients bringing up issues of abandonment, although none of them had literally been abandoned. They feared disconnection from significant people in their lives, no matter how little evidence existed to justify this fear. Sandra never understood the reason for this concern until she discovered later that issues of abandonment were prominent for a great many emotional-subjective people, no matter what their life experience.

Why should abandonment, or at least separation, be such a concern for emotional-subjective people? We hypothesize that this fear is the reverse side of the emotional-subjective gift for connection. Emotional-subjective people feel so linked to others that they register strongly, often both physically and emotionally, any kind of disconnection, even when the break in relationship is momentary and not explicitly expressed.

This experience may be especially common in early childhood, when infants cannot distinguish between themselves and others. As we have said, one way to identify infants as emotional-subjective is to observe how closely they stay connected to the people around them; how they track their parents and others with their eyes; how they respond to others' expressions; and how they react with evident distress when the connection is temporarily broken. Therefore, emotional-subjective people (as infants, as children, as adults) feel moments of disconnection strongly. It is part of the price they pay for the joy and sense of fulfillment they experience when connection is present. Each instance of disconnection contributes to a pool of such experiences, and this pool may grow into pervasive fears concerning loss, separation, and abandonment.

Emotional-subjective people remind us all that we really are participants in one life—that connection is a natural state to be valued and appreciated. They remind us to try to avoid abrupt disconnections, and that it is really preferable if in meetings, phone conversations, or dialogues we begin with a few moments to acknowledge one another in the spirit of camaraderie, and conclude in a personal and agreeable manner.

Memory and Time: The Interplay of Present and Past

Most emotional-subjective people retain extensive and vivid personal memories. Of all the personality dynamics, they are the most able to relive past events in detail, including both the sensory experiences *and* the associated feelings, as if they were happening in the present. This capacity can help emotional-subjective people come to terms with uncomfortable past experiences and eventually release or transform the feelings associated with them. It also enables them to bring the past alive and move listeners to tears or laughter with the vividness and emotional immediacy of their recollections.

Since emotional-subjective people naturally assume that this kind of memory is universal, they may interpret the less substantial memories of mental-physical and emotional-objective people ("How could you possibly forget *that*?"), or the more factual memories of the physically centered, as evidence of a lack of caring. This is not necessarily the case at all. The personality dynamics' experiences and foci of recollection are simply different.

"In remembering people and events, I not only remember my feelings, but I also have a very keen sensory recall. I can bring back the way people looked, smelled, the clothing they wore, the sounds of their voices, the tilt of their heads, the shape of a body, the look in someone's eyes, and all in Technicolor!"

In part, the vivid recollections of emotional-subjective people reflect the richness of their experience in the present moment. Their experience is very much "here and now." There is a constant interplay between the vivid experiences of the present and those of the past, both being incandescent with feelings.

Communication: The Emotional-Subjective Lifeline

For emotional-subjective people, communication serves a far greater purpose than merely transferring information. Its primary purpose is to facilitate and express personal connection. Emotional-subjective people like to communicate in many ways: through words, touch, notes and letters, gifts, eye contact, gestures, and facial expressions. To them, communication is a lifeline, a fundamental necessity, and a great joy.

Even in the most impersonal situations—for example, transferring data to a stranger over the telephone—emotional-subjective people will probably take the opportunity to personalize the conversation. They will at least try to visualize the individual at the other end of the line, sense his or her personal traits, and frame their communication accordingly.

At social gatherings, the emotional-subjective people usually do the most talking—once they have become comfortable. In fact, they often even feel a personal responsibility to help people feel at ease by making conversation and filling silences. But this personality dynamic group is likely to use the most words in any circumstance. This tendency springs in part from their wide range of feelings. For them, clear communication means conveying not only information or thoughts but also the complexities and subtleties of emotions. They also use verbal exchange with others to complete half-formed thoughts, clarify feelings, and translate their many intuitive sensings into cognitive understanding.

In seminars, when we ask for feedback from the different personality dynamic groups about their needs in communication, it is always the emotional-subjective group that compiles the most comprehensive and personalized list. Because this group wants above all to connect with others, they need to feel that other people are attentive not only to their words but also to *them*. They like to receive affirmation that they are being heard through nods, gestures, or verbal responses. If they have difficulty formulating an idea or a feeling, they want the listener to be patient. They know that they will come to clarity, if allowed the time.

When emotional-subjective people wish to discuss a problem, they appreciate a listener who is attentive and empathic and who might offer clarifying remarks. Usually they do not want to be offered solutions. If they want suggestions, they will ask for them.

If emotional-subjective people do not receive the kind of attentive receptivity that enables them to speak their thoughts and feelings fully, they feel that something vital has been denied them. As one of our emotional-subjective friends said, "If this process isn't allowed to happen, I feel it here," and she touched the area of her heart. "It's almost like a physical pain. There's so much inside, and it can't get out!"

Another emotional-subjective friend described his communication needs in this way: "It's the quality of the process itself that matters as much as what is communicated. I want to feel that the other person is sincerely and fully committed to that process. Communication is a dance, and I want someone who will dance with me!"

Communication *is* more of a dance for this group than for the other personality dynamic groups, a dance that is likely to have a complex choreography. For one thing, emotional-subjective people have a natural inclination and gift for communicating through accounts of their own experiences. These personal stories may be full of subjective references, details of feelings, local color, and tangential excursions inspired by something from their own narrative or the interjections of someone else. This multifaceted form of communication may seem unfocused to other personality dynamics, but it has its own logic of emotional connection and usually illustrates a point relevant to the topic under discussion. This is not to say that emotional-subjective people are incapable of a more concise and pointed form of communication when it is required (as in a business setting, for example). But they may need time to think aloud and "free associate" to make their points.

The emotional-subjective communication process is also more complex than that of the other personality dynamic groups in another way. It derives from the emotional-subjective sensitivity to what is *not* said as well as what is said. Even in the simplest exchange, they are engaged in tracking on multiple levels. In the following illustration, Stephen, an emotional-subjective person, converses with Jill as they work on a task. The structure of the exchange from his point of view might be as follows:

Jill: (Says something.)

Stephen: (Hears Jill's overt message. At the same time, he senses a disparity between the spoken words and something unspoken behind the words. He considers his response.)

Jill: (Speaks again.)

Stephen: (Tracks and considers
(a) Jill's overt message
(b) what Jill might be withholding
(c) why Jill might be withholding something
(d) his own response [which he makes]
(e) what he himself withholds.)

Jill: (Responds.)

Stephen: (Tracks and considers all of the above, plus his growing feeling of discomfort as the conversation continues. He also considers whether to address his discomfort directly with Jill; and if so, how and when. Now? Later? He may, at the same time, be gathering further information from details of her appearance, nuances in her demeanor, and consistencies or inconsistencies between her past and present behavior. Weaving together all this information, he shapes his response. And all this happens within a few moments, as they work together on the task!)

This example could pertain to any exchange, whether between a manager and his or her boss or subordinate, a husband and wife, a doctor and patient, two children at play, or a teacher and student. Although emotional-subjective people can experience this multitracking skill as a burden, it enables them to detect the many subtleties in any exchange, whether spoken or unspoken, and to shape their responses accordingly. In this way, emotional-subjective people cultivate harmony among people and achieve the degree of interpersonal connection so vital to them. They are masters of using language both as a tool for good communication and as a means for creating and maintaining positive relationships.

"When I listen to somebody, I don't just listen to their words. I'm thinking, sensing, and planning. I'm wondering if it is the appropriate time and environment in which to make the next comment. And I'm wondering about the kind of comment to make. I think a lot of times it would be better not to be so careful. I often overdo it in trying to find the specific language and tone that will meet the needs of the person I'm talking to."

Words Used Frequently by Emotional-Subjective People

feel	share	harmony	love
feeling	diversity	sensitive	like
artistic	intuition	individual	sense
process	approval	imagine	remember
personally	understand	empathy	Great!...Wow!
connect	need	sympathy	I, me, my
comfortable	gut feeling	subtle	you, your
relationship	inner	coordinate	sad, happy, etc.
how	create	nuance	

Conditions for Learning

Emotional-subjective people learn most effectively under certain conditions. These conditions include:

- a sense of personal comfort in the learning situation;
- auditory emphasis (discussion, personal exchange);
- a sense of personal connection with the instructor (through his or her expressions of personal approval, consistent interest, and honest exchange of feelings);
- affective, imaginative presentations (appealing to the emotions, possibly dramatic);
- clear structure;
- opportunities for communication and learning with others;
- specific activities that promote the capacity for focus (to balance the natural capacity for multifocus);
- specific time parameters;
- opportunities for release of body tension through movement;
- opportunities for creative expression;
- opportunities to identify and process feelings.

When Something Goes Wrong

A meeting didn't go as well as expected.

A communication was seriously misunderstood.

Plans were changed without everyone being informed.

A project or some part of it fails.

How do emotional-subjective people respond to such situations? They usually begin with Step 1 of the following sequence, then proceed as far as the level of their development and self-understanding permits. However, individuals often stop at the earlier steps and rarely reach Step 4.

Step 1

Their first impulse is to "look in the mirror" and blame themselves. "If only I had done this or that, things might have been different!" However irrational from an objective point of view, emotional-subjective people usually feel that they, and only they, are responsible for what has gone wrong. *Often, analysis stops here.*

Step 2

Next, they consider the role that others may have played. They might think, "But she never did advise me properly," or "He forgot to mail the invoices on time," or "They did not fulfill their promise."
Sometimes, analysis stops here.

Step 3

They reflect on the circumstances of the event or situation. They ask themselves such questions as, "Was the cold, damp weather a factor in people's energy being low? Was the poor A/V equipment a major distraction? Did the demands of the market change?"
Analysis rarely continues to this point. But if it does, one more step remains if full understanding is to occur.

Step 4

They take time to examine the situation fully from a perspective that includes all three steps. In doing so, they obtain understanding of the whole story, and learning takes place. At this point, it is difficult to maintain guilt; for they have seen the whole picture. Now it is up to them to act on the insight gained.
It is rare for anyone to engage in all four steps consistently.

Emotional-Subjective Characteristics: A Summary

Qualities
- animated
- individualistic
- communicative
- empathic
- creative (artistic; helping people; new forms)
- relational (making personal connections)
- expressive
- sensitive

Basic Learning Process
- auditory
- lateral
- characterized by dialogue
- interactive with others
- takes in information that has personal significance
- affective (appealing to the emotions)

Management Process

- participative
- collaborative
- communicative
- involved in diverse activities
- may not delegate enough

Values and Affinities

- diversity
- harmony
- regular, significant communication
- connection with people
- organization (connection of people with functions)
- expression of feelings
- creativity

Function

- connect and communicate personally
- organize
- create new forms
- link many parts
- address "people" issues

Interpersonal Relationships

- relational
- verbally expressive
- highly aware of the feelings of self and others
- personalizing

Factors Causing Stress

- lack of opportunity to express feelings
- impersonal or threatening environment
- lack of personal connection
- involvement in too many activities
- exposure to too many stimuli

Body Movements

- often in the horizontal plane (side-to-side)
- *great* variety of movements and postures
- flexible
- variety of facial expressions

Eyes

- expressive
- mobile
- moving between inner and outer focus
- personally connecting

Hands

- *great* many gestures
- used to express or dramatize personal feelings

Trippers and askers surround me,

People I meet, the effect upon me of my early life or the ward and

city I live in, or the nation,

The latest dates, discoveries, inventions, societies, authors old and new,

My dinner, dress, associates, looks, compliments, dues,

The real or fancied indifference of some man or woman I love,

The sickness of one of my folks or of myself . . . or depressions or exaltations. . . .

These come to me days and nights and go from me again,

But they are not the ME myself.

—Walt Whitman

Capacities

Physical-Emotional

- To experience that everything is at once a part-within-a-whole and also itself a whole.
- To respect, understand, and utilize the laws of nature.
- To be fully immersed in the detailed world of matter.
- For systemic thinking and implementation.
- To detach from the material world and gain perspective on one's collected data. This perspective results in the creation of a realizable vision.

- *To be teachers of both detailed systemic thinking (or planning) and the formulation of vision, by example.*

The Physical-Emotional Personality Dynamic: Creating Systems

In December 1992, I and my colleagues were given instructions to put together a preliminary plan for the design of the world's largest semiconductor factory. It was certainly the largest for Intel, in terms of the magnitude of the investment and the sheer square footage of the facility—it was to cover about 200,000 square feet and be five stories high—about 1.3 million square feet in total, including the office building.

I remember walking on the future site with one of the senior vice presidents who had just given us his ideas for the factory, its purpose, and the technology to be manufactured within it. At the time, the location was a parking lot and a large area of dirt on the edge of a mesa overlooking Albuquerque. The next day, I paced out the area I thought the building would cover, and I set a chair where I estimated the building's center would be. Then I sat down and just began to think about something of that size and complexity. I thought about the thousands of people it would take to operate it, the stresses it would put on the existing structure of the organization, and the changes we would need to make. I visualized the processes in the factory, the best way to lay it out, how the people could work relative to each other, and how material could flow most productively. In my mind, I laid a basis for building the factory, designing the layout, and determining aspects of the architecture, given the project's location. I was there several hours and finally snapped out of it only because the sun was going down and it was getting cold.

Almost nine months later, I had the opportunity to stand on the first section of roof. Because it was a five-story building on the edge of a mesa, the view was pretty spectacular. I sat up there and continued my ongoing process of thinking about how the project would unfold.

Looking down the escarpment at the adjacent neighborhood, I thought about Intel's role in relation to the community. The huge building was prominently set where the whole Albuquerque area could plainly see it. This seemed to me a metaphor for how we stuck out, politically and socially. It struck me deeply what our responsibilities were to the community around us. I thought of how our presence would affect people's lives, their drive to work, the economic development of the area, the small businesses, and employment. That was my introduction to the issue of being part of the community and figuring out how we could not only contribute to it, but also be perceived as being part of it.

It's been about two and a half years since I sat up on that roof, and I'd say that since then we've really gone down the path of community involvement. We realized that we needed to listen closely to the people from the community; we formed active community advisory panels, and we turned a significant corner when we started having regular dialogues with groups representing a broad spectrum of people.

Now I feel very good about it, because many people in our organization include community concerns in their thinking. We see our organization both as a community itself, and as a subset of the larger community outside.

To give an example, the area has a diverse population with many Hispanic and Native American people, and one of the things we are trying to do is ensure that the demographics of the community are fully represented in the organization. We are doing that partly through involving ourselves in many educational programs—ranging from those helping at-risk students to those that receive M.I.T. scholarships. We want to ensure that everyone who wants to work here has the educational preparation they need.

To me, building this community aspect is most exciting.

—DAVID MARSING, VICE PRESIDENT/GENERAL MANAGER,
    ASSEMBLY TEST MANUFACTURING, INTEL CORPORATION

Systems Thinking

Systems Thinking: A Metatheme for Physical-Emotional People

Physical-emotional people are natural systems thinkers. Their perceptions are holistic and essentially without boundaries. They experience everything—time, tasks, events, things, people—as interconnected. Their natural focus is not on distinct points or elements, but rather on the general flow of interactions that comprise a whole system of operation. Defining the parameters of any systemic unit often strikes them as artificial and unnatural, since every unit is itself part of a larger whole. They experience themselves, primarily, as an integral part of relational systems, which may extend to their family, their work group, their community, their culture, or humankind, depending on their maturity. They therefore often have less sense of individual identity than of group identity, a characteristic that they share with physical-mental people. They commonly refer to "we" rather than "I."

Physical-emotional people typically offer extraordinary capacities for perceiving how all the elements of a situation, structure, or organization fit or flow together; for assessing events in light of the long passage of time (from past to present to future); and for creating detailed systems of operation in which all the interacting elements are taken into account. Their systemic thinking is usually not limited to theories or models, but worked out in pragmatic detail.

In handling materials, they are often skilled craftspeople with an impressive capacity for detailed work. The following statement of a physical-emotional artisan exemplifies their thoroughness:

> A structure is complete only after it is examined completely, thoroughly, and minutely several times, until no small part is without its unity and application to the whole. Superfluous "extras" are removed unless their utility and value can be shown. It is still easy to add to the task at this point, provided that the addition is congruent with the existing framework of operation, and that it is consistent with the goals which were established in the first place.

As we shall see, the affinity of physical-emotional people for experiencing and thinking systemically finds expression in every aspect of their lives—in what and how they remember, in their relation to their bodies, in their process of communication, in the way in which they handle change, in how they learn, in how they undertake tasks—in everything they do.

Problem-Solving: Undertaking Tasks

When physical-emotional people undertake a task, set about solving a problem, or begin new learning, they follow a process radically different from that of the majority of the Western population. This difference has caused a great deal of misinterpretation of physical-emotional people, especially in organizations and educational institutions.

"When considering important things, like purpose, mission, or objectives, I always want to ask, 'What are the roots of this?' and 'How has this been expressed historically?' That's a way of knowing the real nature of something."

Physical-emotional people take in more data than do people of any other personality dynamic. When they take on a new task or learn something new, they need first to understand the full context of the task—the history leading up to it, any relevant present circumstances, and the required outcomes. Then they accumulate all the data they might possibly need—usually a great deal—with little or no preselection or prioritizing. They immerse themselves in this mass of information, and a remarkable process of assimilation, elimination, sorting, synthesis, and organization takes place. This process seems to be organic—that is, it is a natural process that moves in its own way and takes its own time, like the autonomic processes of the digestive system, independent of the individual's will or ability to consciously direct it. The end result of this process is a comprehensive understanding or a detailed, systemically operational plan. It is only at the end of the process that they can see the structure of the whole and demonstrate how everything fits together.

It is important that others understand this distinctive way of working, for this awareness can prevent much misunderstanding. For example, a young physical-emotional graduate student was preparing her doctoral thesis. She undertook this task in a typical physical-emotional manner: she accumulated masses of information and then allowed her organic, internal process to take place. As the expected first drafts failed to appear, her supervisor grew increasingly impatient and doubtful of her commitment, despite her efforts to reassure him that she *was* in fact working, and the task would be done. Eight months later, she knew she was ready. She sat at the typewriter and wrote the entire thesis without need for revision. Meanwhile, however, her suitability for the graduate program had come into question.

The following story told to us by a physical-emotional manager, Joe, also illustrates this characteristic physical-emotional problem-solving process. His personality dynamic is also reflected in the seamless, fully contexted, detailed, and factual nature of the narrative.

Joe: My wife and I bought a starter home in 1973. It was twenty-four by thirty-six feet and just the downstairs was finished. Two bedrooms, a living room, dining room, kitchen, and a bath. We had one child at the time. Another one arrived in 1974, and it became time to finish the upstairs, which I did myself to save money. I was teaching school at the time, so I couldn't afford to go out and hire anybody to do it. I had done all the framing of the various rooms upstairs, and it was time to do the plumbing, which my wife had been after me for some time to get done.

So one Saturday morning (and this was, oh, it must have been 1976) she said, "Don't you think it's about time you did the plumbing?" I replied, "Well, all right, I've got to get this monkey off my back, so I'd better do it." I went upstairs, and I sat in the framed-in bathroom on a five-gallon can of joint compound, and I started staring at the floor. And I sat there for six hours. I just stared at the floor. Several times my wife came up and asked me, "Well, aren't you going to *do* anything?" I said, "*I am*. I have to understand what I'm doing; I've got to lay this out."

In that period of time, in my mind, I physically laid out and did everything that I was going to have to do. I knew exactly where I was going to cut into the existing water lines; I knew what type of fittings I wanted to get; I had the number of different fittings counted up in my mind; I knew where all of the pipes were going to run; how many holes I had to drill; where I was going to have to notch out the floor joists; where I was going to have to lay a piece of tin or metal over the joists to prevent myself from driving a nail back through the pipe when I put the subfloor back down.

Once I did that, then I was comfortable going out to the hardware store and getting all the fittings and all the miscellaneous tools I needed, and I felt confident that I was going to be able to do it, and do it correctly, the first time. Until I had it all thought out in my mind, and was comfortable with it, I couldn't do the project. I would have been concerned the whole time that I had left something out. So I had to process all of that internally first. Prodding doesn't help me because I still can't take action until I am mentally ready and have thought the whole process through.

David: Did you actually draw a diagram, or anything like that, before you went to work?

Joe: No, I had it all in my mind. I wrote down only what I needed for materials, the various fittings and how many of them I needed; and I took a few measurements to double-check what I had estimated for the lengths of copper pipe, for example. I knew where I was going to put everything; and I knew what the fittings were, so I didn't have to draw a diagram. I actually visualized it. I see sequentially and as a whole, so before I start a job like that, I see where I will cut into the pipes to begin; I see where the T-fittings will have to go in; and I see that because those two pipes are close together, I will have to offset the angle of each of them, so they won't run into one another; I see that I can run them across the ceiling of the cellar, to where I'll take them up through the subfloor; I see where I'll have to notch out all the shelves in the downstairs bathroom linen closet, and run the pipes through with a half-inch separation between them. I can visualize all that. And then I started at one end and followed all the way through in a sequential order. So if this is the first connection, then I'm going to go out a foot, and then I'm going to make a left-hand turn, and then I'm going to run down about three feet, and then I have to make another right-angle turn, and then go straight up, and so on.

David: Is this way of seeing things—as whole systems of operation and then working systematically—part of your general way of functioning?

Joe: Yes, I'm not comfortable just jumping into something. I have to feel that there's a process in place, and I have to get an overview of what the process is going to be. And sometimes that can be a bit of a detriment, because I'm seen as not taking action. I've recognized that in the past and tried at times to be less precise, but it doesn't work for me. I need to have everything planned out to the minutest detail before I start something, so that I avoid mistakes. Sometimes the hardest part of the project is getting started. Once I get into it, it seems to work. But it's very difficult to make that start without having the entire thing visualized.

The implications of working this way in a fast-paced business environment are clear. Let's say, for example, that Maria has just hired Ted, who is physical-emotional, to manage a department in her organization. She knows he is qualified to do the job. Without understanding his personality dynamic, however—and assuming she is not a physical-emotional person herself—she might expect that after a short period of orientation in the department, Ted would start making decisions and giving directions, picking up the information he needed along the way. This expectation could create problems for both of them.

We have found that when physical-emotional people lack enough time to collect, absorb, and assimilate all the information they need in a new situation, the learning process is actually lengthened. With daily responsibilities piling up while he is trying to complete all the internal processing his personality dynamic requires, Ted is likely to feel stressed and frustrated. His manager, Maria, viewing him as progressing slowly for no apparent reason, is likely to become impatient and may well begin to question his competence.

If, on the other hand, Maria is aware of how Ted functions best, her approach might be quite different. Knowing that his learning begins with immersion in the total environment, she might tell Ted to take as much time as he needs—several weeks, or even months—to "settle in." Given the time he requires to absorb the situation holistically, Ted will gain the comprehensive, systemic awareness he needs to do his job most efficiently. When he is ready to take action, he will move quickly, systematically, with a grasp of the systemic functioning of whatever unit he has responsibility for, and probably with a full appreciation of its relation to the organization as a whole. His work will benefit the organization far more than if he were pushed to start making decisions sooner.

It is important to know that in *familiar* situations, physical-emotional people move into action quickly and decisively, though their process is still thorough and methodical.

Time: Continuity, History, and Genealogy

Physical-emotional people experience time and events in a fluid, seamless way. Yesterday, today, and tomorrow flow easily into one another. For physical-emotional people, personal and collective histories are linked in a boundary-free continuum that includes the past, present, and future. LeRoy Littlebear, a leader of the Seven Nations Confederation of Native American peoples, gave a speech to the Constitutional Committee Hearings in Ottawa in January 1992 that eloquently expressed the physical-emotional perspective.[1] He speaks for physically centered people everywhere, whatever their culture.

"As we're talking on the telephone, I'm sitting here looking out at a lake, and I'm aware of the cyclical nature of life, the motion of the Earth and the sun and all the natural processes that link us to what has come before and what will come after. Everything is part of this larger, continuous time scale."

The problem is that you don't understand that we are different . . . or how we are different. For you, time is linear. You never have enough time. For us, this is not so. For us, January 1 is not a celebration . . . it is merely another day.

In your linear thinking, you have the notion of singularity; but we have a holistic way of thinking. We are part of everything that is around us. For us, everything is animate. The land about which we speak is animate and, as such, is part of us. We cannot separate from it. You tell us that you bought our land. How can you sell something that is part of you?

So we ask you to transcend your boundaries. We are generous people, and we are very adaptable.

The temporal frame of reference for those who are physical-emotional extends further than that of any other group. They not only think and talk in terms of continuity, they *experience* it. As the following statement from a physical-emotional person illustrates, they experience themselves and their activities as part of an ongoing process across extended time:

I first noticed this phenomenon some years ago: I'd be out in the woods hunting, and as darkness came on I'd climb a tree. I'd be perched in the tree in the dark, and then about half an hour before sunrise, dawn would start to come. It's quite a magical moment—the light gathers and things gradually become quite distinct. And I'd have this strong feeling: "I've done this before—not just many times but hundreds of times." I feel like I'm actually back there,

---

[1] In our experience, a high proportion of Native American people are physically centered, mostly physical-emotional. This is consistent with our findings that the majority of people from the Far East are physically centered, since the roots of Native Americans are in Asia.

long before recorded history, when we were all primitive hunters and that was all there was. My sense is that there's some part of me that's alive now that was alive then, and under certain conditions I recognize it and say "I'm there!" It feels like it's a physical part of me that evolved then and is with me now, maybe in my brain stem, so there's a continuity.

Because physical-emotional people experience such a deep sense of continuity with the past, an extraordinary proportion of them, from all walks of life, have a great interest in history. It has been fascinating for us to note that so many of the historians whose personality dynamics we have been able to identify are, or were, physical-emotional. Winston Churchill, for example, who was awarded a Nobel Prize for his work as a historian, was of this personality dynamic. "History," he evocatively wrote, "with its flickering lamp, stumbles along the trail of the past, trying to reconstruct its scenes, revive its echoes, and kindle with pale gleams the passion of former days."

Another aspect of physical-emotional people's pervasive sense of continuity with the past is their fascination with genealogy. Most members of this group are interested in keeping track of their ancestry. Many chart their genealogical trees and do extensive research on the lives of their ancestors. It reinforces their sense of themselves as part of one continuous thread. The following family reflection is the kind of story that physical-emotional people love to tell:

> **As I have worked on this book— and writing it has been rather like editing a film for which the photography has been done so generously that there is a great abundance of material from which to choose to make any point— I have rediscovered how it happened that I grew up ahead of my time. In part it came about because during my whole childhood I shared my grandmother's lively relationship to the past and present.**
>
> **—Margaret Mead**

I believe that many of my ancestors were physical-emotional, as I am. In my family, we tell stories about my grandfather. I never knew him to work; all I knew him to do was hunt and fish. To make a place for himself in the community as a young man, he identified things that needed to be done in the community and then did them. He lived in a small, rural town that didn't have a store. He decided it would help the townspeople if they had a general store, so he built one.

He also became a sort of bank. My dad tells the story of how in the old days, when it was hard to make it financially, people would come in for their coffee or flour or whatever, and my grandfather would write up the order, roll it up, and put it in a box under the counter because he knew the people who could and couldn't pay. So he was a kind of a bank. People would pay if and when they had the money.

There's another story about my grandmother. A very poor family with five extremely bright children lived in the town, but they had no money. So when the children went to high school, my grandmother arranged to fix their lunches, and the children would come by and pick up these paper bags and go to school. She did that because it was what that family needed.

My worldview in part comes from my ancestors: my family saw what was needed and put a structure in place that offered service to others.

The Natural World and the Human World

The natural affinity for systemic experiencing that we see in both physically centered groups (physical-mental and physical-emotional) shows up in their unique relationship to nature. It is as if they *know* the river, *hear* the rocks, and *participate* with all living creatures. They experience themselves as part of the same all-embracing system. Even natural disasters, such as fires, floods, and earthquakes, do not seem as upsetting to them as to others, because they deeply know these as normal, inevitable events, expressing nature's need for realignment and renewal. Such events become disasters only to those who regard themselves as separate from the natural system and miscalculate or disregard its forces.

Physical-emotional people feel at one with nature in a way that they would like to feel connected with people. As physically centered people, they have a deep need to feel themselves part of the group, the "tribe." *Family* and *community* are key words in their vocabulary. Yet in the individualized Western world, especially in fast-paced urban environments where this group is so evidently in the minority, they can feel themselves to be "strangers in their own land." This sense is often so customary for them that they are barely aware of it, until they experience the contrast when they have the opportunity to reconnect with nature or are with others of their own personality dynamic. Indeed, many physically centered people have told us how much more "at home" they have felt in the radically different cultures of the Orient, where the great majority of the population is physically centered.

When you walk out in the street, particularly in cities, or ride in elevators, you see that people don't say anything to each other. They don't even make eye contact. I wonder why we don't connect more with one another.

The image that just came to me is that I feel connected with life itself— connected with trees, connected to stones, and connected with living energies. And there's a feeling that all is natural and familiar except for the human species. That is what has been sad—not feeling that energy flow back and forth with people.

I hadn't realized until I participated in a Human Dynamics seminar how not feeling connected has been consistent in my business experience, and even in school with teachers. I've had plenty of attention in my life, and I've been reasonably successful and done well in school, but I've had a sense of separation—of somehow not being recognized for who I am—as if I'm in a foreign country. And there's something profoundly bothersome about that.

> **Before I built a wall I'd ask to know**
> **What I was walling in or walling out,**
> **And to whom I was like to give offense.**
> **Something there is that doesn't love a**
> **wall, that wants it down. . . .**
>
> **—Robert Frost**

Adaptability, Boundaries, and the Difficulty Saying "No"

An apt metaphor for the physical-emotional group may be nature itself. Nature is without boundaries. Sky, water, and earth are connected in a seamless relationship of space and time. Physical-emotional people experience themselves as an integral part of this undivided system.

Like nature, physical-emotional people tend to be very adaptable. What is, *is*. What happens, *happens*. It is easy for them to accept events, things, and people as they are; and they can be extraordinarily enduring.

This is a wonderful gift. On the other hand, it can also be a burden. Experiencing themselves as part of a seamless whole and identifying with the collective can sometimes make it difficult for them to speak with their own voices and to set limits where it is appropriate to do so. Physical-emotional people will often uncomplainingly accumulate a larger workload than one person can reasonably handle, or not oppose an individual or a policy when they are in disagreement, because it feels unnatural for them to say "no." Part of the developmental journey for physical-emotional people is to learn to live in two worlds: a world of integration with everything and everyone, and a world of individual personal consciousness, in which they

"It seems unnatural to me to say 'no.' I've noticed that the tree doesn't say 'no' to the sun or rain or anyone sitting under its branches, it only says 'yes.' I need to remember that I am not a tree, although there are times when my relationship to the tree seems so familiar and profound that I temporarily forget the domain in which I live."

give voice to their own perspectives.

This journey of self-differentiation and articulation may not be easy even when consciously undertaken. One physical-emotional person tells of recently hiring a person he didn't really feel was qualified. "I had listened to my group, who insisted that the person in question was worthy of employment. We hired him, and in one month I had to fire him. It was extremely difficult for him, for the group, and for me. I guess I'm still learning, but it still feels unnatural to say 'no.'"

The Physical Body: Absorbing Sensory Detail

Physical-emotional people seem to continually take in all the sensory information about them, both consciously and unconsciously. Like sponges, their bodies seem to absorb all the details of the physical environment—the objects, the sounds, the light and the lighting, the people, and everything said. They also pick up feelings but, unlike emotional-subjective people, are often unaware that they are doing so.

Because of this comprehensive and continuous process, physical-emotional people can feel overloaded if they do not have breaks from incoming stimuli. It is especially beneficial for them if breaks can be taken outdoors. At the least, when they are in large groups—in a conference room, for example— they might find it helpful to move to one of the corners where they have more space and can take a more objective and comprehensive view of what is going on. It is also helpful for them to be in rooms with natural light and to sit near windows, especially if these look out on a natural environment.

Because this process of absorption is incessant, it is essential for the health of physical-emotional people that they set aside a time and place each day for inner balancing, in which there is a relative absence of stimuli. They need quiet not only for its own sake but also to become conscious of, think over, sort, and sift everything that they have taken in, without distraction. Otherwise, it seems that their physical systems become weighed down with masses of unsorted data, and they can lose energy. Many physical-emotional people we know awaken in the early morning hours to give themselves sufficient quiet time for this process of synthesis and clarification. Some find it helpful to externalize their thinking by writing. All benefit from having the opportunity to process their experiences and information with others.

Indispensable to physical-emotional people is frequent time alone in nature, so that they can resynchronize themselves with the rhythms that are so profoundly their own.

Feedback that we receive from physical-emotional people suggests that the slower rhythm associated with the physical principle is reflected in their having somewhat lower blood pressure and slower heart rate, pulse, and metabolism than the norm. They also seem to have an unusually high tolerance for localized pain. In fact, they seem not to register pain acutely unless their whole body is involved or the situation is extreme.

Memory and the "3-D World"

Because of their dominant physical component and sensitivity to the past, physical-emotional people have remarkably varied and detailed factual memories. They typically have a prodigious recollection of facts, figures, and data related to their work or interests. They also often retain complete full-color memories of environments and recall their personal experiences with a great deal of sensory detail. They can sometimes re-experience their movements, as well as the sights, sounds, smells, tastes, and physical sensations of past activities and events. But unlike emotional-subjective people, they will not necessarily remember their accompanying emotions.

"I can remember lots of details from my childhood. I remember the brook I used to walk over. I can still remember how I hung over the brook. I used to lie down and watch the little skeeters. I can still hear the sounds of the water and smell the smells."

The following account reveals how the past can be re-experienced by a physical-emotional person:

There was one incident when I was about eight years old and I climbed a tree. I can still see myself climbing the tree. The branches were very close together, so it was hard to climb. It was also very tall, and I knew it was somewhat dangerous to be doing it by myself, but I don't remember the emotion, just the experience. I can go through that whole experience of climbing the tree. I went almost to the top. The tree was moving in the wind, and I can still feel the actual movement. I don't know what I was wearing. And I'm not really remembering the exhilaration of it. It's the doing of it. I can redo it.

For me to convey the essence of my memories, it's not as if I would take a video, put it in, and show you that experience. You would have to be moved through the experience with me in some way. There's something about motion in the body that's remembered. There's something about realness.

My memory is about physical movement—about how my feet went up and down. I'm always aware of movement. That's part of being alive. Nothing really is standing still, even though it looks as if it is.

3-D Memory

The following comments on memory are from three different physical-emotional people.

"Three-dimensionality—being able to see the other side of something—that's very real for me. In high school, I was the first person to take mechanical drawing. Doing isometrics from all views was an absolute snap for me. I could look at something, and I knew what was on the other side. For me, being aware of the angles and the three-dimensionality relates to a sense of being in the whole of something. It's as if everything is connected. You can stand at any point in time within a three-dimensional space."

"I've started examining some of my memories, and I notice that I remember things by being in the space again. I know where everyone was by the space they occupied in the room. If we were to talk about something that happened when we first met five years ago, I would say, 'I don't remember who said it, but it came from over here.' It's like being in the environment again and knowing in what part of the three-dimensional space something happened."

"I remember things from an early age, and I see them as if I were in a movie. I don't necessarily remember what people said, but I'm quite sure I can remember many details. One example was when we were living in Cedar Rapids, Iowa, when my younger brother was a tiny infant and I was about one and a half years old. I remember my mother first showing him to me. I also remember a year or so later, when I was about three, painting my brother with oil paint. I can recall the scene clearly today. We were 'playing' under the sleeping porch of my grandmother's house. I can see under the house, in all its details. There were boxes and crates and old bicycles, and we got into the paint. It was cream color. I first painted some of the orange crates, and then I thought, 'Gee, I think I'll paint Jackie!' So, I did! I painted his clothes, face, and hair; and he thought it was funny. Mom didn't. I knew she was upset, but I was too little to be punished. When I recall that scene, I know I can also turn around in my memory and see the back-yard, the garage, the garden, and the trees, as in a movie."

Communication: Patient and Practical

Physical-emotional people generally prefer to listen—and speak only when they feel their message is needed. When they do express an opinion, their ideas tend to be practical, detailed, and related to the deeper purpose or context of the task at hand. They are usually patient listeners, absorbing every word. Because they tend to remain quiet until they have something to say and don't take action until they have completed their plan internally, others may sometimes radically misinterpret their quietness and stillness as "nothing going on."

The content of this group's communication process tends to be concrete and practical, emphasizing facts rather than feelings, and the achievable rather than the speculative or fantastic. Because words serve as concrete objects and reflect systematic thought, physical-emotional people formulate spoken statements with care. Statements to physical-emotional people need to be made with equal care, because they tend to take words literally and use them as a basis for taking considered action.

The natural rhythm of physical-emotional people's communication is even-paced and deliberate. Indeed, they are often interrupted by others (especially emotionally centered people) who find their pace overdeliberate or who mistakenly believe a pause to mean that the speaker has finished what he or she has to say. Physical-emotional people may also seem to be "slow," because they need time to extract required

"When we [a group of physical-emotional people] got into our dialogue this morning, it struck me that a natural pacing occurred. We were in the same rhythm. It was the same feeling I have when I am in the woods—things are happening naturally, interlocking and building as they should. It happens so rarely when I am with people. If it were to happen more often—that would be an ideal world!"

data from their vast bank of accumulated information. When they do speak, their statements tend to be either factual and concise, or factual and very detailed—depending on who their audience is, the amount of information they feel needs to be conveyed, and the listener's willingness to adapt to their rhythm.

Often they like to use a story or anecdote to convey the richness, complexity, and interconnectedness of what they wish to communicate. It is not natural for them merely to make points, because points for them are always part of a larger whole. In addition, they are uncomfortable with an exchange of abstractions—they prefer concrete examples.

> "If I'm asked, 'Tell me the most important points,' well, my mind doesn't work that way. I end up telling little stories. I find when I'm teaching in a case-oriented business school that the only way I can really answer a profound question is to tell a story. But I find that many students can't handle a story. They say, 'Just tell me the answer—give me the three points!' Well, there aren't three points!"

Sometimes others can even interpret physical-emotional people's silence or deliberate speech or action as slow-wittedness, a judgment no more valid for a physical-emotional individual than for anyone else. This misinterpretation can lead to grave consequences.

Many children in classrooms have been mistakenly labeled "slow learners"; many talents in organizations have not been recognized, used well, and rewarded; and many physical-emotional people have felt themselves to be somehow inferior, because their distinctive processes of thinking and communicating have not been understood. Physical-emotional people are commonly extraordinary resources of information, systemic thinking, and practical skills. But these may remain unknown to others because they are not reflected in ready communication.

Organizing Ideas

"I catalogue ideas in gestalts, not by topics. This sometimes makes my retrieval of information slow and difficult. My mental 'file folders' are labeled according to the whole experience I have had.

"Emotionally centered people are different. They're like painters when they talk—dabs here, dabs there. What they say is like a vector in a computer program pointing to a whole library of data or experiences. They hop around to different places. It's very difficult for physically centered people to work that way. The emotionally

> centered get frustrated with us because we do our thinking inter-
> nally and just tell them what our conclusion is."

It is a common error in Western culture to believe that speed and intensity of speech indicate superior intellect or capability. We need to attend
carefully to the statement of one young physical-emotional manager who,
though brilliant, had experienced his full share of frustration. In describing
his communication process to his colleagues, he explained, "You need to
understand that I process *every* word you say. Therefore I am always a little
behind you. Know that in my silence there is much activity."

The word "context" holds enormous significance for physical-emotional
people. In written or oral communication, they like to give and be given
detailed background information that "sets the scene." This information
may include historical data, topographical data, personal data, details of
current circumstances, the parameters of the topic of communication, and
the purpose of the communication. In describing an event, presenting a
project, telling a story, teaching, explaining, or directing, the establish-
ment of such context is vital to their discourse. This detailed scene-setting
takes more time than other personality dynamics customarily require; but
once it is established, it will contribute significantly to the success of the
communication.

> When somebody I don't know is trying to communicate with me, I need to
> know who they are, where they come from, what their background is.
> Otherwise I have difficulty in knowing how to receive their messages.
>
> I find it ironic that in a business school they worry so little about context.
> "Let's put it into context," and then they write three paragraphs. Well, you
> can't put things in context in three or four paragraphs. You've got to tell some
> more stuff!

One way to shorten this process in business encounters is to provide physical-emotional people with advance information in writing to set the context. They value written communication for its precision and the time it
allows for consideration.

Clear and Detailed Communication

The written communication that physical-emotional people favor is clear, factual, and detailed. The following note was written by a physical-emotional friend to one of our colleagues, instructing her on making changes to panels that he had originally constructed for displaying information about the learning processes of the different personality dynamics.

DEAR SHARON:

I'm told that you will be the lucky person to perform this task. Don't worry; it's very, very easy. First you must visit an art supply store, the kind of place that sells paints, brushes, colors—things an artist might use. Ask them for a can of their strongest spray adhesive (for example, I use 3M Super 77 spray adhesive; no CFCs because we already breathe quite enough of that junk). Take it home, or to the place you work. Spread plenty of newspapers on the floor, and make sure there is lots of ventilation! Put the new "learning begins" statement on the newspapers, face down, and spray the back side according to the directions on the can of adhesive.

Now, my adhesive can says to immediately put the sprayed thing in place for the strongest bond; yours may be different, so again, follow directions. The important thing is having someone help you do the final placement on a piece of large paper.

Of course all this would not be necessary if the protective spray I used before did not dissolve the black ink, but we learn so many new things every day! Hope you and yours are well.

Yours,
FRANK

Words Used Frequently by Physical-Emotional People

time	accuracy	whole	details
concrete	history	holistic	facts
complete	literal	delegate	data
context	precise	group/team	methodical
action plan	system	consensus	reliable
immersion	systemic	past	story
utility	practical	real	silence
experience	absorb	three-dimen-	nature/natural
experiential	specific	sional	we, our
continuity	organic	do	

Teams: Working Toward Consensus

Because of their inherent sense of identification with "groupness," physical-emotional people have a natural affinity for teamwork and a desire to create consensus. They enjoy working with others in a cooperative atmosphere of common purpose, and group participation gives them the opportunity to serve as an integral part of the whole.

They typically bring to groups qualities of groundedness, practicality, and patience, and their gifts for seeing systemic interconnections and creating detailed, systematic plans. Their pace will probably be more deliberate than that of their emotionally centered colleagues, and they are likely to be less talkative. As they listen, they absorb everything that is happening and every word that is being said, so they are usually able to summarize meetings with great reliability. They also filter out the emotional content to arrive at a clear understanding of the facts. They themselves usually have a great deal of factual information to offer.

"I prefer to think things through by myself, rather than in a process of exchange or debate. Because I also tend to think in terms of whole systems, much inner assembling needs to be done before I am ready to state my conclusions."

Physical-emotional people will probably be able to contribute their best to meetings if they are provided with as much relevant information as possible beforehand; and they may well make their best response to what transpires if they have time afterward to assimilate all that takes place. This response might be written to team members or given at the next meeting.

Because physical-emotional people sometimes have difficulty expressing their own opinions, it might be helpful if the team asks them for their views, provided they are not pressed to reply immediately but can respond later if they prefer. In general, the more deliberate the pace and the more systematic the team's process, the easier it is for them to make their contribution.

Because they are patient and persistent, and value consensus, physical-emotional people often make effective arbitrators.

The Language of Ironwork

There exists in the world of blacksmiths a universal language spoken through the tools while working at the anvil. When a smith needs help on a particular piece, he calls for an assistant known as a striker, signaling him not with his voice, but through a rapid series of hammer taps on the anvil. These ring out like a piercing solo, insisting on being heard over the din of the smithy. Once the striker is poised in front of the anvil with a 12 lb. sledgehammer in his hands, the smith pulls the bar of glowing hot iron from his forge and places it firmly on the anvil. He delivers a precisely placed blow that is immediately followed by the striker's sledge landing in exactly the same spot.

Without words of instruction, these first two blows mark the tempo of the striking to follow and dictate at what force the strike shall beat. A beat is not missed as the following succession of blows, only fractions of seconds apart, continue in a finely orchestrated rhythm, all the while coaxing the form to life that is held within the hot iron's volume. No matter where on the iron's surface the smith cares to work, the striker will follow, returning a mirrored reflection of the smith's direction. The exchange is continued until the bar loses its softening heat and the smith glides his hammer along the anvil face as a motion to rest. Timeless in its message, this particular dialogue has been the dominion of smiths since the first lone craftsman realized that teamwork was more effective than solitary enterprise.

—*Tom Joyce*

Change: Thinking Things Through First

Physical-emotional people deeply know that although formulating an idea for change is simple, implementing it is often an intricate and time-consuming process with far-reaching consequences, both evident and hidden. They therefore weigh carefully any suggestions for change before they accept them and move into action. They naturally want to examine closely the lessons of the past and evaluate in some detail the consequences for the future before they embrace any idea for initiating change and move into action.

Oren Lyons, the contemporary Native American chief of the Onondaga Nation, is physical-emotional. He explains that his people, in making decisions, use a point of reference seven generations into the future. Looking at this kind of temporal frame of reference, it is easy to see why physical-emotional people do not undertake change lightly. Change can be particularly difficult for them if it does not flow naturally from past to present to future, but involves an abrupt shift in policy or direction.

For example, one physical-emotional manager said,

> When the new CEO arrived, he instituted a lot of change that affected everybody in the organization. It was a *whole* change, connecting vision to implementation, and strategies to people issues. The purpose, utility, and direction of the change was clearly stated. He took into consideration the past, respected the present, and projected a better future. He went to extreme pains to make certain that the change process was communicated to everyone. I was excited about the whole process—I had no difficulty with it at all.
>
> I have difficulty with the kind of change that feels partial—when someone changes just one process and presents the change as, "This is the way we're going to do this from now on." If I don't understand *why* we need to change a current system, if I'm not included in the change process, or if people don't realize that one change often involves a systemic redesign of a whole project, I am *very* uncomfortable. This happens a lot.

No other personality dynamic group has such a capacity for seeing the total impact of decisions in both the short and long run. Feeling the weight of the implications of change for the whole system, physical-emotional people want decision-makers (themselves or others) to consider all the ramifications of a change carefully and to plan its implementation systematically. As far as possible, they want to avoid subsequent alterations because they know that changing a part often requires making adjustments to the whole. Physical-emotional people have another reason for not accepting change quickly—the apparently autonomic nature of their thinking. It is as if the body itself has to assimilate and find comfort with a new idea before they can take confident action. Once this process is complete, and they have internally accepted and integrated the idea for change with all its detailed ramifications, physical-emotional people will move into action quickly, methodically, and with total commitment.

In Western cultures, many physical-emotional people suffer intense stress because others neither share their attitudes toward change, nor understand their process in adapting to it. They are sometimes even judged to be conservative, stubborn, set in their ways, or resistant to change, although none of these labels is necessarily accurate. But physical-emotional people do require answers to such fundamental questions as, "Is the proposed change appropriate in the light of past experiences, current needs, and long-term consequences? Can we *really* pull it off, given current reality and the resources available? What do we need practically and in detail to make it work?"

In addition to considering these questions carefully, the best way others can help physical-emotional people to process change is to provide them with the *time* they need to consider, assimilate, plan for, and adjust to it. This may mean giving them advance notice about an impending change, preferably in writing, including as much data as possible on the reasons for the change, the actions needed to implement it, the goals sought, and the anticipated impact. This will help them to contribute their characteristic gifts—assess the value of the change and its long-term consequences realistically, raise issues of practicality, and plan its implementation in careful detail.

Conditions for Learning

Physical-emotional people learn most effectively under certain conditions. These conditions include:
• utility of the learning made explicit;
• considerable context provided;
• clear, systematic, concrete, and detailed presentation;

- clear parameters for assignments (*specific* instructions for what, why, where, when, how);
- kinesthetic emphasis in a "hands-on" environment (opportunities for learning by experience, demonstration, and involvement of the whole body);
- deliberate pacing;
- sufficient time allowed to absorb, assimilate, and distill data, complete tasks, and formulate responses (whether spoken or written);
- concentration on one topic at a time over an extended period, rather than many different things in a relatively short time;
- periodic checks to ensure that sufficient data is available;
- avoidance of singling out from group;
- a relaxed atmosphere.

When Something Goes Wrong

A meeting didn't go as well as expected.

A communication was seriously misunderstood.

Plans were changed without everyone being informed.

A project or some part of it fails.

How do physical-emotional people respond to such situations? They usually begin with Step 1 of the following sequence, then proceed as far as the level of their development and self-understanding permits. However, individuals often stop at the earlier steps and rarely reach Step 4.

Step 1

In this step, physical-emotional people establish as far as possible the facts of the *concrete situation* ("What went wrong?"). At the same time, they ask themselves what *they* did or did not do that contributed to the problem. They define what went wrong in terms of work and workmanship, emphasizing their own role. Self-blame is common at this stage.

Often, analysis stops here.

Step 2

They enlarge their perspective to include *other people's* actions. For example, "He did not give me all the data that I needed. She did not complete the first phase of the project. The boss did not share his new plan with the rest of us." As with Step 1, they evaluate the "others" in terms of work and workmanship.
Sometimes, analysis stops here.

Step 3

The *situation*, *self,* and *others* are all examined. Now, however, if the individual is sufficiently personally conscious, he or she sees the people involved as unique, with their individual ways of experiencing, thinking, feeling, and functioning. This is different from viewing people only in terms of their capacity to work. This step brings valuable new data to the situation.
Analysis rarely continues to this point. But if it does, one more step remains if full understanding is to occur.

Step 4

At this stage, physical-emotional people step back and take the long view, including all the information derived from the preceding steps. This full picture shows them the relationships among everyone concerned and offers a springboard for solutions. They have learned something useful about themselves and their colleagues and achieved a balanced understanding of what went wrong and how to fix it.
It is rare for anyone to engage in all four steps consistently.

Physical-Emotional Characteristics: A Summary

Qualities
- still, grounded
- calm
- enduring
- adaptive
- receptive
- practical
- objective

Basic Learning Process
- systemic
- interactive with task
- taking in much detailed data
- extensive internal processing
- hands-on experience (kinesthetic)
- absorption over time

Management Process

- delegate tasks easily
- share the parts within the whole
- need freedom to set own schedule
- process much information—may need time to reach decisions
- may need help with personalized communication and "people issues"

Values and Affinities

- practicality
- turning ideas into reality
- detailed planning, producing, packaging
- factual communication
- cooperation
- the natural world
- continuity
- interest in how things work
- systematic thinking and problem-solving

Function

- translate plans into actuality
- ensure practicality
- link present with past *and* future
- undertake detailed practical work
- bring stability
- take whole systems into account

Interpersonal Relationships

- serve needs of others
- accepting
- calm
- reliable
- may need help in expressing feelings and in personal exchange

Factors Causing Stress

- insufficient factual data
- overload of accumulated data and memories
- insufficient time to process data and make responses
- insufficient time alone, especially in nature, to reconnect with natural body rhythm
- lack of clear parameters and directives for tasks and responsibilities

Body Movements

- relatively still
- movements small and slow
- often in the sagittal (forward/back) plane
- relaxed and "grounded" posture

Eyes

- regarding
- diffuse focus

Hands

- gentle, slow, soft gestures often used to describe function

To be recognized and accepted by a peregrine, you must wear the same clothes, travel by the same way, perform actions in the same order. Like all birds, it fears the unpredictable. Enter and leave the same fields at the same time each day, soothe the hawk from its wildness by a ritual of behavior as invariable as its own. Hood the glare of the eyes, hide the white tremor of the hands, shade the stark, reflecting face, assume the stillness of a tree. A peregrine fears nothing he can see clearly and far off. Approach him across open ground with a steady unfaltering movement. Let your shape grow in size but do not alter its outline. Never hide yourself unless concealment is complete. Be alone. . . . The hunter must become the thing he hunts. Persist, endure, follow, watch.

—John Alex Baker

Physical-Emotional & Physical-Mental

A Brief Comparison

Whereas the emotional principle is the principle of individual self-expression, the physical principle is the principle of the group ("groupness"). Identified strongly with the group, the two physically centered personality dynamics (physical-emotional and physical-mental) are more alike than are the two emotionally centered groups, whose members show greater individuality of expression.

As an aid to distinguishing between the physical-emotional and physical-mental personality dynamics, we outline below some basic points of likeness and difference between them.

Key Similarities

- Both groups think systemically.
- Practical matters come first.
- "The way things are" and "what works" are two principles that guide their actions.
- They are highly attuned to their physical surroundings and to the overall context of any situation.
- They are deliberate in their thinking, communication, and activity.
- They collect and process large amounts of data.
- They see words almost as physical objects: useful items that are dependable, believable, and stable. They can be uncomfortable with imprecise, abstract, or emotionally laden language.
- Because of their group identification, they sometimes have difficulty expressing their own thoughts, feelings, and opinions.
- They appreciate the past and the maintenance of continuity.
- They are often interested in history, and its implications for the present and future.
- They possess amazingly retentive memories for facts, environments, and situations.
- They prize craftsmanship.
- They learn new material most readily through hands-on experience and demonstration.

Key Differences

The two physically centered groups also show several important differences. These differences generally stem from the nature of the connection of the physical principle to its secondary principle in each case. For example, the close connection between the physical and emotional principles in the physical-*emotional* group means that they process a multiplicity of connections among the data in which they immerse themselves. The close connection with the mental principle in the physical-*mental* group means that they naturally have a somewhat more detached perspective and manipulate their data more selectively.

Let's look at a few of the resulting distinctions by revisiting the story of Joe, a physical-*emotional* manager, (see pp. 157–158), and comparing Joe's problem-solving approach with that of Don, a physical-*mental* manager.

- Joe takes in *all* the data relevant to any undertaking, without pre-sorting. In the beginning, every piece of data has equal value and equal weight. After he has gathered the data, he begins a largely autonomic process of assimilation. In this process, he sifts the emotional material from the facts, works through all ambiguities, and begins to make natural connections.

  Don, on the other hand, consciously selects and sorts information from the beginning.

- Joe's process is almost completely internal. It takes its own time and moves in its own way.

  Don does not keep a whole complex process in his mind. He uses diagrams, models, notes, key points, and structures to help him along the way. He directs the process more consciously in terms of time frames and procedures.

- If Joe's process is interrupted, it may take him some time to "get back in the flow."

  Don will probably be able to get back in the flow more easily, especially as he will probably have recorded his process in some form.

- For Joe, structure emerges at the conclusion of any project.

  For Don, some structure is created in the beginning. "I remember that when I attended lectures at the university, I needed the lecturer to begin with some kind of an overview—it could be in diagram form—to give me a sense of how the teaching was going to unfold. It gave me the opportunity to set up a kind of internal indexed filing system for organizing information as it came at me. Without some outline or structure at the beginning, I was lost."

- Joe's final response to a problem is likely to be operationally detailed.

  Don's response will probably be more "lean" and strategically oriented.

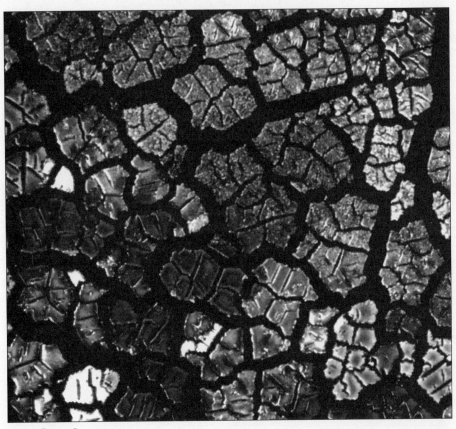

Capacities

Physical-Mental

- To perceive patterns in the complex interplay of events.
- To create and implement strategic, systemic models.
- For order, efficiency, and simplicity of form.
- To link the objective data of things with the subjective data of people.
- To value love as the highest law in the universe.

- *To be teachers of strategic, systemic thinking and compassion, by example.*

The Physical-Mental Personality Dynamic: Pattern Integrity

9

I was recently asked to help a management team at a Fortune 500 company clarify their alignment around a new vision for the product development process. At times the team members appeared to agree on what they wanted and needed, while at other times they expressed divergent views. As I heard the managers share their ideas of what was important in the product development process, I quickly began to see that different perspectives were being mixed into one jumble.

So I drew a matrix to attempt to graph the team's perspectives. The matrix differentiated between desired future reality, current reality, and the multiple levels of perspective for each. At the top level of the matrix was the *overarching vision*, which articulated the overall goal of the new initiative. Below that were the team's *mental models*, the assumptions they had about the product development system that would enable the vision to be realized. The third level was about *systemic structures*, the concrete systems and processes that would operationalize the vision. The fourth level was about *behavior over time*—how the new product development process would unfold. And finally, the bottom level was about *events*—specific, observable events that would illustrate the realization of the vision.

This matrix, which I named Vision Deployment Matrix (VDM), provided immediate clarity to the group. Everyone saw that they were in total agreement at the level of vision—and close to total agreement at the level of mental models. The divergence of views grew, however, as we progressed through the next three levels: systemic structures, behavior over time, and events. This pattern made sense to the team when they realized that the specifics at the lower levels were more dependent on each participant's local conditions. They didn't necessarily *need* to agree on every level.

Creating this matrix helped the team see that they had a high degree of alignment where they should, and it allowed them to acknowledge the different views at the other levels that were appropriate. With that insight, the team's sense of alignment around the overall vision increased dramatically.

—DANIEL H. KIM, CO-FOUNDER, MIT CENTER FOR
ORGANIZATIONAL LEARNING

Pattern Integrity

Pattern Integrity: A Metatheme for Physical-Mental People

"Pattern integrity" is to the physical-mental group what "creating systems" is to the physical-emotional group. Stemming from the close relationship between the physical and mental principles, physical-mental people seem to have an inherent capacity to see and experience patterns. Their physical centering ensures that they pick up and assimilate large amounts of factual data; the close relation with the mental principle gives them sufficient perspective on their data to see the interplay of factors and events across time, and so discern patterns. The patterns may exist in any number of forms and on any scale—for example, in computer programs, machines, the universe, gardens, paintings, musical compositions, scientific undertakings, historical events, the infrastructure of cities, or the behavior of organizations. They see patterns in the inner workings of a watch, a car, and in the interaction of players, rules, and elements in a game. They experience patterns in the complex interplay of events when walking in nature, seeing and feeling the sun; noticing its reflection glinting on leaves or shimmering on lakes; aware of the wind's movement and its effects on leaves, grasses, trees, and one's own skin; sensing the deeper patterns of terrain, weather, altitude, vegetation, and animal and human life interacting over time.

Physical-mental people have a fundamental awareness that all phenomena are the result of the organized interplay of ener-

> The sea lies all about us. The commerce of all lands must cross it. The very winds that move over the lands have been cradled on its broad expanse and seek ever to return to it. The continents themselves dissolve and pass to the sea, in grain after grain of eroded land. So, the rains that rose from it return again in rivers. In its mysterious past it encompasses all the dim origins of life and receives in the end, after, it may be, many transmutations, the dead husks of the same life. For all at last returns to the sea—to Oceanus, the ocean river, like the ever-flowing stream of time, the beginning and the end.
>
> —*Rachel Carson*

gies and forces, held together and governed by specific laws or rules, and forming patterns that combine and interact in increasingly complex ways. They naturally think in terms of subsystems of systems related to larger systemic wholes.

For this group, therefore, utilizing patterns is essential for comprehending the world and functioning in it. Physical-mental people not only perceive and think in terms of patterns, they also use a language of patterns to communicate—for example, through graphic representations such as maps, diagrams, and working models, or in the abstract language of mathematical equations. Their spoken communication itself tends to be patterned, often systematically conveying considerable amounts of interrelated facts and information.

When given data, physical-mental people typically assemble and reassemble it until they see patterns and systems, and useful meaning emerges. In the face of new information or unexpected events, their immediate instinct is to try to accommodate or incorporate the idiosyncratic into the larger, systemic pattern they perceive. If they cannot accomplish this integration, they conclude that there is discord, conflict, and disorder in the system—and they will instinctively try to fix it!

Seeing systemic patterns gives physical-mental people the frame of reference they need to take constructive action. When they see how an arrangement of patterns and relationships works to achieve a *purpose*, the patterns become the infrastructure for a model. The model they then create is the most efficient and effective they can devise as a guiding mechanism in planning for action.

This capacity for thinking in terms of patterns seems to be related to a strong spatial awareness, the ability to think and visualize three-dimensionally, and the sense of time's continuity from past to present to future. There are unfolding patterns of events across time, and there is a pattern in the multiplicity of interactions in any moment, as the following example describes.

"My natural inclination is to see patterns in terms of wholes within wholes. Seeing whole systems that are part of larger systems, and then seeing one in the context of the other, perhaps makes me a natural systems thinker. I can never see just an isolated part without asking the questions, 'What is it a part of? What is its *purpose*?' and, 'How is the system it is a part of related to the larger environment?'"

When I drive, I am conscious of the complex pattern of events around me. I simultaneously watch many cars ahead; keep aware of the traffic all around; sense subtle changes in speed, flow, rhythm; and adjust accordingly, so that we all remain part of the same flowing pattern. At the same time, I am aware of the functional pattern of the car itself—the interaction of all its mechanical parts—

and I'm aware of myself in interaction with them. I register at once subtle changes in the sound or feel of the car, almost as if I were sensing those changes in myself. So I usually anticipate problems with either the traffic or the car.

Strategic Planning, Prioritizing, Systematizing: Natural Gifts

The pragmatism of the physical principle, combined with the far-seeing perspective of the mental principle, can also be seen in this group's emphasis on *purpose*. In any endeavor, physical-mental people are always asking, "What is our purpose?" With this as their guideline, they prioritize with relative ease, evaluating data or prospective actions in light of their relevance to the established purpose. The same interplay of principles in the personality allows physical-mental people to be both strategic *and* tactical planners. They are typically able to see the broad movements required across time to achieve ultimate purposes; and, at the same time, because they think systemically, they are commonly able to plan the practical steps to get there. They often refer to their "macro" and "micro" modes, and their ability to switch between the two—macro when they open up to look at the big picture and micro when they narrow their focus to concentrate on small details.

Physical-mental people plan with care because they are aware of the systemic consequences of decisions and actions; and they plan alternative scenarios because they know that the future will bring unexpected factors into play. Frequently, they produce a series of charts that lay out the goal, the current situation, the events and trends from the past that led up to it, and one or more plans for moving systematically from the current situation to the goal. The complexity and degree of detail in the charts depends on the breadth of the endeavor—for example, on whether the goal is to help someone plan his or her career, or to create a conference for a thousand people, or set a company's course for the next five years. In any case, the outcome will be a plan for moving systematically and *with maximum efficiency* from point A to point B.

Depending on the maturity of the individual, however, the plan may contain a weakness. Physical-mental people sometimes undervalue or even omit issues relating to people as individuals. They tend to include people in their planning in terms of their function (the role they play), rather than as sentient human beings with personal feelings, reactions, and needs. As physical-mental people mature and gain awareness of the more subjective and emotional part of themselves and others, they increasingly include these considerations in their thinking and planning.

Strategic Consumption

"The presence of a strategy or at least a reason for doing almost anything is very important to me. If I see that somebody is operating without one, I feel something is wrong or missing. 'What do you mean you're just *doing* it?' Whatever way I do something, I will have thought about it beforehand and will continue to think about it. I keep asking myself, 'Is what I'm doing now consistent with my purpose?' It's such a natural process for me that I find it hard to believe that *any* action can be taken without a clear strategy.

"For example, I've come to realize that even when I'm eating, there's an overriding strategy. Before eating a particular meal, I might decide to save a piece for a particular reason. Another time, I'll try to match foods and make sure that I end up consuming all the different pieces together. The constant is that it's not a mindless process like, 'Okay, whatever's there, I'll just eat,' unless I'm really distracted. Usually, if somebody were to ask me mid-stream, 'What's your strategy for eating this dish?', I might have to think about it, but I would probably actually have one. It wasn't until somebody asked me, 'How do you eat corn?' that I could describe my systematic, kernel-by-kernel 'strategy,' which I had used consistently for years, and give my reasons for eating corn in that particular way."

This physical-mental person went on to say that he is part owner of a business organization where he is largely responsible for determining the company's goals and planning the strategies to achieve them. "The strategic steps I offer are *always* methodical. Whether it's eating corn or running a business, it's all one story."

Solving Problems: Knowing How Things Work

Physical-mental people are typically deeply interested in how things work, whether the things are machines, societies, mathematical constructs, or the systems of nature. They always seem to have in mind the question, "What is the pattern (or what are the intermeshing patterns) of operation here?" From childhood on, in their quest for the answer, they typically exhibit an irresistible urge to take things apart and (often) reassemble them. Their next question is, "How can we make this work better?" One physical-mental person we know cannot go into a store or office without observing or inferring the systems of operation; calculating income and profits based on the type of merchandise, location, clientele, and so on; assessing the quality of service; and mentally creating alternative systems to ensure greater efficiency and profitability.

A corollary of this interest is the compulsion to solve problems. Physical-mental people typically see the world through the lens of actions to be taken or problems to solve. This pull is so strong that they often feel compelled to tackle problems that are not necessarily their responsibility. For example, they might wonder why others do not notice a client waiting for service, or why a group seems unable to figure out how to organize an activity, or why an individual seems unable to cope with a task; when to them the solution (or at least the process for achieving a solution) is obvious. While other personality dynamics might simply offer ideas to get things moving or ask questions to help the individual or group gain insight into why they are stuck, physical-mental people are more inclined to work out and offer a complete systemic solution.

In some instances this effort might be appreciated, but sometimes the people being helped feel left out of the process and in some way diminished. Again, with experience and maturity, physical-mental people learn how to best apply their problem-solving gift. In any case, in seeking solutions to problems, they view the issue systemically and try to create a pattern of operation for solving not only the particular circumstance, but problems of that nature in general. The steps they follow are as previously described for strategic planning: establish the goal; understand clearly the current circumstances and the pattern of events leading up to them; and out of this comprehensive grasp of the situation, devise a step-by-step system of operation for achieving the goal.

Maps, Charts, Diagrams, Models

Physical-mental people use maps, charts, diagrams, and models as a set of interrelated visual tools through which to record, study, remember, and communicate complex two-, three-, or otherwise multidimensional interrelationships. For example, it is easy for them to understand and use three-dimensional scale models for something like a building project and to grasp more abstract representations such as the network diagram of a new computer system.

If the subject matter is too complex to be represented accurately by a diagram and the work warrants the time and effort, they create a model. A model may take the form of a physical representation, a mathematical equation, a computer program, or a spoken explanation. Physical-mental people find carefully crafted *combinations* of maps, diagrams, and models especially interesting and informative—for example, they would probably derive great satisfaction from a relief map of the earth on a revolving globe that is set on its angle of inclination, with natural resource and population distribution represented.

Indeed, physical-mental people seem to love maps of all kinds. They use and create them with great relish. We know one person who purchased at least 20 maps in preparing for a trip to Alaska. She ultimately knew more about Alaska than many people who live there. She knew all the roads, each trail, and most of the sights, and prepared an extraordinarily clear and detailed itinerary.

> "Whenever I am going to a new place, I like to study maps of the area, starting with the broadest appropriate scale. If it is a far-off place, a global or national map may be best to see how an area relates to where I live and to other places I have been. Then I look at a state or regional map to situate myself at a finer scale; then a city map, which includes my physical arrival point (airport, railway station, or highway) and the place where I will be staying. Finally, I look for detailed maps and information on specific locations I plan to visit."

Efficiency appeals strongly to physical-mental people, so they appreciate maps as tools for ensuring that they navigate smoothly and reach their goals. Maps also help them visualize locations, anticipate problems, and create alternative strategies. Maps seem to meet a deep need in physical-mental people for spatial orientation.

The following maps[1] were drawn by a Japanese woman named Ryuko, who wanted to help Sandra find her way to an important meeting. They indicate the level of care and detail with which physical-mental people like to guide themselves (or others) to a given goal and maintain a clear sense of their location in space.

---

[1] These maps were originally hand drawn. They have been technologically re-created to make them legible on a smaller scale.

Dear Dr. Seagal:

I don't know which is the best way to come here from your home. I hope one of these meets your requirements.

Sincerely yours,

Ryuko

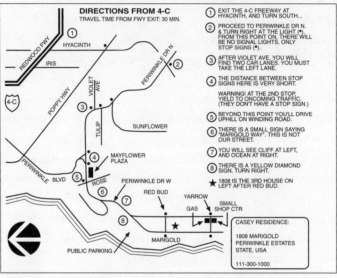

DIRECTIONS FROM 4-C
TRAVEL TIME FROM FWY EXIT: 30 MIN.

1. EXIT THE 4-C FREEWAY AT HYACINTH, AND TURN SOUTH...

2. PROCEED TO PERIWINKLE DR N. & TURN RIGHT AT THE LIGHT (•). FROM THIS POINT ON, THERE WILL BE NO SIGNAL LIGHTS, ONLY STOP SIGNS (•).

3. AFTER VIOLET AVE, YOU WILL FIND TWO CAR LANES. YOU MUST TAKE THE LEFT LANE.

4. THE DISTANCE BETWEEN STOP SIGNS HERE IS VERY SHORT.

   WARNING! AT THE 2ND STOP, YIELD TO ONCOMING TRAFFIC. (THEY DON'T HAVE A STOP SIGN.)

5. BEYOND THIS POINT YOU'LL DRIVE UPHILL ON WINDING ROAD.

6. THERE IS A SMALL SIGN SAYING "MARIGOLD WAY". THIS IS NOT OUR STREET.

7. YOU WILL SEE CLIFF AT LEFT, AND OCEAN AT RIGHT.

8. THERE IS A YELLOW DIAMOND SIGN. TURN RIGHT.

★ 1808 IS THE 3RD HOUSE ON LEFT AFTER RED BUD.

CASEY RESIDENCE:

1808 MARIGOLD
PERIWINKLE ESTATES
STATE, USA

111-300-1000

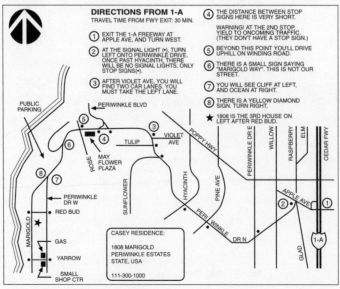

DIRECTIONS FROM 1-A
TRAVEL TIME FROM FWY EXIT: 30 MIN.

1. EXIT THE 1-A FREEWAY AT APPLE AVE, AND TURN WEST.

2. AT THE SIGNAL LIGHT (•), TURN LEFT ONTO PERIWINKLE DRIVE. ONCE PAST HYACINTH, THERE WILL BE NO SIGNAL LIGHTS, ONLY STOP SIGNS(•).

3. AFTER VIOLET AVE, YOU WILL FIND TWO CAR LANES. YOU MUST TAKE THE LEFT LANE.

4. THE DISTANCE BETWEEN STOP SIGNS HERE IS VERY SHORT.

   WARNING! AT THE 2ND STOP, YIELD TO ONCOMING TRAFFIC. (THEY DON'T HAVE A STOP SIGN.)

5. BEYOND THIS POINT YOU'LL DRIVE UPHILL ON WINDING ROAD.

6. THERE IS A SMALL SIGN SAYING "MARIGOLD WAY". THIS IS NOT OUR STREET.

7. YOU WILL SEE CLIFF AT LEFT, AND OCEAN AT RIGHT.

8. THERE IS A YELLOW DIAMOND SIGN. TURN RIGHT.

★ 1808 IS THE 3RD HOUSE ON LEFT AFTER RED BUD.

CASEY RESIDENCE:

1808 MARIGOLD
PERIWINKLE ESTATES
STATE, USA

111-300-1000

Time and Continuity

The two physically centered groups are similar in experiencing time as continuous. Both groups share a respect for and an interest in the past, and both view present events as a natural consequence of all preceding events. More than people of any other personality dynamic, they know that to fully understand the present and plan for the future, it is necessary to understand the past. Much of what is written about the physical-emotional personality dynamic in this regard (pp. 159–162) applies to both physically centered groups, and we recommend that you consult those pages for a general understanding of the physical-mental person's relationship to time.

There are, however, some distinctions between the two groups. For example, the span of historical time that physical-mental people refer to is usually not so extensive. They go back only as far as needed to identify and understand patterns pertaining to a present situation. Also, because the mental principle relates to the future, as well as to a more detached perspective, physical-mental people can usually see more quickly the connections between the patterns of the past and those of the present, and project multiple future probabilities and possibilities. This ability contributes to their capacity for both effective long-range strategic planning and adjusting course in response to changing circumstances in pursuit of long-term goals.

The following comments by a physical-mental person illustrate the capacity for persistently pursuing a goal over time:

> I remember when I was about six or seven years old. I was sitting on my father's knee, and he was talking to me about what I wanted to do when I grew up. I said that I wanted to be an electrical engineer. As I look back (I am now an engineer), I see that I actually laid plans down throughout the years toward that goal. It has been the same for me in so many other areas of my life. I created steps to achieve the things I wanted to accomplish, and most of it happened even in the time frame I wanted. This is surprising to me, but it's been a consistent pattern.

Memory: A Systematic Filing Process

Physical-mental people are second only to physical-emotional people in their extraordinary capacity for remembering past events in full sensory detail, and in their encyclopedic memory for facts. However, there are some

distinctions. Because physical-mental people are more selective about what they take in, their memories are also more selective. They remember more what they *choose* to remember and tend to accumulate extraordinarily detailed knowledge about topics that are of immediate interest or might serve future purposes. Their recollections may take the form of images, maps, charts, or diagrams. They also seem to have readier access to their information than physical-emotional people, because they have "filed" it in sets and subsets. A conscious sorting process has taken place. The more often the "file" is consulted, the more detailed and voluminous the information available.

Physical-mental people typically recall past experiences, even those of distant childhood, in extensive sensory and environmental detail and in the context of a sequence of events, enabling listeners to share vividly the experience of being in the physical situation. They will not, however, recall the accompanying emotions; these will be implicit in their account.

Their recall of past events also has a remarkable spatial quality. Many physical-mental people have given us accounts similar to the following:

> I seem to have simultaneous views or perspectives on any situation I remember. One is usually from within—what I saw and took in during the experience. The other view (sometimes there are several others) is of the whole scene or parts of the scene, as if I were a third person looking on and seeing myself in the context. These views coexist and simultaneously interact to give a fuller understanding of the situation than any one view could give independently.

These memories remind me very much of how I read and understand architectural drawings. When I look at a floor plan, an elevation, and a section drawing of a building, I get a much more complete understanding of what that space or building is or will be like. This deeper understanding is more than an addition of the parts; it's synergistic. The views or perceptions in my memory seem to work in a similar way.

"I remember heading up to my cousin's cottage, which was probably about the distance of a city block away from ours. There was a worn path right from our place to his. I can remember almost every little bump along the path. I can remember the kinds of rocks, large and small, and every inch of the terrain because I used to run over it so much in my bare feet. It's as if my feet remember it all! Events in which my physical body was directly involved have strong memory for me."

The Physical Body: Sensing the World

Like their physical-emotional counterparts, but to a lesser degree, physical-mental people absorb a great deal of the sensory data around them, including awareness of their own location in the environment and their spatial relationship to all the objects and people around them. They record most of the words that are spoken and include in their data the *observable* feelings of those present.

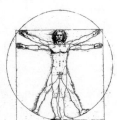

Although physical-mental people are able *to a degree* to filter out what might not be of service to them, they can be subject to sensory overload. They need time to sift through, clarify, and synthesize the large amounts of data they absorb; identify what they need to discard; and organize what they choose to retain. One way they do this is by processing information and experiences with others, often with one or two selected confidants. Most of all, however, they benefit from taking, or being given, consistent breaks from the incessant incoming stimuli, and having time alone in a quiet, unstructured environment for solitary processing and "just being." Time in nature is especially healing and renewing for this group, and physical exercise also helps.

As with the physical-emotional group, some evidence suggests that the blood pressure, heart rate, pulse, and metabolism of physical-mental people are likely to be slower than those of the other personality dynamics. Moreover, both groups apparently have a high tolerance for pain. In fact, they seem not to register localized pain readily and can therefore easily disregard pain unless the whole body is involved or the condition is extreme. They also show a remarkable capacity for endurance.

Two Different Rhythms: One "Real," One "Not Real"

A distinguishing feature of being physical-mental, expressed to us by many physical-mental people, is the experience of living in two distinct rhythms—a fast rhythm associated with the activities of the mind and a slower rhythm in the body. They seem to experience these two rhythms either distinctly or concurrently; but, in the latter case, accompanied by a sense of discrepancy and unease.

Although they recognize the need for both rhythms, most physical-mental people identify the slower rhythm as more basic, more like "home." They identify this rhythm as literally more natural—more akin to the rhythms of nature itself, "organic." The faster rhythm is identified with the world that people have created, with its exchange of ideas, calculated interventions, fast pace, and induced changes. Though they can participate very well at this mental level, the rhythm feels at odds with their more natural, deliberate pace, and it becomes extremely stressful over extended periods of time. The qualities of these two rhythms are so profoundly different for physical-mental people that many of them have referred to the slower mode as "real" and the faster mode as "unreal."

"My head belongs in the business world, and, while I like it, it goes too fast. What I really like to do is get my dog and go down to the ocean for a long walk.

"I also love to work on quilts, to shop for fabric, to knit mittens for my friends' children. This I do in my own time. There's a natural rhythm I am attuned to."

In a business setting or classroom, or when interacting with emotionally centered people, physical-mental people are usually obliged to operate in their faster mode. Their capacity for endurance enables them to maintain this pace for considerable periods, but without quiet time to be alone and revert to their more organic rhythm, they can begin to feel exhausted, overwhelmed, and "unreal" themselves. They experience tension and lack the satisfaction of feeling they have contributed their best work. They benefit if they have contrasting periods during each day to be quiet, assimilate all they have taken in, and resume their more natural rhythm. They need, at least, to find this kind of balance in their lives as a whole. Many do so by engaging in a craft (good artisanship is a strongly held value), by building, tinkering with machinery, or otherwise working with their hands. Most often they express a profound need to spend time in nature. Connecting with nature, they regain connection with the "real" part of themselves.

One physical-mental person, now working in a challenging position at a multinational corporation, has experienced two contrasting eras in his working life. For 14 years, he worked in the depths of forests as a woodcutter. He felt very much in tune with himself in this occupation but entered the corporate world to better meet the economic demands of raising a family and financing his children's education. The life he now leads is intellectually satisfying and offers practical advantages, but to him it is still not "real." Like many physical-mental people, he knows that corporate life, with its fast pace and artificial environments, though mentally satisfying, is not where he thrives best physically and spiritually. He creates his balance by taking advantage of the opportunities offered by the company's location in Maine to live in a rural setting, go sailing, and work on his house.

The following is an excerpt from a tape-recorded conversation among three physical-mental men (we have heard similar discussions in which physical-mental women were involved) in which they discuss their need to find a way to accommodate the schism they experience between the fast rhythm of the mind and the slower, more natural rhythm of the body. All the men are "successful" managers in their organizations.

> "When I'm out fishing, I can easily lose track of time. In fact, I can lose track of *everything*; I become part of nature. It's easy for me because *this* is the real world."

Don: In the ideal world I would love to farm as a baseline and then come into the community from time to time to talk and relate. Not too long ago, I could have retired to one of the islands off Vancouver, had a place to grow a garden, and been almost self-sufficient—and that would have been enough. Now I need a better balance. But it would be great to have both.

Claude: I could be far more satisfied doing physical work—could be wood-cutting, probably not farming—but something physical. Building, for example.

John: And teaching mathematics in the evening!

Claude: Or physics—or something like that. There'd have to be something challenging mentally. But I would like my work to be more physical. Sitting behind a desk for eight hours is not one of the things I enjoy most.

Don: You almost have to craft a job that has these components. I've certainly seen those combinations more readily available in some parts of Japanese society. The position of craftsman in their culture is very interesting. Here, it is a kind of hobby. In Japan, crafts are even financially very successful. It is more than a manual task—it's the expression of life through their craft. Crafts are valued as much there as we value the work of fine artists here. I see the happy marriage of these two parts more often in Japan.

In Western cultures, many physical-mental people are under great stress. Their most natural rhythm and pacing are not that of the majority, and their systematic way of working and impersonal way of communicating have not been understood.

Relationship to Nature
The continuation of the discussion sheds light on physical-mental people's relationship with nature and its forces.

John: When I lived way out in the woods, I'd leave my little shack at night—the woods are more alive then—and I used to sit up against a tree and watch the moon, watch *that* half of the world. There's a lot going on out there! It's all quiet. The owls are amazing—no noise!

Don: I lived in Vancouver for two years near Stanley Park, which is at the head of English Bay. There was one particular huge storm—several large ships were anchored in the harbor, and the storm got so bad that they started to drag their anchors. I remember walking out to Stanley Park, and the wind was blowing so hard that I had to hold onto a tree to stay upright. I watched two tugboats going out, fighting the current, trying to stop a ship from grounding on the beach. I could have stayed there all night. It was just fabulous! I loved it!

John: When storms happen, I go down to the beach. Sometimes it's so bad that people are evacuated. I remember once holding onto a signpost and being blown horizontal—and I weigh a lot! It held me off the ground! It was great!

Don: I find that when I'm in that kind of situation, I have a sense of knowing where the limits are.

John: Yeah. Nobody has to tell you not to walk in the lee side of a tree!

Claude: I feel a sense of danger when I get to the point where I'm pushing the envelope. I don't think we're foolhardy, but when the elements become somewhat severe, there's something tantalizing about that. It's more than curiosity—it's almost a need to go out and be a part of it!

John: Yes—because this is *real*! It's beyond the mental realm. *This* is *real*. Here's the excitement!

Don: Claude, I know you were in Los Angeles during the big earthquake in '94. What was that like?

Claude: It was more of an intellectual experience, because I was in bed and not outdoors with my feet on the ground. I had to stay in the house because I had a young child who needed help sorting out what was happening. In that type of situation, it's more a matter of making sure everything's OK, and if it's not, you see that things are taken care of. I have about fifty strategies that kick into action at the same time. That's all mental work—there's nothing physical about it.

Don: Something I'd like to do before I leave this world is to be near a lava flow. Just to feel that! There's something about the movement of the flow that I'd like to experience first-hand. I'd also like to experience being close enough to feel the heat. Not to be burned—but just to feel it. There's something about the relationship of its movement, its color and the tactile experience, that would somehow be a link to profoundly understanding it. This is the marvel of reality for me.

What I Love

We asked Sue, one of our physical-mental friends, to relax, take her time, and speak about what she loves. The following is less than one-third of her tape-recorded response. It not only attests to physical-mental people's affinity with nature and their capacity to absorb and remember sensory detail, it also demonstrates their capacity for processing and articulating systemic wholes. The communication itself is densely patterned.

Sue is describing the environment in which she spends her vacations.

"The shape of white pine trees, the way they all twist around to point east, the clumps of moss so green and soft, the texture of the rocks, the way they change in color. If you look at the ground through a lens, it looks like a cluster of jewels.

"Sunlight sparkling on the waves like diamonds on a blue cloth. The sound of the wind in the pines. The water lapping on the shore. The smell of juniper and chives. The song of the white throat sparrow, the Canada bird, the calls of the loon. The way the clouds go puffy along the horizon. The scent of hot rocks juxtaposed with the scent of water.

"Cardinal flowers, white water lilies, little white violets in early spring, the wild iris in early summer. The frogs twanging in the ponds at night, the grinding call of the bull frogs. The sound a canoe paddle makes lifting up from the water when it's calm. The ripple and gurgle of water under the keel when you're sailing. It sort of chuckles along. The wild roses, the lacy froth of cherry blossom in the spring, the emerald tufts of grass growing along cracks in the rock in June and early July, the same pale gold later on. The shapes of the islands and the rocks, the way they curl and twist. The channels between the islands.

"The herons, gulls, and terns. Shapes and textures of leaves and branches. The lichens and fungus. The sound of water on the shore. The arrangement of the rocks along the shore of the bay, like a country in miniature. I remember once going across the bay in winter. It had been very calm when it froze and the ice was very clear and you could see down to the bottom. There were great long cracks and the ice was gulping and moaning. It was all right because you could see the ice was over a foot thick, but it felt weird. Another year we came and there was snow on the ice and little frost curls like feathers all over. It seemed sad to walk on them and destroy them. When the water is frozen it's so quiet, the stillness is uncanny. If it's a calm day with no wind, there's no water noise, and that seems abnormal.

"In summer there's always the sound of the water and the wind. The clouds are wonderful in winter. There's an amazing variety of color like great piled up bruises; greens and grays and yellows. I suppose the seasons really have their own colors there. The winter is green and white. Spring is blue and green. Deep blue. Light greens and dark greens. As summer moves toward fall it becomes gold and green and pale blue. When the autumn is well under way it's deep blue and green. Sometimes there are the northern lights and they can be magnificent. They pulse, wax, and wane. Sometimes they go around the whole sky. The stars are wonderful. So many, so bright and clear. In June there are fireflies darting about. Little flecks of light pulsing and fading. In August there are shooting stars.

"One of the best sensations is swimming and feeling the water ripple over your skin like cool silk. Nothing between you and the water. Follow that with lying on smooth, warm granite and letting the warm air dry you.

"The wonderful quality of the light at dusk. The sun is getting low and bathes everything with a purple gold mantle. It's just magical. It's so rich. If you have the right kind of clouds at sunset, usually a mackerel sky, it will just incandesce in crimson. Beautiful. The blue fades to gray. . . ."

Communication: Factual, Practical, and Purposeful

Physical-mental people appreciate communication that is factual, concrete, and practical. And because they are always listening for what action they should take, they like to have the *purpose* of the communication clearly established from the beginning. Not only do they ask themselves as they listen what action might be required of *them*, but also, because they think in terms of the group, "What do *we* need to do? How do *we* take action?" They also benefit from being given an overview or "executive summary" of the communication at the outset, so they can orient themselves to what follows. Because they know that they involve themselves fully in any endeavor to which they commit, this summary helps them to determine their degree of involvement—whether to offer solutions, delegate, ask for details, or take up the matter later if necessary. If they decide to become personally involved, they will want considerable context and detail.

Their natural rhythm of communication is even and unhurried, and they prefer dialogue to be conducted in this fashion, with each person speaking in turn and room allowed for deliberation. They experience this relaxed rhythm as creating a space in which the participants are more fully present, all that needs to be spoken gets spoken, and ultimately the group has a sense of having engaged in something real and complete.

This mode of communication can strike emotional-objective people, especially, as too slow and over-concerned with details; it can stretch their patience and make them restless. Emotional-subjective people may also have difficulty, finding the process uncomfortably impersonal. Both emotionally centered groups may have difficulty with the physical-mental tendency to ask probing questions in order to verify facts, gather reliable data, and clarify more lateral communication. Emotional-objective people may feel that this impedes their forward movement, and emotional-subjective people may feel that they are being judged. The intent of physical-mental people, however, is to gain sufficient understanding to be able to make their own most useful contribution. Once they trust another's expertise and reliability, they usually become less exacting.

As much as they like to discuss and debate issues, they may find it difficult to be in discussions that do not move consistently toward practical solutions. Physical-mental people sometimes think people of other personality dynamics get lost in the *process* and lose sight of practical *purposes*; however, as long as they envisage the potential for payoff, physical-mental people can stay a course with extraordinary patience, focus, and tenacity.

Unless they feel they have something useful to say, physical-mental people are often silent. In their desire to be of service, however, they can go to the opposite extreme and be overzealous in conveying information. They take questions seriously. To quote one physical-mental manager,

> "I need to be *told* if no action is expected of me, if someone just wants me to listen or be empathic. Otherwise my listening is in the wrong place."

At home, my daughter will tell me, "That's enough, Dad. I don't need the encyclopedia right now. I just want to know what time it is, not how to fix the watch!" Or my kids will say to me, "Dad, I want the one-minute, five-minute, or thirty-minute answer." They have learned to specify how much data they want.

Charts, diagrams, tables, models, as well as a summary of key points (perhaps in bullet form) are all effective aids to communication with physical-mental people. It is often a good idea to precede face-to-face communication with written material, allowing the person enough lead time for assimilation and thought. Physical-mental people usually appreciate written communication because of the opportunity it affords to be precise, present detailed information in an organized way, and consider issues carefully before making a response.

Words Used Frequently by Physical-Mental People

purpose	experience	do	group
details	plan	work	represent
pattern	model	current reality	consensus
method	map	past	synergy
practical	location	future	three-dimen-
specific	whole	action	sional
outcome	system	facts	mechanics
strategy	systemic	continuity	macro/micro
concrete	holistic	reliable	unreal
precise	time	nature	
context	real	organic	
efficient	complete	abstract	

Systemic Realignment: The Physical-Mental Approach to Change

Physical-mental people experience change in two ways. One way is by making the quick adjustments often required to fit into the fast-paced, "unreal" world of business and society. However, changes of this kind often feel artificial and disjointed to them, like blindfolded rides on a roller coaster.

Over time, these rides can wear them out.

The other kind of change they experience is related to the rhythms of the "real" world of nature, where change is organic. Species mutate, rocks erode, seasons shift, and cells renew themselves; but there is always the stability of continuity and systemic unfolding. Physical-mental people are intimately attuned to this kind of change. They are like sailors constantly making subtle adjustments in course and rigging in response to the shifting patterns of winds, waves, and currents. This kind of change feels comfortable to them. They can also easily accommodate "macro" change—a complete change of destination—if the way in which the shift takes place respects a systemic pattern of operation they can understand. Physical-mental people know that a successful passage depends on weaving both the micro and the macro changes into systemic interrelationship.

When a proposed change is substantial or involves an abrupt shift in direction, physical-mental people, like the physical-emotional, want time to carefully consider the change and its ramifications. Because of their capacity for systemic thinking, they know that change in one part of a plan or operation affects the whole, and that the whole needs to be taken into account. In addition, because of their inclination toward the concrete and practical, they link proposed change to its consequences not only for key strategic factors but also for multitudes of practical details. They understand the complex consequences of change and the time and labor involved in its implementation. They ask such fundamental questions as, "Is the proposed change appropriate in light of past experience, current needs, and long-term future effects? Will it help meet our purposes? Can it *really* be achieved, given current reality and the resources available? What would be required, in practical detail, to bring about the desired results?" If the change is proposed by others, they want to know that the basic homework has been done and that the decision-makers will not change their minds once change has been initiated, unaware or uncaring of the complexity of the consequences. Physical-mental people know that it is often not so difficult to formulate ideas for change, but putting them into operation is intricate, time-consuming, and consequential.

Both physically centered groups have an intrinsic need and capacity to see the total effects of decisions in both the short and the long term. Not surprisingly, therefore, they adopt change cautiously. As a result, they are sometimes judged to be conservative, stubborn, set in their ways, and resistant to change. This is not an accurate perception. They are usually not opposed to change, provided they are convinced it is necessary in order to reach long-term goals, they know that the means for successful implementation are available, and they are assured that a detailed step-by-step plan of operation will be created. Once these criteria are met, physically centered people will move into action quickly, methodically, and with total commitment.

Conditions for Learning

Physical-mental people learn most effectively under certain conditions. These conditions include:

- purpose for the learning made explicit;
- structured outline and considerable context provided;
- clear, systematic, and concrete detailed presentation;
- opportunities for "learning by doing" (kinesthetic emphasis);
- instruction supported by models, diagrams, and charts;
- careful pacing, with sufficient time to absorb, assimilate, and distill data, complete tasks, and formulate responses;
- opportunities for reflection and solitary work;
- opportunities to work with others after assimilating details and preparing models.

When Something Goes Wrong

A meeting didn't go as well as expected.
A communication was seriously misunderstood.
Plans were changed without everyone being informed.
A project or some part of it fails.

How do physical-mental people respond to such situations? They usually begin with Step 1 of the following sequence, then proceed as far as the level of their development and self-understanding permits. However, individuals often stop at the earlier steps and rarely reach Step 4.

Step 1

They first focus on the situation itself, assessing it in terms of its significance. If the situation has value for them, they immediately assume responsibility for fixing it. Their attention is on the problem itself, as if they are looking through a microscope set at maximum magnification.

Often, analysis stops here.

Step 2

In taking personal responsibility, they begin to widen their field of vision and focus on the quality of their own actions in contributing to the problem. They objectively examine the situation *and* their role in it, screening out emotional content.

Sometimes, analysis stops here.

Step 3

As they broaden their field of vision, the "playing field" grows. They take the human system fully into consideration. They include in their analysis such factors as the personal maturity of others, distinctions in their ways of functioning, and the role that feelings and attitudes may have played. They see the world of people as well as the world of things—a far richer process than before.

Analysis rarely continues to this point. But if it does, one more step remains if full understanding is to occur.

Step 4

They examine the situation from a perspective that includes all three preceding steps. In doing so, they grasp the whole story, and learning takes place.

It is rare for anyone to engage in the whole sequence consistently.

Physical-Mental Characteristics: A Summary

Qualities

- still
- grounded
- calm
- enduring
- adaptable
- objective
- receptive
- practical
- efficient

Basic Learning Process

- systemic
- interactive with task
- taking in much data, in considerable detail
- internal processing
- hands-on experience (kinesthetic)

Management Process

- delegate tasks easily after initial plans have been structured
- need freedom to set own schedule
- process much information—may need time to reach decisions
- may need help with personalized communication and "people issues"

Values and Affinities

- systemic thinking
- interest in how things work
- practicality
- translation of ideas into actuality
- efficiency
- concreteness in planning, producing, packaging
- factual communication
- task orientation
- cooperation
- continuity
- nature and the natural

Function

- conduct long-term strategic planning
- create detailed diagrams and models
- translate plans into actuality
- ensure practicality
- link past, present, and future patterns
- undertake detailed practical work
- take into account the whole—work with whole systems
- put systems in place to ensure efficient functioning
- solve problems

Interpersonal Relationships
- serve others' needs
- accepting
- calm
- reliable
- objective
- communication largely related to practicalities
- may need help expressing feelings and connecting personally

Factors Causing Stress
- accumulation of data and memories in the body, which can lead to physical ailments
- insufficient time to process data and make responses
- insufficient time alone, especially in nature, to reconnect with natural internal rhythm
- unremitting immersion in fast mental rhythm
- emotion-laden communication

Body Movements
- relatively still
- movements small and slow
- often in the sagittal plane (forward/back)
- posture conveys a sense of relaxation and groundedness
- little change of facial expression

Eyes
- regarding

Hands
- movements are gentle, slow, soft
- often used to describe function

Man is a pattern integrity.

He is like the knot tied in a rope.

He is not the rope.

I'm going to splice a piece of manila rope to

a piece of cotton rope and then splice the

other end of the cotton rope to a piece of nylon rope.

I'm going to make the very simplest

knot that I know. The rope has not done this,

I have done it to the rope.

I can slide this knot along . . . I slide it along the

rope and now it leaves the manila

and now it's on the cotton. I keep sliding it

along and now it's on the nylon.

So . . . and suddenly it's off the end.

We say the knot was a pattern integrity, it wasn't

manila, it wasn't cotton, it wasn't nylon.

Cotton and nylon and manila;

any one of them are good to let us know

about its shape, what its pattern was,

but it was not that; it had an integrity of its own.

—Buckminster Fuller

Part III:
Human Dynamics in Action

In this third section, we present Human Dynamics in action—some examples of the many ways to use Human Dynamics in both personal and organizational development.

Chapter 10, "Communication and Team Learning: Beginning Tools and Practices," focuses on ways of improving communication within a team setting. Some topics include "Talking Each Other's Language," "Communication Rhythms," and "Handling Confrontation Effectively." This chapter also contains exercises for the development of personal and interpersonal skills.

Chapter 11, "Organizational Applications," presents examples of the use of Human Dynamics programs in business and healthcare organizations, specifically London Life Insurance Company, Digital Equipment Corporation, and Intermountain Healthcare System.

Chapter 12, "The Developmental Continuum," describes the developmental path for each of the personality dynamics. We use short "stories" to illustrate personality integration and the difficulty of consistently expressing transpersonal qualities when the personality is *not* integrated.

The final chapter, "Visions: Looking Ahead," gives accounts of some of the work in progress in research, education, and East/West bridge building. We also identify potential areas of medical and other scientific research, in which we can build on our current understandings to further probe the why and wherefore of human development.

Communication
and Team Learning:
Beginning Tools and Practices

One of the most significant contributions of Human Dynamics is the understanding it affords of people's distinctly different communication processes and needs. Understanding these distinctions enables people to make better connections with one another, whether in the context of the workplace, the family, the community, or the classroom. When people are aware of their own needs in receiving communication, they can guide others in communicating with them most effectively. When they are aware of another person's communication needs, they can adapt their own approach to connect well, maintain harmony, and ensure the quality and effectiveness of their exchanges.

Understanding differences in communication needs and processes is crucial in organizational settings. In this "information age," the unimpeded, undistorted flow of communication throughout an organization is essential for good performance and even survival. Deft and harmonious teamwork is also essential, but many teams break down or limp along because the members are misreading one another's messages. Differences become sources of disharmony, rather than of complementarity and mutual enrichment. Further, understanding the communication processes of different personality dynamics can play a pivotal role in determining the success of sales or other presentations to clients, customers, or audiences. Teaching or training is also enhanced when instructors not only understand the learning processes associated with each personality dynamic (and adapt their teaching methods accordingly), but also recognize the distinct communication needs of each student and use their understanding to make a better connection. Similarly, the value of these insights for couples and families is obvious. Many relationships stagnate or fail because couples misinterpret one another or are unable to develop a sense of sustained connection.

For a detailed analysis of each personality dynamic's communication processes and needs, we encourage readers to refer to the sections on communication in part II (chapters 5–9). In this chapter, however, we would like to make some additional observations applicable to all of the personality dynamics.

First, as chapters 5–9 explain, people of each personality dynamic have words or phrases that tend to crop up in their discourse with unusual frequency (for example, mental-physical—*perspective*; emotional-objective—*good idea!*; emotional-subjective—*feel* or *feelings*; physical-emotional—*context*; physical-mental—*purpose*). But the various personality dynamics also use words a little differently and may even mean different things by the same word. Thus effective dialogue depends not only on paying attention to one another's words, but also on taking into account who's saying them. For example, when an emotional-objective person and a physical-emotional person say in reference to a task, "I'm finished," he or she may mean something very different. The emotional-objective person is likely to mean, "I've brought this project to a point where I feel it's good enough that I can move on. If it turns out to need adjustment, I can come back to it." Whereas the physical-emotional person probably means, "I've completed this project down to the last detail, and everything is in place for smooth running from now on."

Similarly, when a mental-physical person says, "I like clear communication," and an emotional-subjective person uses the same words, the two people probably have something very different in mind. The mental-physical person probably means, "I like words to be used meticulously in accordance with their dictionary definition and to be expressive of a logically connected sequence of thought." Whereas at least part of the emotional-subjective person's message is almost certainly, "I appreciate communication in which feelings are out in the open, and there are no hidden agendas."

Exercise: **Confirming Intended Meanings**

What is said is not always what is meant, and what is heard is not always what was meant (or said). Practice reflecting the meaning you perceived back to the speaker to check for congruence with the intended meaning. Simply ask, "Did you mean that . . . ?" This practice is especially valuable in light of the distinctions among the personality dynamics. For example, if someone says, "We should follow that up," the implications of the remark will be different, depending on the personality dynamic of the speaker.

Communication Rhythms

We can see another distinction among the personality dynamics in what we might term the rhythm in communication, as depicted by the following chart.

RHYTHM IN COMMUNICATION

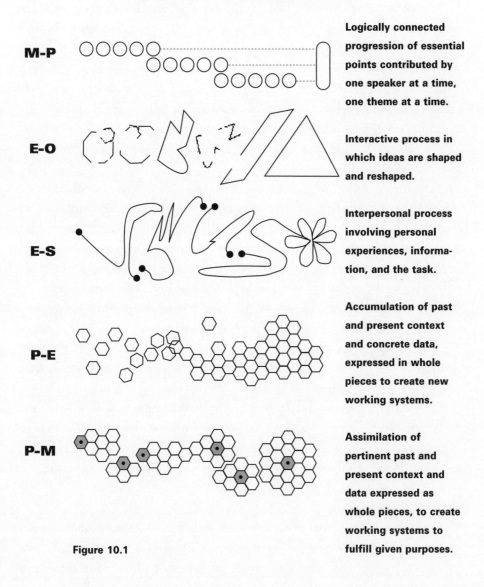

M-P — Logically connected progression of essential points contributed by one speaker at a time, one theme at a time.

E-O — Interactive process in which ideas are shaped and reshaped.

E-S — Interpersonal process involving personal experiences, information, and the task.

P-E — Accumulation of past and present context and concrete data, expressed in whole pieces to create new working systems.

P-M — Assimilation of pertinent past and present context and data expressed as whole pieces, to create working systems to fulfill given purposes.

Figure 10.1

We might demonstrate the differences in the various communication rhythms by comparing how each of the five groups would approach a particular task, say, the development of a new training strategy for their organization.

Mental-Physical

Mental-physical people will tend to discuss the issue in the abstract. They will speak one at a time, clearly and precisely, each person making essential points in a logical, orderly fashion. They will want to clearly define the words "develop," "new," and "training." The pacing of speech will be even, with periods of silence for internal processing. After considering all the points, they will probably finish by establishing guiding principles for the training strategy and laying out a clear, long-range plan.

Emotional-Objective

The emotional-objective process will be more interactive. Someone will start by quickly offering an idea for addressing the issue, and zip!—someone else will be stimulated to respond with another idea. This may in turn trigger someone else's idea, to which the first person may react by reshaping his or her original thought. The degree to which a participant holds on to an idea will depend on whether he or she has been thinking about it for years, a few days, a few minutes, or formulates it while speaking. In general, expressing an idea is just a way of *beginning* for emotional-objective people. They usually appreciate having their ideas either expanded or challenged, so long as they feel an openness on everyone's part and see that forward movement is maintained.

This interactive process of shaping and reshaping will continue until the group concludes with a plan that offers immediate actions and a general direction for the future. The pacing will be much more variable than with the mental-physical group, and the delivery often staccato and intense.

Emotional-Subjective

The emotional-subjective process is likely to start with someone giving a dramatic account of a personal experience as a participant in a training program. The others will follow the story empathically, living the experience as if it were his or her own. Then someone else will respond, "Well, let me tell you what happened to me! . . ." and everyone will follow *that* journey. They will continue this highly interpersonal process, each responding subjectively both to the other people and to what they say. The discussion will flow back and forth among the speakers, sometimes in this direction, sometimes in that, but always with the participants maintaining connection. To those of other personality dynamics, this process may seem chaotic, but in fact emotional-subjective people track the process perfectly. They will eventually reach creative, multifaceted conclusions that take into account the personal needs of all the participants in the training programs.

To experience the discussion as complete, they must feel that they have not only developed an appropriate plan but also shared a satisfying interpersonal process.

Physical-Emotional

The physical-emotional rhythm, on the other hand, will have an even and deliberate quality. It may start with someone making a historical reference, such as, "Fifteen years ago, we inaugurated such and such a program. . . ."

Each person will lay out in detail a whole piece of information, to which others will methodically add more whole pieces of information, setting context and establishing continuity between the past and the present as they go along. They will speak one at a time. There may be frequent silences, as the group members consider their information and, eventually, potential courses of action. The flow of their discussion will be steady, and the content will be linked, giving a sense of accumulating weight to their deliberations. To those who are not physical-emotional, the process may seem overly detailed and methodical; but if allowed sufficient time, the group will eventually produce a highly practical and comprehensive plan of action.

Physical-Mental

The physical-mental process will combine characteristics of the physical-emotional and mental-physical personality dynamics' processes. As with the physical-emotional group, the pacing of the conversation will be even. Usually one person will speak at a time, laying out a whole piece of information. They, too, establish context and accumulate factual data but in less detail than the physical-emotional group. Their thinking is geared more selectively to the end purpose, which they like to clarify early. They therefore tend to speak and reach conclusions more rapidly than the physical-emotional group. They will produce clear strategic plans including models, diagrams, and charts that set long-term structures in place.

As with the mental-physical group, their language will be precise, and the flow of their discussion logically linked.

The Implications of Diversity

One of the most dramatic parts of Human Dynamics training programs occurs when the members of the different personality dynamic groups explain to one another their respective communication processes and needs. It becomes evident that each personality dynamic has, to a degree, misinterpreted the others. At the very least, each has been frustrated by the others, and each has caused the others pain. This is because each group's communication needs and processes are unique: they differ with regard to pacing; need for detail; need for personal connection; valuing of feelings versus factual data; preference for a highly interactive, multidirectional process as opposed to a methodical, logically connected, linear process; and so on. Recognizing that someone else's communication process is a purposeful function of that individual's inherent "way of being," and not a personal peculiarity or affectation, can come as a considerable shock. On the one hand, the realization may illuminate years of misunderstanding; on the other, it shatters any illusion that another's basic communication process will change easily. As one woman blurted out in a seminar when both of these revelations dawned on her, "You mean . . . that's the way he *is*?" (referring to her husband of some 30 years).

The question then is, how do we use this new awareness of the diverse communication needs to facilitate communication; avoid misunderstanding; and promote harmony, community, and collaborative endeavor?

One step is to see how inextricably the various communication processes are linked with each personality dynamic's unique capacities for contributing to the collective good. Figure 10.2 shows the links between each personality dynamic's communication needs and the function each naturally plays in an organization (or family, or community).

COMMUNICATION NEEDS RELATED TO FUNCTION

PERSONALITY DYNAMIC	COMMUNICATION NEEDS	FUNCTION IN ORGANIZATION
Mental-Physical	Clear Objective Logical Precise	Evaluate objectively Maintain clarity Articulate principles Make long-range plans
Emotional-Objective	Direct Goal-oriented Giving general picture Responsive: involving interplay of ideas	Move events forward Innovate Create models Make short-range plans
Emotional-Subjective	Personally connecting Sensitive to feelings Sincere (real feelings expressed) Process-oriented	Address "people issues" Take feelings into account Communicate personally Organize Create new forms
Physical-Emotional	Considerable context and detail Concrete and factual Practical Allowing sufficient time for response	Create systems Ensure practicality Operationalize Ensure continuity
Physical-Mental	Purpose clearly established Sufficient context and detail Concrete, factual, structured Allowing sufficient time for response	Plan strategically Make models Create systems Operationalize Ensure practicality and continuity

Figure 10.2

Mental-physical people's need for objective, clear communication is related to their gifts for thinking logically, setting structure, identifying values and principles, and maintaining perspective. Similarly, emotional-objective people's directness and preference for discussing the general picture, rather than detail, springs from their inner imperative to keep things moving forward. The more personally expressive communication of emotional-subjective people relates to their ability to organize and motivate people and maintain harmony. The emphasis of both physically centered groups on giving and receiving concrete data is linked to their ability to create and operationalize practical, systemic plans.

Recognizing that these processes and capacities are expressions of the same fundamental infrastructure in the personality, and are profoundly expressive of who the person *is*, suggests two strategies. One is that we need to let one another know our communication needs. The other is that we must all try to adapt our own natural way of communicating to meet others' needs. This requires willingness and attentive effort; however, it is a noble, compassionate, respectful, and pragmatic endeavor that pays dividends not only in the formation of close, harmonious relationships, but also in time and energy saved and higher productivity.

Exercise: Walking in Another's Shoes

Practice "living" another personality dynamic for a time (during a meeting, for example). For example, you might choose to:

- Slow down.
- Speak more deliberately.
- Speak with enthusiasm and emphasize important words.
- Practice connecting with others more personally by sharing something you normally wouldn't.
- Focus on one thing at a time.
- Pause before speaking.

Notice how you feel. Is it different? Does the experience change your perceptions? Will it change your future behavior? What have you learned from it? Ask others for feedback. Did they notice anything different about you or your participation?

As a general principle, one way of connecting with others is to entrain with their rhythm. Rhythm is primordial; one cannot change someone else's communication rhythm. But we can all learn to accept another's rhythm and adapt our own as best we can when we are with someone of another personality dynamic. With conscious practice and maturity, our rhythmic range expands. This practice applies not only to rhythm; we can learn a lot about others and enhance our communication skills if, in general, we consciously try to "walk in the other person's shoes."

Talking Each Other's Language

We would all do well to remember the following points in communicating with personality dynamics different from our own:

Mental-Physical

When communicating with mental-physical people, it is not particularly suitable to engage in elaborate personal processing. Work through any needs you may have for personal processing *before* you talk with them. That way you will have a clear sense of the purpose and direction of your communication, the questions you need to ask, and the outcome you expect. The more objective and clear you are, the more your listener will hear and understand you and be able to exercise his or her own gifts for clarity, objectivity, and focus.

We all must learn to give mental-physical people the time they need to consider what we say, and we must also be patient in answering their questions. It is often useful to ask mental-physical people if they have finished speaking before responding; their pauses do not necessarily mean that they have finished talking, but that they are pursuing a line of thought and formulating their words.

Because mental-physical people do not usually express their feelings, and because they think internally and nonverbally, you may find yourself wondering exactly "where they are at." If you wish to know, simply ask such questions as, "How does that make you feel?" or "What do you think about that?"—then allow time for a considered reply.

To connect most deeply with mental-physical people, listen for their values and principles, and communicate with them accordingly. Their deep feelings are related to their values.

Emotional-Objective

With emotional-objective people, *follow the movement* of their ideas. Avoid getting caught by one idea or taking every word literally. Their words are like improvised music, forming patterns and structures that flow and dissolve and keep moving. Their statements are not necessarily completed thoughts, but contributions to a creative interactive process in which we are all invited to participate.

Emotional-objective people are typically interested in the direction you are taking, the reasons for it, and how you expect to accomplish your goal. They also want to know about the people involved, your time frames, and the expected outcomes. They appreciate interactive brainstorming that yields a rich array of options, and they enjoy asking questions in a process of mutual inquiry. They focus on external problem-solving rather than inner exploration. They will ask for detail if they need it.

Emotional-Subjective

You will make your best connection with emotional-subjective people when you allow yourself to become more personally available, more personally revealing, even more personally vulnerable. *Follow their feelings* rather than their words, for usually their feelings are threads that connect one statement with another. We all must learn that when people of this personality dynamic talk about a personal problem, they usually do not want brilliant solutions as much as attentive listening and consistent empathic support. Given these, they will come to their own solutions as they speak. When they want suggestions, they will let you know.

Emotional-subjective people have a deep need to maintain a sense of harmony and personal connection while they pursue goals and address problems. They want to establish a comfortable atmosphere in which the process of communication can be enjoyed—even when it is highly results-oriented. If they feel that participants are fully committed to a mutual process of sincere exchange in which feelings are fully expressed, the group will be rewarded with their full engagement and the release of their creative energies. Remember that emotional-subjective people will always be aware of any attempt to pretend interest or attentiveness. If you do not have time to be fully "with" them, they would rather postpone a conversation than engage in a less satisfying process.

Physical-Emotional

With physical-emotional people, try to relax your body and enter into their communication rhythm. Feel your contact with the ground. Allow the silences to be as pregnant as the words. Physical-emotional people will probably want to lay out a complete context for any issue. Allow this, without interruption. If you are not sure whether they are ready for you to enter or re-enter the conversation, ask! Allow pauses at the end of any statement before you respond. This will help you align with their rhythm and ensure that they have finished what they want to say.

Utility and *continuity* are key words for physical-emotional people. They need communication to be concrete, detailed, and systematic. They also want to know how the present moment is linked to the past. They often like to communicate in the form of stories, because stories give context, convey reality, and provide a sense of the connections and interactions among the elements in any situation.

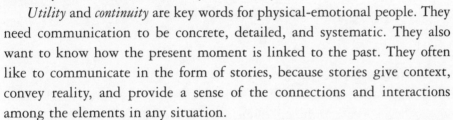

Allow time for a detailed exchange. Remember that every word you say will be assimilated and processed; so try to make your language as clear as possible, without unnecessary elaboration (especially of an emotional nature). Be thorough.

Physical-Mental

With physical-mental people, it is equally important to be pragmatic, factual, and grounded. Establish the *purpose* of the communication first, and then set the relevant context. Let them know early in the communication the outcome you want, including any actions on their part—they will be listening especially for actions to take. Be as structured, succinct, and methodical as you can. Set the key points clearly, and be prepared to offer considerable factual detail, either verbally or in written or diagrammatic form.

> ## *Exercise:* **Changing Habits**
>
> Our habits have been created out of countless repetitions. The more deeply ingrained a pattern, the harder it is to change. The following practice is exceedingly simple in structure, but surprisingly challenging to use.
>
> Identify a behavior you want to adopt or stabilize, or a quality you wish to nurture in yourself. For example, you might decide that you want to allow a colleague to speak without interruption, or you may decide that you will practice a personal development exercise every morning. Whatever behavior you select, repeat it consistently over a 21-day period. If you forget your practice, *you must begin again at Day One!*

Avoiding the Judgment Trap

Remember that each personality dynamic is often misinterpreted by the others, so be aware of these judgment traps. Here are the classic misunderstandings to watch out for:

Mental-Physical
Aloof, not caring

In fact, it is through their capacity for detachment and perspective that mental-physical people frequently show their caring. They are impersonal by design. Their gift to us lies in their impartial and objective viewpoint and their sense of what is essential.

Emotional-Objective
Pushy, controlling

Emotional-objective people light the fires of new endeavors. They challenge us to move and change. Their capacity to initiate can be remarkable. See this quality as an offering rather than a problem. Their gift to us is their willingness to step forward into new territories without a road map.

Emotional-Subjective
Touchy-feely

The emotional sensitivity of emotional-subjective people is one of their most valuable assets in accomplishing the difficult task of fostering positive relationships. Their gift to us is their willingness to use the lessons of their own subjective experience to create and maintain harmony among people, communicate empathically, and provide personal support.

Physical-Emotional
Too slow; needing too much detail
This group records and stores more data than any other personality dynamic. Systemic by nature and embodiments of continuity for us all, they work carefully and methodically and with vast amounts of detail. They remind us all of the value of careful craftsmanship, systematic planning, and cooperative endeavor.

Physical-Mental
Not personally caring; needing too much detail
The physical-mental group is second only to the physical-emotional group in the vast amounts of data they record and store. They show their caring, in part, through using their information to create fully operational systems that work efficiently for everyone.

Exercise: Self-Questionnaire for Understanding Others
The following questions can help you objectively assess a relationship with which you may be having difficulty, and take appropriate action to improve it. In particular, these suggestions may help you better understand the other person in light of what you now know about different personality dynamics.

Characteristics
1) What are the essential characteristics of your colleague?
2) How are they distinct from your own characteristics?
3) How does this distinction create tension for you?
4) Are any of the characteristics that create tension for you also characteristic of yourself? (Sometimes we are most disturbed by something we see in others that is, in fact, an undesirable and possibly unconscious characteristic of our own.)

Continued on next page

Communication

1) How does your colleague receive and give out information?
2) What kind of information does he or she seek?
3) What is his or her rhythm of speech? Pacing of speech?
4) How much does he or she speak? Listen?

Acquiring Information

Which of the following describes the needs of your colleague in acquiring information?

1) A precise, thorough, clear, purposeful, and logical overview
2) An innovative idea or structure for creating forward movement
3) A personally relevant and personally felt dialogue in which feelings are valued
4) Context that includes the past and that lays out a "whole picture" in a detailed, concrete, and methodical manner

Stress

1) Under what circumstances does your colleague get stressed?
2) How does he or she handle stress?
3) How does his or her response to stress affect you?

Positive Qualities

1) What positive qualities does he or she manifest?
2) What are this person's major strengths?
3) What can you learn from your colleague?

Personality Dynamics

1) What do you think is the personality dynamic of your colleague?
2) What is your personality dynamic?
3) What changes need to occur for you to feel more comfortable in this relationship?

Taking Action

1) What steps will you take to foster the changes you identified in 3) above?
2) If you have taken a step, how has it affected the relationship?
3) What will be your next step?

Handling Confrontation Effectively

One communication exercise we undertake in seminars is to have the different personality dynamic groups consider the question, "If someone needs to confront us about an issue, how should they go about it so that the process is as satisfactory and productive as possible?" We ask the groups to discuss the following points:

1) How should the communication be initiated?
2) How can the process unfold most comfortably?
3) How should the process conclude?

The groups then share their conclusions. The following responses constitute typical feedback from the different personality dynamic groups. *However, before reading them you may find it useful to consider these questions for yourself. What you learn may help you when you need to confront someone else. It may also help you convey to someone else how they can best communicate with you.*

Basic Rules

Of course, some basic rules apply to all of us, regardless of personality dynamic. For example:

- Ensure that the dialogue takes place in privacy.
- Be factual.
- Avoid blaming. Focus on the issues, not the person.
- Take responsibility for your own feelings. For example, say, "When you did this, I felt rejected," rather than "*You* made me feel rejected," or "*You're* so rejecting!"
- Focus on what needs to be done, or on what could be done together to improve matters, rather than simply giving directives.
- Allow space for the other person's responses, and be attentive.
- Maintain a tone of respect.

Although some of the following preferences that characterize the different personality dynamics clearly apply to business rather than family situations, most offer pertinent guidelines for any context.

Mental-Physical

- Because we prefer to focus on one thing at a time, select an occasion when there is sufficient time for us to focus solely on your issues.
- A written statement ahead of time on the nature and significance of the issue might be helpful. It provides us the opportunity to think about the situation beforehand.
- In presenting the issue, be as direct, factual, objective, and logical as possible.
- Give us an overview. Explain the issue's importance, its ramifications, and your purpose in raising it.
- We will hear you if you *tell* us about your feelings and what is causing them. We may shut down if you *demonstrate* them too strongly.
- If we do not respond emotionally, don't assume that we don't care. We will show that we have taken your concern to heart by involving ourselves in resolving the issue.
- Confirm with us any assumptions you have about our thoughts, feelings, or intentions. Because we do not always express these outwardly, you may misinterpret us.
- Give us time to share our perspective.
- Clarify issues regarding feelings. What are your feelings? What have we done, or failed to do, that catalyzed them?
- Work with us to agree on a principle (or principles) for proceeding that will probably apply to many other situations.
- We will most likely reach mutual understanding if the conversation focuses on the values involved—your values, my values, and the values that have been violated.
- We will make any necessary behavioral changes if we see the value in doing so.

Emotional-Objective

- Set a time to talk when we are free to give you our full attention.
- Be direct and straightforward.
- Please remember, however, that we are not necessarily as tough or self-assured on the inside as we may appear to be on the outside. Respect our feelings.

- Be aware that we identify ourselves with our work, so begin with genuine acknowledgment of our good work (if possible) before you present your issues.
- Remember that respect is one of our primary concerns, so please treat us with respect.
- State your concern rather than your perception of the solution.
- Start with the assumption that our intentions are and have been good.
- Let us explore *together* ideas for future action, and then agree on the steps to be taken.
- Know that we are open to being left with a challenge.
- Try to raise everything that is concerning you *now*, because we do not like to revisit issues. We want to reach mutual understanding, agree on future steps, and move on. However, we will be glad to meet again, after an appropriate period of time, to assess whether our agreed-upon course of action is working.

Emotional-Subjective

- Create a relaxed atmosphere for our conversation.
- Understand that we are usually hard on ourselves, so you do not need to be hard on us.
- Be honest, sincere, and direct.
- Do not generalize. Give concrete examples of the problem.
- Allow us space to identify and express our feelings.
- Please respect those feelings.
- We will probably need to process our feelings to clarify our thoughts. We may not express ourselves with total clarity as we engage in this process, so please be patient and don't take every word literally or hold anything we say against us.
- We need to feel that you are fully attentive. As we proceed, let us know that you are really hearing us.
- Talk in terms of "we," not "you."
- Tell us how we can help you.
- Don't patronize us, judge us, or withdraw.
- Ask questions if you are not sure you understand us.

- Don't provide ready-made solutions, but allow solutions to emerge from our dialogue.
- Allow sufficient time for this process; it will be worth it.
- Before ending the conversation, ask how we feel, and if we feel that everything that needs to be said has been said.
- Be open to postponing conclusions. We may feel that there is more to be said but have gone as far as we can for the moment.
- Keep the door open for further dialogue and exploration of solutions. We will continue to process our conversation, and may have further insights or observations to share.

Physical-Emotional
- Present the context for our conversation *in advance*, and in person. Let us know
  —the issue;
  —your perception of the current reality;
  —how the issue affects you;
  —how it affects the "big picture" (our shared interest).
- Be as concrete as possible. Provide specific examples.
- Don't push for an immediate response. Set a time with us for future discussion so we can consider the situation and prepare our response.
- When we do discuss the issue, allow sufficient time for a full exploration of the situation.
- Check with us to ensure that we have all the data needed to fully understand the situation from your point of view.
- Be patient in coming to a solution. Our goal will be a mutually satisfactory solution that will endure over time.
- We want to conclude with a clear understanding on both sides of
  —what you will do;
  —what I will do;
  —how these steps will resolve the issue and benefit our common interest.

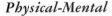

Physical-Mental

The physical-mental requirements are the same as those of the physical-emotional, but with the following nuances:

- When presenting the context in advance, be sure to include either a written or spoken statement of *where we have come from* and *where we need to go.*
- Work with us to reach a solution that includes *strategies and structures that will serve our common purposes.*

Exercise: Distinguishing Between Interpretation and Fact

We all need to learn to distinguish between a personal interpretation and a fact. Human Dynamics helps us to understand and release many misinterpretations of ourselves and others that we may have held as "facts." However, old behavioral habits can be stubborn. Here are some steps for cultivating new habits:

1) Ask yourself, every day, whether your perception of another person is a fact or simply a personal interpretation. Just posing this question puts you on the road to distinguishing between the two. For example, suppose your supervisor consistently gives you projects without providing certain information that you need in order to complete them. This irritates you, and you suspect that he or she is lazy . . . or incompetent . . . or is deliberately withholding information to prevent you from succeeding. So the question is, are these suspicions based on facts—or are they merely your interpretation, with no real basis in truth?

2) Begin to identify and work with the interpretations you are making. Write the facts regarding the exact behavior that irritates you. Then review what you have written and delete any *interpretations* of the behavior. For example, "She dumps the project on me without giving me the details I need" (a fact); "She's trying to trip me up" (an interpretation); "He doesn't look me in the eye when he hands me a project" (a fact); "He doesn't trust me" (an interpretation).

Continued on next page

3) Because one's own interpretations are sometimes difficult to see, ask a friend to review your list with you.

4) When you have clearly identified the facts, write your interpretation of them on a separate sheet of paper. If you have several different interpretations, write each of them on a separate page. Begin each statement with the words, "I interpret this behavior to mean . . ." For example, "I interpret this behavior to mean that she resents the amount of time I need to gear up for a project." Or, "I interpret this behavior to mean that she thinks I can't do the job."

Does this process change your interpretations or yield insights into the situation? You might realize that your interpretations of your supervisor's behavior share a common theme—that she doubts that you can do the job, for example—and that, in fact, you yourself have some self-doubt about your abilities in this role. Or you might perceive the behavior as consistent with his or her personality dynamic—and not personally directed at you. Check out your interpretation(s), or your new insights, with the individual concerned. In a spirit of objective inquiry, you might say, "I'm not certain if I have understood the following correctly. May I check it out with you?"

Conscious Team Learning

Hardly any endeavor of significance was ever achieved without teamwork. As organizations become more and more decentralized in their effort to anticipate and respond to change, teams gain more and more autonomy and are increasingly required to be responsibly self-directed.

Yet good teamwork is relatively rare, one of the reasons being that people are unaware that different personality dynamics exist and that the representatives of each group have distinct perspectives, communication needs, pacing, processes of learning and problem-solving, and affinities for certain functions.

Figure 10.3 indicates the customary patterns of each personality dynamic while moving from the initiation of a task or project to its implementation.

Clearly, mental-physical people proceed in an orderly way, with a con-

ACTIVITY RHYTHMS

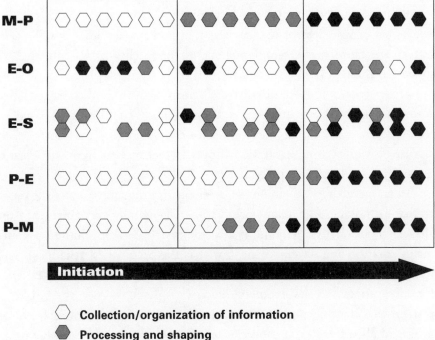

Initiation

⬡ Collection/organization of information
⬢ Processing and shaping
⬢ Action/implementation

Figure 10.3

sistent and evenly distributed investment of energy in collecting information, processing it, and finally taking action.

For emotional-objective people, work tends to be an experimental process. They like to move into action as soon as possible on the basis of minimal data, process the results, make the necessary adjustments, and move into action again. Through repeating this process, they eventually evolve an effective operation.

The multiple activity rhythm lines indicate the complexity of the interpersonal and intrapersonal processing that characterizes all the endeavors of emotional-subjective people. In fact, the diagram could contain any number of layers to reflect the intricacy of this process.

Physical-emotional people need the most time in the beginning, for they collect the largest amount of information, especially if the task is new. Once they have collected and extensively processed the data, their plan will be completely ready for implementation, and they will move quickly into action.

Physical-mental people's activity rhythm is similar to that of physical-emotional people, except that they gather and process less data. They too can move rapidly into implementation, once they have collected and processed the necessary data and formed their strategic plans.

Unawareness of these distinctions hampers team performance. As each team member works to satisfy his or her own needs, conflicts arise. In a classic team process, none of the members can understand why the others are not "hearing" him or her. Frustration builds, sometimes to the point that the group may not be able to proceed.

In fact, the diversity among the personality dynamics offers the opportunity for outstanding teamwork. Human Dynamics recognizes not only that each personality dynamic is a whole system with unlimited potential for integration and development, but that the personality dynamics *together* form a larger, more comprehensive system that also has unlimited potential for integration and development. Each complements the others, like the instruments in an orchestra. The ability to take advantage of each person's gifts and affinities depends on the team's awareness and understanding of the various personality dynamics. If each team member understands the personality dynamics' unique capacities, respects the communication needs and problem-solving processes of each, and makes conscious use of their complementary gifts, then the team can truly fly!

Exercise: **Process Checks**

Another useful tool for enhancing teamwork is the "process check." Essentially, the method entails stopping a discussion periodically to allow a few moments for each member of the group to reflect on and share his or her response to the discussion. The following process check is based on one used in Human Dynamics seminars.

One person in the group keeps track of time. Every 20–30 minutes, he or she stops the discussion and the team members ask themselves the following questions:

1) How am I feeling about myself . . . about others in the group . . . about the process?
2) Am I successfully fulfilling the function of my personality dynamic with the group? If not, why?
3) What can I do to contribute more fully?
4) What can I do to facilitate the functioning of others?

Each participant shares the salient points with the group before the discussion is continued.

In sharing their experiences, the team members must be honest and direct while maintaining respect for team harmony. They need to convey what was positive as well as what was uncomfortable; and they need to keep positive connections by using such expressions as, "It was really helpful to me when you said . . ." or "Although you are comfortable with. . . , I would have liked it better if . . ." Team members must also keep their communications in the first person—own the responsibility for what they say. For example, "When you interrupted so abruptly, I felt that my opinion wasn't being considered." "When we got into so much detail, I felt we lost momentum." "I felt I could have contributed more, but I couldn't find a place to jump in."

Aware of each other's thinking and feeling, the team members can make individual or collective adjustments to improve their process.

If timing, pacing, problem-solving process, language, and so on are all distinct, how *should* a team begin its process of working together? Is there an optimal way? Should the team begin with the function of the mental-physical people—with an overview of the assignment, clarifying the vision, defining the terms, and setting structures for proceeding? Or should the team begin with the physical-emotional people, and build from the ground up? Or do they support the immediate move of an emotional-objective member to the flip chart?

In our experience, it's best to allow the process to unfold naturally by *accepting* the beginning efforts of everybody—*listening* to everyone, and *noticing* how the process itself wants to move. Provided everyone is aware of what is happening, the group can keep things from becoming chaotic. *Everyone recognizes that this is only a starting point and will be prepared to accommodate all points of view as the process unfolds.* So long as the process includes all perspectives, beginnings can take any form.

Yet another question arises: If a team lacks one or more of the personality dynamics, is its effectiveness doomed? No. But again, the key is consciousness. If the members know that one of the personality dynamics is not represented and understand what this means, they can resolve to do their best to compensate collectively for the missing function(s), or they might decide that one of the members should assume the major responsibility for this function.

One of the most profound applications of Human Dynamics in organizations has been the *conscious creation* of teams of mixed personality dynamics. Teams that are already intact, of course, benefit hugely from training in understanding and using the personality dynamics that they comprise. But to knowingly fashion teams of mixed personality dynamics and matching maturity levels, and to provide them with training, has been, as one manager put it, "a quiet but real revolution." Such a team will have vision, purpose, structure; innovative thinking and forward momentum; concern for its own harmony, sensitivity to the implications of its work for other people, and creative and intuitive capacity; respect for the past while moving into the future, the ability to think systemically and practically, and the consciousness to integrate and fully use these gifts. Focus such a team on anything—strategic planning, reengineering, marketing, new product design, training—and you have the benefit of five equally valuable points of view and five equally valuable creative systems able to work synergistically to get results. Most important, the collective process becomes generative, with each member continuously gaining self-knowledge and learning about the others—*which means learning about humanity in general.* The group becomes a small "learning organization" or "learning community," whose collective learning and output can prove prodigious.

A lesson to be learned by teams of all kinds, whether a project team in a corporation or the "team" of the family, is that a qualitative *process* leads to qualitative *results*. In fact, a qualitative process is *itself* a qualitative result. In a qualitative process every voice is heard, every way of being is respected, and the gifts of every personality dynamic are fully utilized. As a result, team members find the experience deeply satisfying and enjoyable, *as well as* productive.

Moreover, the team's plans and decisions are more likely to bear fruit because every participant feels invested and will do his or her utmost to see them fulfilled. Finally, the team members establish a reservoir of trust and goodwill that provides an invaluable foundation for continuing collaboration. Without a qualitative process, teams may see short-term gain but will pay a high cost in stress, dissatisfaction, lack of trust, hidden agendas, reluctance to collaborate, and depleted energy. Deep satisfaction with workplace relationships is not only desirable in itself; it produces spectacular, practical results.

A Word on Leadership and Teams

Western cultures have typically given the leadership role to emotional-objective people. Certainly in the culture of the United States, we tend to value the gifts and affinities that emotional-objective people bring: capacities for risk, challenge, change, innovation, and short-term planning. Our experience in large corporations is that the majority of CEOs are emotional-objective people. We also see that many people in corporate cultures attempt to emulate the emotional-objective pattern, whether they are emotional-objective or not.

This is unfortunate for a number of reasons. First, it is unhealthy for those individuals, and it denies organizations the creative energy that can be derived from people living who they *are*. Second, the concept of *one* kind of leader or one "way of being" having more value than another is false. If any other personality dynamic were given this status, it would be just as false. All the personality dynamics have leadership capacity, though each will express their leadership differently. All the personality dynamics bring equal (though different) gifts. Each personality dynamic *needs* the others.

In fact, the concept of a single leader upon whom all depend is flawed. Ideally, leadership should be a team function in which all the personality dynamics participate. This is the only way to ensure the inclusion of multiple and complementary perspectives. These points have major implications for working successfully in a global society. When the five personality dynamics work together as a leadership team, they constitute a microcosm of the human macrocosm. They represent all of humanity. If this small world can work together well, there is hope for the future of the whole.

Organizational Applications

The power of Human Dynamics lies in its practical usefulness. Our purpose in pursuing our work and writing this book is much more than simply to present interesting new knowledge about human functioning. It is also to present a tool for enabling individuals and organizations to achieve their extraordinary potential. Our efforts have been divided between continuing investigation of the human systems we have identified, and developing programs for putting what we learn to practical use.

This chapter describes some of the ways in which Human Dynamics has been used in organizations. One of the unique characteristics of the work is its versatility. Because Human Dynamics is concerned with basic understanding of how human beings function individually and collectively, it has almost limitless applications. This quality has occasionally made it suspect; some people wonder how a single set of understandings can be so diversely applied. But that is the nature of foundational discovery—it is *foundational!*

Claude Teisinger was responsible for introducing Human Dynamics to Dow Chemical Corporation when he was manager of its factory at Long Beach, California. He has written,

For many years, we have trained our personnel in the human relations area— in listening, managing conflict, presentation, and so on. Most of the training is directed toward dealing with one set of circumstances and is normally appropriate for or needed by a small percentage of the people attending.

Based on my extensive experience with Human Dynamics, an understanding of the basic functioning of people allows a person to self-construct solutions *when dealing with people in virtually all circumstances.* This understanding eliminates the need for almost all of the "how to deal with humans" courses that are aggressively used in most organizations today. Working at the *root* of any problem or opportunity is always superior to implementing symptom solutions, so I have personally introduced Human Dynamics training as *the* method for bringing organizations together and assisting people in organizations in their personal exchanges with others.

Shooting all the ducks in the flock with one shell may not be as much fun as traveling all over the country looking for a shot, but it sure makes sense if your business is shooting ducks.

In addition to the economic advantage of such foundational training, there is a learning advantage. Each successive application of the work flows out of an already established set of understandings and experiences, so that the learning is progressively deepened for each individual while the spread of applications in the organization flows naturally and consistently. This fortifies the learning on both an individual and an organizational level, providing a common language and common frame of reference.

The tangible applications of these tools are often relatively simple—a new way of beginning a meeting, a slight modification to a training format, a stated acknowledgment of the value of seeing a particular situation in different ways—but these relatively simple acts reflect deeper changes in the attitudes, perceptions, and interactions of the people involved. As one seminar participant explained a year after an initial program,

Human Dynamics has allowed me to see every single encounter with another person through a different lens than I had before; it's a lens that allows me to view people more positively and with more understanding. Simply, it has changed the way I see and interact with other people and greatly enhanced the effectiveness of those interactions.

The understandings and tools of Human Dynamics have been applied by business organizations since 1983 to a wide variety of efforts: team building, communication, project planning and management, leadership development, change management, individual and team learning, sales, and valuing of diversity. The common thread connecting all these efforts is the need for greater understanding of human functioning and for enhanced practical skills in human interactions.

Diversity

Before describing in some detail the specific experiences of some major organizations in applying their Human Dynamics training, it is appropriate to refer back to the theme of Peter Senge's foreword and to say a few words about the application of Human Dynamics to the issue of diversity.

When we participated recently in a discussion with the Diversity Team at Shell Oil Company, the chairperson at the meeting, Renata Karlin, identified two main approaches to the issue. One approach looks at the issue in terms of such distinctions as race, culture, gender, religion, etc. The other is more concerned with distinctions in how people *are* and how they function, regardless of other distinctions.

Clearly Human Dynamics falls into the latter category. We have found that Human Dynamics programs, even when not directly addressing the issue of diversity, have a double value in this area. First, they bring people together by demonstrating the practical and synergistic value of diversity as shown in the *distinct* personality dynamics. But they also bring people together by demonstrating the *commonalities* that exist *within* the personality dynamic groups, regardless of distinctions in age, race, culture, and gender.

In Human Dynamics seminars, when the participants have identified their own personality dynamics, they break up for a period into their different personality dynamic groups to explore together their common attributes and experiences. This is always a wonderfully affirming experience for the participants, in which they discover together that they are not alone and that their way of being is really OK! And sitting together discovering their fundamental similarities may be men and women of all ages, people of various ethnicities, people of different professions, and people at different levels in the organization. As a woman in an emotional-objective group once exclaimed, "Look at us! I'm from Malaysia, we have an African-American male, an Asian male, a Hispanic male, and two Caucasian females. We've come from such *diverse* backgrounds and yet we have *so much in common!* It's just fantastic!"

People discover, in fact, that in some very basic ways they have more in common with others of the same personality dynamic than they do with people who may be of the same nationality, ethnic background, etc., but of another personality dynamic. In light of this experience, the old divisions seem not to be the point. The people have experienced one another at a more fundamental level of relationship.

The question may be asked, "But are you not simply substituting or adding new sources of division among people?" The answer is "No," for two reasons. One is that all the patterns of the different personality dynamics are woven from the same three principles—mental, emotional, and physical—common threads that bond humanity. The other is that the distinctions in functioning are constantly demonstrated to be equally valuable and interdependent, each an enrichment of, and source of inspiration for, the others. People naturally emerge from the seminars seeing *all* other people with new and more appreciative eyes.

This is *not* to say that the other approach to issues of diversity is not valid. But in addressing issues of diversity and diversity training, our recommendation would be to first lay down a training that enables people to experience their inherent commonalities, and at the same time discover for themselves the extraordinary *value* in difference, before addressing issues of biases because of distinctions in race, gender, etc. The latter approach, if it is still deemed necessary, will be much more agreeable and effective if built on a foundation of respect and appreciation for people as they *are*.

In reading the following accounts of the use of Human Dynamics in organizations, therefore, it needs to be recognized that although the training programs may be nominally addressing other issues, diversity training is always happening!

Managing Change

LONDON LIFE INSURANCE COMPANY

The following account outlines the flow of the various applications of Human Dynamics within London Life Insurance Company since 1989. It also provides a detailed description of how London Life has applied Human Dynamics as a key to effectively managing change and undertaking massive retraining in the use of computer technology across the organization. Glenn Pridham, who is responsible for corporate development and training at London Life, saw at once the potential value of Human Dynamics for his organization. Being a visionary (and mental-physical), he drew up a multiyear strategy for applying Human Dynamics at London Life—the company is now in the seventh year of his plan.

Context

London Life Insurance Company is a financial services company of 5,500 people and assets of $10.4 billion. With over 14 percent market share, London Life is the largest insurer of Canadians.

Human Dynamics first came to the attention of the training and development department in 1988 as a result of a mandate from the company president to make training more effective by better understanding how people learn. Since that time, Human Dynamics has become a foundational model for much of the company's corporate training. More than 3,000 people within London Life now understand and use Human Dynamics to some degree. Additionally, programs have been offered to spouses, local schools, and community groups.

The first Human Dynamics program was introduced to the company in 1989, as part of an executive leadership development program. The idea grew out of research showing that a prime distinguishing feature of effective leaders is that they know themselves well. Over the span of two years, nearly 400 senior managers took part in the course to develop leadership skills and build self-understanding and understanding of others. They responded with such enthusiasm that a version of the course was offered across the organization.

The same managers later attended a Human Dynamics program for applying understanding of distinctions in communication and problem-solving processes to team functioning.

A Human Dynamics workshop with a team building application was eventually offered across the company, attended wherever possible by intact teams or groups of people who needed to collaborate. To quote Glenn Pridham, "We continue to do a great deal of Human Dynamics training toward qualitative team functioning. This has given our company a tremendous advantage."

The next major application came with educating London Life trainers in the diverse ways that people learn. As Glenn Pridham said,

We took the approach that trainers needed to be facilitators of learning, not merely expounders of a topic or demonstrators of a skill. In order to make the training *optimally effective for every learner*, they needed to understand the learning processes of the different personality dynamics.

Human Dynamics eventually became a key component of *all* management training at London Life, including courses on project management, negotiation skills, and coaching and counseling.

Highlighted Applications and Results
Management of Change

More recent applications of Human Dynamics at London Life have centered on the management of change. Like most other companies, London Life has faced an increasingly competitive market in which continuous change must become a way of life. After a costly failure with a large-scale change project 10 years ago, London Life sought better ways to manage the complexity of implementing change. Its key finding, after considerable research, was that *most change efforts fail because they lack focus on the people issues involved in change.*

Human Dynamics has played an instrumental role in defining those people issues and showing how they can be addressed. London Life trainers now deliver four change management courses—Implementing Change, Sponsoring the Change, Mastering Change, and Handling the Stress of Change—in which Human Dynamics supplies key elements. One crucial understanding that these trainers have reached is that learning and change are inextricably linked. In Glenn's words,

> External competition for customers drives change. Change drives learning. In any organizational setting, learning is driven by the need for its people to frequently acquire and apply new knowledge and skills for the benefit of the organization. Often, we must give up (perhaps "unlearn") old work habits, old ways of working with technology, etc. Learning can be viewed as an internal process of change within each individual.
>
> Human Dynamics allows us to understand that resistance to change is often just a matter of unanswered questions and unmet needs. Reactions to change are sometimes perceived as resistant. But once people's questions about change are *appropriately* answered, they can accept change. We tend to communicate information about change through our own perspective. Human Dynamics has shown us that while everyone asks the same questions—who, what, where, when, and how—we ask them for different reasons, and we need different answers. By highlighting legitimate and recognizable patterns in the

personality dynamics, Human Dynamics allows us to shape different approaches to people, greatly improving the success of the change process.

The course on Handling the Stress of Change, for example, teaches managers of a change process to understand what causes stress to the different personality dynamics. Moreover, it helps anyone who has to navigate change (essentially everybody!) to recognize their own needs and take care of themselves appropriately. One benefit of these courses is that people feel not only that their needs are legitimate, but that their organization acknowledges and makes every effort to meet them.

Wendell Davidson, one of the company's Human Dynamics facilitators, makes two points with regard to the change seminars:

> So many people at London Life have been exposed to Human Dynamics through other workshops that we can easily build on their existing knowledge to manage change effectively. And since the different personality dynamics are present in the change courses, we provide them with opportunities to group together and formulate for themselves their needs with respect to change. Then the groups inform each other. We simply facilitate their discoveries and understanding. The result is that they *own* their learning about themselves and each other. They are not simply accepting something we tell them.

Technology Learning

Like many other organizations, London Life has faced a major challenge in training people to use new technology. London Life executives recognize that efficiency and customer satisfaction depend on technology competency. Typically, people approach new technology with a great deal of anxiety (and, in many cases, resentment at being required to change). Also, the training is typically conducted in a standardized manner, and many employees fail to make the grade. They may lose their jobs or have to be relocated—in either case, they are replaced by someone who will need training in the new position as well as the new technology. This process can eat up a huge amount of time and spawn much disruption, and the organization may suffer staggering losses, both financially and in employee satisfaction and morale.

Aware of these pitfalls, and in light of their previous costly failure, London Life executives prepared carefully for their company-wide retraining projects. As a primary strand of their strategy, they tailored their training methods to the needs of the individual learners, using the advanced training of their Human Dynamics facilitators in the Human Dynamics "Learning and Teaching" program. They have applied this knowledge in two ways: they have presented curricula with a variety of options available to suit the learning processes of the different personality dynamics; and they have made available "technology learning coaches."

More than 200 technology learning coaches have been recruited from across the company, selected both for their expertise with the technology in question and their ability to relate to people. Their role is to coach, mentor, and nurture the learner. They undergo an intensive workshop in which they receive training in coaching and active listening skills, in the nature of change, and particularly in the distinct change and learning processes associated with the five personality dynamics.

Technology learning coaches are then assigned to a group that needs to implement change involving technology and typically stay with the unit through the entire "learning curve." The coach knows the personality dynamic of everyone in that group and therefore knows how each person learns and reacts to change.

Before the new approach to training was widely adopted, there was some skepticism at London Life. The company undertook a pilot project, using technology coaches trained in Human Dynamics. In the words of Wendell Davidson,

> At the beginning of the project, the leaders identified people they felt would not be able to make it through this change into the new environment. They were certain that half the group or more would have to be replaced by others with the right aptitudes, skills, and motivations. As it turned out, *everyone* who participated in the project succeeded. Though some participants elected to retire or move into other areas of the company, everyone was empowered to move into the new technology era. The significant thing for me is that we were able to manage the process so that everyone *had* a choice. I can't think of a more powerful message than that.

As a result of this and similar pilot projects, the company launched broad-scale retraining.

Retraining the District Sales Division

During a 14-week period, London Life trained 2,160 sales and customer service people from sales offices all over the country on personal computers. They required specific training on the technology platform that the reengineered business processes would use. The training focused on the essential tools of word-processing, presentation, and spreadsheet software; most of the learners had no prior exposure to personal computers. Fifty-four technology learning coaches provided the training. Earline Philips, coordinator of the technology learning project for the district sales division, describes the project:

> We ask the technology learning coaches to look for a person's personality dynamic in order to know how that person likes to learn: Is it hands-on, do you want me to guide you through this, do you want to read and I'll just be around the corner if you need to ask questions, or do you want to work together with someone else?
>
> The coaches became good at switching gears based on the preferred approaches to learning. They got so good at it, they could shift gears automatically and go into the mode they knew would work.
>
> The regional vice presidents, ultimately responsible for the sales representatives within the organization, were absolutely thrilled. They received many comments on how patient, knowledgeable, kind, and understanding our coaches were. It's the best response we've ever had. And because of the effectiveness of the approach, there was an immediate high level of skill available, which saved tens of thousands of training dollars.
>
> It also made some lasting relationships. The salespeople say to themselves, "I've developed a relationship with one of these coaches, and if I'm really stuck with a related problem I'm going to call that person." Wherever they are in the country, they feel they have a friend and a resource to turn to.

Apart from everything else, the experience has been a training in consciousness about the learning process that both learners and coaches can take everywhere. The participants also felt seen and respected for who they were. The value of this in terms of goodwill and loyalty within the company is beyond reckoning.

Large-Case Reengineering

One reengineering project at London Life known as "Large Case Reengineering" involved a department of 75 people who handle group life and health insurance benefits for companies with more than 400 employees. This department processes approximately 20 percent of London Life's revenues. Dan Rutledge was assigned to work with this department as technology learning coach. When he started, the entire unit had attended the appropriate change management courses and had learned about the different needs of the personality dynamics with regard to learning and change. However, the in-house training program that was already in place did not meet the needs of the different learners. It was a self-paced, facilitated process involving independent study in a room with six or seven other students and a facilitator. This system worked well for some people, but others came back saying that they couldn't learn in that environment—there was too much distraction, they had no opportunity to discuss the material with others, some felt uncomfortable asking questions, and others had difficulty in learning primarily from a book.

Dan introduced a far more flexible system. He found some video courses with complete, straightforward explanations and interesting graphics. The format of the course involved watching a video segment, then reading the same portion from a textbook. The book had the same graphics and the same information as the video. There were also exercises to do on the computer. In addition to reading, therefore, the course offered visual and auditory training, and the opportunity to reinforce new learning with hands-on practice. The course was offered in a room equipped for two people to work simultaneously.

Dan shares his observations,

Each student utilized the video training to suit their particular learning needs. For example, there was an emotional-objective person who went to the room and only watched the video; I thought he had essentially just gone in, sat back, and watched TV. I wondered, how can I challenge his learning process and really not come across in a negative way? I decided to stop by his desk in two or three days and try to help him apply some of the things he learned. When I stopped by, I found that he was actually very excited about what he had learned. He showed me half-a-dozen different things he could do based on what he'd seen in the videos, all of them immediately applicable to his job.

It turned out that for emotional-objective learners, just going in and watching the video was an effective means of learning, as long as they could immediately apply the learning to their jobs. Most emotional-objective people didn't read the book, and they certainly didn't do any of the practice exercises. Yet they came away with a great learning experience and were delighted that they got everything they needed.

Another person was physical-emotional. She booked both sides of the room so that she could concentrate by herself. She told me that she had not been able to learn anything in the training room with six or seven people in it, but in the smaller room she *had* learned because she was able to repeat a section of the tape six times without being embarrassed. She kept rewinding it until she had learned it. She said, "I took my time and I learned it thoroughly. I listened to every video, I read every line in the book, and I did every exercise on the computer."

This particular woman helped change my mind about how people learn. I used to get frustrated if people didn't get something the first time, and I was really frustrated if they didn't get it the second time. Now I say to myself, "Well, maybe this person is physically centered; and if so, she's going to learn it much more thoroughly; and she's going to remember it a lot longer than I will." So the experience is having an impact on me as a trainer.

One of the physical-mental men told me that he loved the course. He watched only the first fifteen minutes of the tape, then read the book and did the exercises on the computer. He almost completely left out the video. I couldn't imagine it, but that's how it worked for him.

Emotional-subjective learners sometimes booked the space together. They would stop the tape, and discuss how what they had just seen related to their jobs. "We can use that in this way, and we can use that on this account," and so on. They fed off each other and built wonderful ideas. They came out of each session raring to go, asking me, "How do we do this? How do we get this started?"

I had thought my biggest challenge would be to get the people to apply the training to their work and become more productive. But that wasn't an issue—as long as the training was delivered in a way that was effective for them.

Rethinking Curriculum Design

London Life is trying another approach to teaching basic technology to large numbers of people: actually creating a different curriculum for each personality dynamic. The goal is to discern the learning needs of a specific personality dynamic and tailor the whole approach accordingly. The company is doing this by combining their Human Dynamics training with input from staff members representing the different personality dynamics.

For example, Kim LeBlanc coordinated a five-member team of emotional-objective people. The team designed a two-hour curriculum for teaching emotional-objective learners how to use a word-processing software package for creating a business letter and designing tables. Other teams are devising teaching approaches for the other personality dynamics.

Kim describes the process for piloting an emotional-objective curriculum:

We started with six or seven learners. I explained to them what the learning would be about, and that the approach would be quick and to the point. I said, "This demonstration will take less than one minute." Then I quickly talked them through it while another person operated the software. We kept the demo short because we found that two or three minutes bored emotional-objective students. Then we built something in the software called a cue card. Instead of reading instructions from a piece of paper, the students were given step-by-step instructions on the PC screen for using a template. The cue card was in bullet form, without a lot of words.

Kim's team also tailored the learning environment to the emotional-objective learner. Lined paper and pencils were provided, but the desks were cleared of nonessential objects. The curriculum leaders for each personality dynamic tried to make everything in the room relevant to the course and the learner.

Wendell Davidson observes that the adjustments required to accommodate the different personality dynamics are often small. "One of the powerful aspects of the Human Dynamics system is that it gives you a framework for making specific changes in training and curriculum design that may be quite small but have a large impact."

Glenn Pridham again:

Through all these efforts, we're building a technology platform that enables London Life people to do their jobs very differently in the future. The learning of basic technology has become infinitely easier with the Human Dynamics approach, because it tells us so clearly how people learn. Understanding the basic patterns of learning as individuals and as an organization, we have been able to help our people master technology much more quickly than anyone else.

Future Directions

London Life will continue its various Human Dynamics–based trainings and is planning to add a new module designed specifically for salespeople. Like new technology classes, sales presentations are most effective when tailored to the personality dynamic of the potential client.

Further down the road will be a new module for job specific trainers (OJT), which will build on the concepts learned through technology coaching.

Glenn Pridham sums up London Life's experience with Human Dynamics:

The Human Dynamics work has benefited our entire culture. It has caused one of the best kinds of revolution possible—a quiet, steady, and enduring one. It has been instrumental in giving us a competitive edge.

Learning Environment

DIGITAL EQUIPMENT CORPORATION, NETWORKS ENGINEERING

The following account of the use of Human Dynamics at Digital is based largely on a report by Chris Strutt, a Human Dynamics facilitator who joined Digital 23 years ago as a software engineer, and is now a consulting engineer. For the past decade Chris has focused on the connection between business results and the human side of organizations; it is in this arena that she sees both the root causes of failure and the greatest leverage for success.

Chris traces for us a fascinating journey of learning that began in 1987 and continues to the present. Her story tells us how, in response to persistent problems in quality and customer satisfaction difficulties, the Networks Engineering group moved from fixing symptoms, through problem-solving, to the removal of root causes. The story is a salutary one for any organization.

Context

Human Dynamics was introduced into the Networks Engineering group in 1993 after six years of grappling with problems in quality and customer satisfaction. At that time Networks Engineering consisted of about 1200 people, who designed and built hardware and software products that link computers, enabling people to work together no matter what systems they use or where they are located.

In 1987, complaints about product delivery times and quality had come to the attention of the group. The group immediately responded by fixing key elements of the development process, writing new process guidelines, delivering workshops on quality and development methods for project managers, and instituting monthly project reviews by senior management. These strategies did improve quality and time-to-market (TTM), but in the process they revealed much deeper issues: a marketplace shift, with customers now wanting systems solutions as well as products; and a dramatic growth spurt within the company that intensified internal complexity.

In response to customer demand, the group began thinking about producing families of products and systems. By 1990, it became evident that much more than just development strategies had to change. The group began to apply the tools and concepts of systems thinking to all aspects of work team functioning, and now paid at least as much attention to relationships *among* the pieces—including products, processes, people, teams, groups, and the company itself—as to the pieces themselves.

Through thinking in systemic terms, the group became aware of a deeper and more pervasive issue underlying TTM and quality problems—the lack of a shared vision to provide direction for the whole. The group took steps to engage 350 of its key employees in building a shared vision, which drove investment decisions for new products and gave everyone greater clarity and context for their projects.

It was clear to the group that they could survive only by functioning as a "learning organization," as described by Peter Senge in his book *The Fifth Discipline*—that is, "an organization where people continually expand their capacity to create the results they truly desire . . . where people are continually learning how to learn together."

The group practiced new ways of collaborative decision-making on projects and programs, focusing on inquiry, reflection, and surfacing assumptions which, when brought to consciousness and articulated, might be revealed as incorrect. With this emphasis on conscious teamwork and collaboration, Networks Engineering reached one more level of discovery: they could only address those issues that were actually put *on* the table. However, in the classic manner described by Chris Argyris in his book *Overcoming Organizational Defenses*, many issues remained safely buried below the tabletop and were consequently "undiscussable." People's words did not always match their actions or their knowledge. Not the least of the undiscussables were instances where projects ran into difficulties but no one was willing to acknowledge the problem. In fact, it was the deeper, human issues of lack of trust and poor communication that lay at the root of the TTM and customer satisfaction problems.

People's words did not always match their actions or their knowledge. In fact, it was the deeper, human issues of lack of trust and poor communication that lay at the root of the TTM and customer satisfaction problems.

There was, at this time, an atmosphere of crisis in the organization. Considerable downsizing was anticipated, and people felt helpless and afraid. Indeed, August 1992 saw the launching of two years of restructuring, downsizing, and cost containment. Networks Engineering expressed an additional concern: "What are we doing for the survivors?" The results of research on downsizing in large corporations were clear: only a fraction of the companies returned to profitability, and, of these, an even smaller fraction ever returned to previously enjoyed levels of employee productivity and morale. The preceding several years' work with some systems thinking and learning skills had taught the group an important lesson. As Chris puts it,

> The most fundamental obstacle to improving product quality, customer satisfaction, and hence profitability lies in the absence, avoidance, or breakdown of authentic connection and communication among human beings.

Human Dynamics at Digital

At the urging of Chris Strutt, Digital introduced Human Dynamics training to Networks Engineering in 1993 with two key goals: (1) to revitalize the group's employees and reconnect them so as to rebuild an atmosphere of openness and trust; and (2) to enhance team communication skills so as to accelerate decision-making and action for business success.

Both of these approaches address root causes of TTM and quality deterioration. According to Chris, "The expectation was that with connections and trust built up through Human Dynamics, we would be able to work back to the critical undiscussable issues and get these most difficult issues out in the open as they arose, so that they could be rapidly resolved."

The work with Human Dynamics began as a grassroots effort: initially only two people were sent to be trained and licensed as Human Dynamics facilitators. In May 1993, the first workshop at Digital was delivered, receiving an evaluation from participants of 5.5 out of a possible high of 6. That same month, a workshop was delivered for the new Networks Group vice president and his newly forming leadership team. As a result, the team learned to recognize, understand, and appreciate the special gifts that each of them brought to their work—knowledge that proved essential over the next several months as the group established Digital's core networking business.

Word spread, and enough anecdotal evidence of the effectiveness of Human Dynamics training accumulated to draw the attention of the late Peter Conklin, corporate consulting engineer, then serving as leader of Digital's "Engineering Excellence" program. Conklin saw the importance of this work in engineering. In January 1994, he funded the training of four new facilitators, and Human Dynamics became an official educational program under the auspices of Digital's "Engineering Excellence" program.

Over the next four months, the company offered four to five workshops per month, each one facilitated by two in-house Human Dynamics facilitators. Workshops were delivered to teams who were focused on delivering a product, service, or some other set of results. By their nature, these teams were diverse, comprising members from across numerous organizational, functional, and hierarchical boundaries.

Chris was very encouraged by the number of requests for workshops:

> Our past experience shows that the best indicator for the value or usefulness of any new technology is the level of continuing demand. Since the Human Dynamics work began as a bottom-up effort, and continued as a middle-across effort through the "Engineering Excellence" program, we knew that no one was seeking a workshop just because they were being pressured by upper management.

As the groundwork in Human Dynamics was being laid, Digital continued to struggle to get back on its feet financially. Starting in May 1994, the company endured the severest belt-tightening yet. Among many things, it put an immediate stop to most expenditures for training. Overnight, the Human Dynamics program came to a halt, and five of the six Human Dynamics facilitators left the company. Yet although no new people were being trained in Human Dynamics, those who had been trained continued to use their understandings within Digital.

By late 1994, the company entered the final stages of its restructuring. It now employed about 60,000 people worldwide—half its original size. The moratorium on training expenses began to lighten. After a seven-month hiatus, a Human Dynamics workshop was delivered in December 1994. As before, word spread, and more requests for workshops came in.

Margaret Ledger, the new manager of Digital's technical competency development group (TCDG), began to see Human Dynamics as essential for project team leadership and operation across the company. With support from key people in the newly formed business segments, Margaret incorporated Human Dynamics into the TCDG's core curriculum, to be delivered on demand across the company alongside cutting-edge technical training in areas like C++, Object-Oriented Design, and Windows 95. Three new facilitators were trained, and by 1996, more than 800 people across the company had received Human Dynamics training. The demand for workshops remains steady.

Highlighted Applications and Results

To date, applications of Human Dynamics at Digital have focused primarily on individual and team functioning. Themes that have emerged consistently are that (1) employees raise undiscussable issues more and more easily; (2) teams have progressed past limited mental models, assumptions, and judgments; and (3) individuals are reporting a greater level of honesty and trust on teams. Much evidence for these gains is anecdotal, but its consistency makes a powerful statement.

John Adams, now retired, was former vice president and technical director for Networks Engineering. He believes that Human Dynamics treats undiscussables not so much as a complex organizational problem but as a basic issue of interaction between people:

One particularly difficult issue was people's unwillingness to discuss a problem or delay in a project. Now, that seems to be significantly diminished. That was the goal—to have fewer surprises. We can't prove the correlation, but we know that once we began working with Human Dynamics, problems became easier to discuss.

The following stories describe some of the ways Networks Engineering applied Human Dynamics within teams.

Balancing Perspectives for a Systemic Result

As part of a major restructuring exercise, one engineering group manager at Digital had to merge two different software engineering groups (totaling about 350 people) and create a new organizational structure. He gathered a diverse set of people from the two groups—the managers, some technical leaders, and some other key individuals, who together formed a cross-section of the new organization. Because they had all attended a Human Dynamics program, he asked them to group themselves according to their personality dynamics. Then each personality dynamic group developed its own proposal for the new organization. He knew that each group would bring a unique and crucial perspective to the task.

One group took a long-term view, concerning themselves mostly with guiding principles and overarching goals. Another group emphasized short-term results, flexibility, and responsiveness to change; their proposal included the most innovative ideas. Yet another group focused on the people of the organization, their relationships, the merging of the two cultures, and how to engage everyone in the process of restructuring. The fourth group attended mostly to the facts of the situation and the actual data available; they presented the most pragmatic and detailed alternatives.

After all four groups had heard and discussed each others' proposals, two people from each of the four groups were asked to work together to produce a synthesis of the proposals. As a result, the manager was presented with a balanced analysis for guiding the new organization.

Balancing Teams

A key person on a Digital product development team that had received

Human Dynamics training had left the company. She had been deeply appreciated by the team; they knew that it would be hard to find the right person to replace her. One of the team members, Barbara,[1] says that much of the subsequent team discussion focused on personality dynamics— "What are the personality dynamics already in the team? What would we need for balance?" Eventually they selected a replacement who accepted the position.

Barbara remembers,

> At one of the first meetings, the engineering manager, who is emotional-objective; the new team member, who's physically centered; and I, an emotional-subjective person, sat together. The new person had put together this long, typed list of issues, with many questions about deadlines and all kinds of specifics. The engineering manager looked at her and said, "I am so happy that you've joined the team, because we really need you to keep us on track." It was a wonderful moment of appreciation. In the past he might have rolled his eyes and looked at me as if to say, "She's going to kill me with all of these questions and details." But he and I both knew how much we needed someone like her to balance the team.

Increased Productivity and Creativity

A key product's profitability was dwindling alarmingly. A team of 16 creative people from business, marketing, and engineering was asked to come up with alternatives for injecting new life into this product. Before jumping into the task, the team took the time to review the communication needs, problem-solving processes, and task orientation of each personality dynamic. They also agreed to use "process checks"—a mechanism for periodically checking that the team is using the gifts brought by each personality dynamic.

Eight weeks later, the team produced exciting results that led directly to new product development that is now recognized industry-wide as award-winning Internet collaboration software. Its members state that they could not have achieved such innovative and high-quality results without

---

[1] The name of this person has been changed.

their understanding of the personality dynamics. They know that without the process checks, conflicts that arose would have become undiscuss-ables—talked about one-on-one in the hallways and never resolved. Instead, the team equipped itself to handle issues openly in a nonthreatening, non-personal, and productive manner.

One member of the team commented that she had recently participated in another project that had been totally derailed because issues were not handled directly:

> I saw a fundamental difference in the way the members of this team approached their functions. What I saw evolve was a degree of trust and a capacity for sharing that allowed a different level of creativity and reframing to be achieved. It impacted more than just how we worked together—it broke down barriers in our thinking.

New Product Development

Debbie Falck (an emotional-subjective person) was one of the original team members. She is currently part of a group that focuses on visual design. Recently she was demonstrating a new interface for a virtual workspace to one of her colleagues who is physical-mental:

> I'd been creating a lot of prototypes for what this might look and feel like; we were talking about networking and virtual reality space, and I was flipping from one screen to the next and showing these abstract, provocative images—dreamy kind of stuff—like what you see when flying through clouds at twenty thousand feet. And she looked at it and said, "Well, Debbie, that's great, but where would I put my printer?" That just sent me right out the window!
>
> But then I thought, that's wonderful, she's right—what a difference from my way of thinking. And I realized that as we design interfaces, we need to come up with a menu offering a variety of presentations to meet the needs of the different personality dynamics. My guess is that what she would create as a workspace on her computer would need to be much more structured, perhaps more realistic, than my workspace. That really has implications for how we create products.

A New Language

After learning about Human Dynamics, when people in Networks Engineering have conflicts or problems with each other, they often tend to explain them in Human Dynamics terms. As John Adams noticed,

> An example might be the shift from saying "so-and-so is micromanaging me," to "so-and-so is physical-emotional and sometimes his request for detail drives me crazy, but I understand that it's his way of building a complete picture from which a decision can be made." The first statement is very subjective and difficult to discuss; the second one provides more objective language and allows the participants to have an effective dialogue about the amount of information each needs in order to make a decision. The fact that there's a vocabulary for dealing with those conflicts as soon as they manifest themselves acts as a tremendous safety valve.

Tailoring Communication

Owing to the continuous shifting of roles during the restructuring at Digital, one group vice president faced a reporting structure that changed four times in this period. Fortunately, she knew her own personality dynamic and that of each new manager. From her Human Dynamics training, she could attune to the different communication preferences and the way each personality dynamic approached problem-solving and decision-making. She tailored her communication accordingly, consciously adopting the language and questions through which to connect with the others most quickly and effectively. As a result, she continued to get the kind of support she needed despite the many changes in the hierarchy above her.

As another example, a program manager needed a technical leader to make some critical decisions. She knew her own personality dynamic and his, and she was aware of the potential points of conflict in their communication processes. Whereas she naturally approached issues by building up from the details until the structure emerged, he identified the principles and structure first and then filled in the detail as needed. Knowing this, she designed her communication to best suit *his* process, starting with the structure first. As a result, they made

> One group vice president faced a reporting structure that changed four times in this period. Fortunately, she knew her own personality dynamic and that of each new manager. She tailored her communication accordingly, consciously adopting the language and questions through which to connect with the others most quickly and effectively.

their decisions in one 15-minute conversation. Without this understanding, the two might have struggled through endless arguments and discussions to reach a conclusion. Even if the result had been the same, the cost—in terms of time, energy, and loss of goodwill—would have been much greater.

Future Directions

Chris Strutt sees that a key strategy for sustaining the use of Human Dynamics is to establish more frequent and regular mechanisms for sharing experiences and offering "refresher" seminars. She believes that these sustainment activities are especially crucial at Digital, because there is so much change and movement of people from team to team.

Other Human Dynamics applications for the future include exploration of different teaching and learning processes, leadership development, individual development, and the planned creation of balanced teams. In Digital's first experiment with balancing teams, Networks Engineering assembled several teams to visit customers in Europe, Australia, and the U.S. The group contained a functional mix—business, marketing, and engineering—but, explains Chris,

> We made sure we had a mix of personality dynamics also. The project involved a process of inquiry about the contexts in which the customers were operating, and it was vital for us to have the fullest picture possible. We felt we needed the perspective of as many of the personality dynamics as possible.

In reflecting back on the journey that Networks Engineering has undertaken in the last eight years, Chris says:

> Every step has been important and necessary. But the greatest leverage seems to lie with Human Dynamics. Had we known eight years ago what we know now, we would no doubt have introduced Human Dynamics in parallel with the basic reengineering of our planning and development processes. In other words, we might have better balanced symptom fixing with root cause removal. All of the subsequent trainings would have been enhanced and made more potent by first laying a foundation of Human Dynamics awareness.

Cultural Transformation

INTERMOUNTAIN HEALTHCARE SYSTEM

In no setting is stress higher, good teamwork more critical, and harmonious relationships with "customers" more desirable than that of a healthcare provider. Human Dynamics has been introduced into a number of hospital settings with the goals of improving teamwork, reducing staff stress, and enhancing the quality of interaction and communication with patients. Human Dynamics was first introduced to Intermountain Healthcare System in 1994.

Context

Intermountain is an integrated health-service network with 24 hospitals, a health-plan division, and numerous physician clinics. It is regional in Utah and in the contiguous areas of Wyoming and Idaho. Within the healthcare industry, Intermountain is recognized as a leader in continuous quality improvement in the clinical setting.

Like other healthcare organizations in the country, Intermountain faces monumental changes and challenges. As part of its response, it has redesigned work in several areas and explored the concepts of the learning organization. Its goal is "to offer seamless, patient-centered care across its integrated network of facilities." Human Dynamics was initially introduced to Intermountain to focus on the development of self-managing teams and cultural transformation.

Highlighted Applications and Results—
Ambulatory Surgery Redesign Team

Sixteen people were offered the opportunity to participate in a new team that would redesign the ambulatory surgery process for five facilities in the Salt Lake valley. The team included people from several departments, disciplines, and facilities. Some of the people knew one another, but had not worked together before.

Before they began their work, the team members attended a four-day Human Dynamics workshop, with the purpose of understanding and appreciating their individual differences in order to increase effectiveness of a redesign initiative. They then began applying what they had learned about themselves and each other in a variety of ways.

Committing Fully

The team members started off by agreeing to contribute fully the gifts inherent in each of their personality dynamics. This involved understanding that some conventional ground rules—such as "only one person talks at a time," or that people stay seated—might need to be amended from time to time. Such rules may actually impede the process of some personality dynamics; more important, they miss the point that team members need to allow one another to do whatever they need (such as walking around the room, taking a short break, reflecting without jumping into the discussion) to make their unique contribution. "Contributing fully" needs to be defined by the individual and not by group pressure. The questions for each individual become, "How can I contribute my function to the group? How can I best allow each of the others to contribute *their* function?" and "How can I best communicate with each team member?"

For Diane Kelly, work design project coordinator who served as the internal consultant to the group, this joint commitment proved a key experience:

> People would ask periodically, "How are we doing? Are we bringing our gifts?" It wasn't overdone, but there was a general level of intensity and participation, of being present to the process, that was quite striking. Anyone who has ever worked with groups would have noticed it immediately.

Diane also observed how the workshop had predisposed the group to begin with this level of commitment:

> It's very honoring because it says, "This is you; you are whole, your pattern has internal logic. You are the way you are supposed to be, and you have a unique and vital contribution to make."

Monitoring the Process

The team used Human Dynamics in some very basic ways. For example, it took time at the beginning of a meeting to ask, "What, specifically, do we want to achieve today, and who is the best person to lead us through this process?" And it had each participant in turn express his or her needs for information, for processing, for time to reflect. This discussion made the decision-making steps more explicit.

The group also stopped at intervals to "check in" about how they felt about the process and their own contribution to it. Process checks gave the group a mechanism for calling a time-out when the process and task weren't meshing.

Correcting Assumptions

Naturally, difficulties cropped up occasionally. The group's task was stressful because it had implications for so many people. Diane described how an ongoing issue surfaced strongly in one particular meeting.

> We had a physical-mental person who is quite knowledgeable about clinical procedures. She sometimes formulated solutions to problems by herself, then came to the meeting and announced them. Others, particularly the emotional-subjective individuals, assumed that she did not value their input, so they felt excluded and they retreated. Around one issue regarding patient care, the tension became so high that several people left the room. The team recovered well, however. They examined their various reactions honestly and objectively at the next meeting.

The physical-mental woman realized that, because others were not coming to the meeting armed with conclusions, she had assumed she was the only one who cared about the issue. The others realized that she did not think her conclusions were the only ones possible. The discussion revealed the assumptions that had been made and their contribution to the conflict. It also became evident that much of the misunderstanding was due to her preference for thinking things through alone, compared to the emotionally centered preference for highly interactive problem-solving.

Surfacing Undiscussables

As they discussed some stressful encounters, Diane observed that the team became ever more trusting of one another and comfortable verbalizing thoughts that would have previously been left unspoken. Someone might say, for example, "I really feel disengaged from this process because I don't think we've finished that last point at all." And the response they would typically get would be, "Okay, let's go back and do it." Most important, they were able to use the objective language of their different ways of processing to explain areas of misunderstanding rather than engaging in personal blame.

Using the Whole Team's Resources

Meetings are often dominated by those who speak the most; some people are excluded simply by the pace of the conversation. One of the significant contributions of Human Dynamics is that it encourages an environment in which *all* personality dynamics can offer their strengths. Diane gives an example:

> One physically centered woman was particularly quiet during meetings. It would have been easy for me and other emotionally centered people to drown her with the quantity of our talk, or discount her as uninvolved. Because we were careful *not* to do this, she added so many key pieces! At one point, she defined the whole surgery process from the patient's point of view. She used maps of her unit to first trace the existing patient flow and then how she saw the new way.
>
> It was the most impressive before-and-after description I've ever seen of how redesign could impact patient flow and staff efficiency. She was able to visualize all of the interrelationships of people and functions, as they relate to the physical space that the patients and staff move through. It brought the change alive in a way that process charts and flow diagrams can't. We would have lost all that if we hadn't allowed her the space to contribute as she naturally can.

Conclusions

The team completed the first phase of their project *in approximately one-third the allocated time.* Diane reports that they are certain they would not have been able to work as efficiently and speedily without the Human Dynamics training. She saw the group move from not believing they could make a difference to becoming very proactive. They took ownership of both the *process* and the *outcome.* Numerous comments, from within and outside the team, suggest that the group was more self-regulating than any other team. Occasionally they called for a coach to help them, but for the most part they functioned as their own managers in achieving their goals.

Shock Trauma Intensive Care Unit

The shock trauma unit at Intermountain has an unusually low staff turnover rate. Many of the staff have worked together for 10 years, some for more than 20 years. As one nurse observed,

> After you know people for that long, you don't cut them any slack. It's hard to change how you perceive them and interact with them. I think we all found after the Human Dynamics seminar that it became easier to accept one another, because we did see each other in new ways.

The unit was already a high-performance group, but Vicky Spuhler, nurse manager of the unit, reported that the understandings they gained through Human Dynamics took them to the next level of performance. They began to see that certain assumptions about behaviors had become problematic.

Changes in Perception

The seminar insights represented major changes for several staff members in particular. One example was a nurse who identified her personality dynamic as mental-physical. Other nurses and staff had questioned her commitment to the unit and her colleagues because she was focused intently on her own work and didn't seem to notice what was happening around her. She didn't offer to help others on the floor unless she was in charge of the unit. But according to Vicky,

> Betty explained to the group that it was natural for her to focus all her attention on one task. She said, "I don't feel a need to find out what everyone else is doing unless I'm in charge. I just give my full attention to my patients and their needs. That's my way of contributing. But if you want my help, you only have to ask me. I'll be there." Other mental-physical people identified with this tendency toward more solitary functioning and explained that it in no way implied a lack of caring about their colleagues.

Everyone came back from the discussion understanding Betty in a new way; indeed, they almost felt apologetic about the earlier conclusions they had drawn. Now, instead of feeling resentful toward her, her peers are able to use her skills—all they need to do is ask!

Managing Oneself, Coaching Others

Penny O'Malley, an independent consultant, and Dorothy Weber, an internal consultant, both licensed Human Dynamics facilitators, have been responsible for delivering the Human Dynamics work at Intermountain. They have conducted coaching sessions with the nurses to help them identify and acknowledge those behaviors of patients, family, nursing staff, or external circumstances that trigger their most stressed, least mature behavior. Because these triggers and reactions are explored in the context of personality dynamics rather than individuals, no one has difficulty acknowledging the issues, and the staff can explore ways to defuse the stress. They ask, "What would it take to get me back to feeling more balanced and able to contribute my gift?" The answer may be a moment of silence, taking a few deep breaths, or being able to voice one's feelings to a colleague.

"A major outcome of working with Human Dynamics," explains Dorothy, "is the ability to deal with behavior in a positive framework." Numerous anecdotes from shock-trauma staff members report that they see patients or families in a new light and are applying their Human Dynamics insights to the ways in which they interact and share information with them. Here are some examples:

Sometimes a patient or family repeatedly asks the same question. Instead of becoming irritated, I now realize that the problem may be that I am answering from the perspective of my own personality dynamic and missing their question entirely.

We now frequently notice how the physically centered patients and their families ask practical, data-driven questions, as compared to the more personal concerns of the emotionally centered. And we are beginning to realize that these patterns provide us with information about the tone and language in which they can hear us best. Recognizing that people have different needs, I now ask families directly, "What would be helpful to you in understanding your situation? How can we best support you during this difficult time?"

Future Directions

Intermountain plans to explore further applications of Human Dynamics to direct patient care—to issues of assessment, patient education, family interactions, and wellness. It will continue to benefit patients indirectly through its sustained effort to strengthen individual and team performance and to develop coaching and mentoring skills. As Penny O'Malley sees it, "The ultimate goal within healthcare is to help practitioners coach patients to reduce stress, to improve their health, and to increase the quality of their lives."

Intermountain Healthcare also plans to measure the effectiveness of Human Dynamics in several ways. While measurements to date have been largely anecdotal, based on self-reports or the observations of change agents and group facilitators, questionnaires were completed by workshop participants immediately following the training and again several months later. According to Dorothy Weber, the results have been overwhelmingly positive. "We were confident we were going in the right direction when we received consistent reports that three months after the seminar, people were still feeling the impact and working with the understandings."

In Summary

We have come to regard Human Dynamics as crucial "basic training." As David Marsing from Intel pointed out in Chapter 1, it complements technical training, helping ensure that people are functioning at their best both individually and also collectively, in teams, as a community, and as a community within a community.

As Glenn Pridham from London Life has shown, it can ensure that training of all kinds, including technical training, is optimally effective. The London Life experience also demonstrates how the basic Human Dynamics understandings can be woven synergistically into every developmental program, because the same distinctions in the personality dynamics are always present, always needing to be taken into account. Once people have had the initial program, a seminar on change management, teaching and learning, stress management, or sales will build on the same set of basic understandings. This not only has advantages of economy, it also has learning advantages. The learning is progressively deepened for each individual while the spread of applications in the organization flows naturally and consistently. This fortifies the learning on both an individual and an organizational level.

In telling the story of the Networks Engineering group at Digital, Chris Strutt reaches the conclusion that other trainings will be more effective if Human Dynamics training is laid down first. This has been our consistent experience. It is obvious, for example, that training in conducting effective dialogue, negotiation, and conflict resolution will be enhanced if the participants first understand the interplay of the personality dynamics. In fact, it is often unawareness of the distinctions among the personality dynamics that is creating the difficulty in these areas. It is also obvious that training in such disciplines as Total Quality Management, strategic planning, and systems thinking will be lacking if the human system, the one that creates all the other systems (with the exception of nature itself), is left out of the equation.

Everywhere there is a critical need for tools to develop skills in communication and cooperation. This is nowhere more apparent than in the extreme context of a hospital, as the Intermountain Healthcare story indicates. The capacity to communicate effectively among the staff and with the patients can save lives. We expand upon Human Dynamics' role in healthcare in the final chaper of this book, where we begin to examine the link between personality dynamics and wellness.

With the increasing complexity of skills needed in business today, it is clear that we need a framework for understanding and utilizing the one interface that is integrative to the whole. There is *one common denominator* that links everything to everything else. It is the human system.

As people are the vessels of human experience, they are also the architects of human expression. ***Therefore, the first system to be consciously understood and trained must be the human system itself.***

The Developmental
Continuum

T he personality dynamics that Human Dynamics identifies are not sta-
tic theoretical constructs, but living systems capable of infinite development. Anyone can expand the expression of his or her mental, emotional, and physical capacities. Each personality dynamic has a unique developmental journey, a journey that has two major aspects: development of the
integrated personality, and *transpersonal* development. Development of the integrated personality involves nurturing and integrating the mental, emotional,
and physical principles in their more ordinary forms of expression, such as a
clear, objective mind (mental); a "good heart," with the ability to create satisfying relationships (emotional); and the ability to take effective, practical
actions (physical). The integrated personality demonstrates a balanced expression of all three principles. Transpersonal development, on the other hand,
involves nurturing and integrating the three principles in their higher, more
spiritual form of expression, such as vision (mental); deep compassion (emotional); and actions that are directed by vision and compassion, in the service
of the collective good (physical).

Although both of these developmental aspects actually exist together,
we distinguish between them because so often they seem to function sepa-
rately in people. Many people are satisfied with their personality development, and are unaware of a more profound dimension to their existence.
Others may be attuned to the transpersonal dimension, but cannot make its
qualities effective in their daily lives because the mental, emotional, and
physical principles are not sufficiently developed and integrated at the level
of the personality. *Both the personal and transpersonal aspects need to be consciously
developed and integrated for anyone to realize his or her full human potential.*

Human Dynamics permits us to recognize the developmental journey
unique to each personality dynamic in both these dimensions, and allows us

to design tools and practices to facilitate moving along each path. In this chapter, we describe the developmental journey for each personality dynamic.

The Integrated Personality

In Human Dynamics, the name of each personality dynamic reflects the two principles most naturally integrated in the person's consciousness and behavior ("mental-physical," "physical-emotional," and so on). But of course, the third principle, the remaining strand, is always present. For the mental-physical group, the third principle is emotional; for the emotional-subjective (emotional-physical) group, the third principle is mental; and so on. Although this third principle is always active in each of us, it is often not consistently integrated with the other two principles.

The integration of the third principle constitutes the direction of growth for all five personality dynamics.

To give an example, mental-physical people experience life through the mind (mental), and they usually focus their attention on the concrete, external world (physical). While the interplay of these two principles is usually readily apparent, the expression of the emotional principle is often much less evident. Part of the direction of growth for mental-physical people is to cultivate expression of the emotional principle, to become more aware and appreciative of the inner life of feelings, and to learn to connect with others more personally and intimately.

The same kind of continuum exists for all of the groups. In fact, *it is the integration of the third principle that constitutes the direction of growth for all five personality dynamics.* For example, emotional-objective (emotional-mental) people have strong feelings about their ideas, which they produce in abundance. When the third principle (physical) is integrated, they also *do* something with their ideas. The integration of the physical principle ensures that their capacity for forward movement is tempered by a willingness to slow down, respect the past, and work patiently with others to bring ideas to fruition.

For emotional-subjective (emotional-physical) people, the mental principle is the third principle. The mind, of course, is always active, but when the mental principle is fully integrated, the emotional-subjective person's gifts of sensitivity, connection with others, and multifocus are stabilized by capacities for detachment, perspective, and single focus. These allow the individual to see objectively, as well as to feel, and to *respond* to events and situations rather than merely *react*.

Integration of the mental principle also defines the direction of growth for physical-emotional people, enabling them to gain perspective on the vast amounts of data they gather, impose an organizing structure, and maintain a specific as well as inclusive focus.

Finally, the direction of growth for the physical-mental personality dynamic, as for the mental-physical, is integration of the emotional principle—adding to their affinity for group life a capacity for personal consciousness and individual self-expression; and to their focus on the concrete and practical, awareness and valuing of personal feelings and a greater capacity to express them.

PERSONALITY DYNAMIC	PERSONAL INTEGRATION
Mental-Physical	Emotional
Emotional-Mental (Emotional-Objective)	Physical
Emotional-Physical (Emotional-Subjective)	Mental
Physical-Emotional	Mental
Physical-Mental	Emotional

Personal development involves development and integration of the third principle.

Figure 12.1

To understand the developmental process, we all need to know that the integrated personality is *inherent* in the less developed personality. It is not so much a matter of "adding on" new capacities as it is bringing capacities to life and encouraging them to bloom. By understanding this potential, people can help each other to move forward in their integration. For example, we can help mental-physical or physical-mental people to widen their natural affinities if, while speaking with them in their "own" objective language, we take opportunities to emphasize the importance of feelings. Similarly, we can help an emotional-objective person to grow by encouraging him or her to write down the consequences of an action that he or she proposes. And we can all aid our own integration by learning from our life experiences and by undertaking personal development exercises (see Chapter 10, "Communication and Team Learning: Beginning Tools and Practices").

Transpersonal Integration

Achieving personal integration by no means signifies the end of the developmental story. As we mentioned earlier, every individual's makeup includes a transpersonal dimension that is of another order than the personality—more fundamental, essential, and spiritual.

People in whom the transpersonal dimension is active are typically suffused by qualities that we can all recognize but often find hard to describe—qualities such as grace, compassion, kindness, gentleness, or a visionary capacity. When people are transpersonally developed and personally integrated, such qualities are consistently reflected in their actions, and their lives are consistently oriented to serving the common good. As Figure 12.2 indicates, the mental, emotional, and physical principles all have their transpersonal as well as personal expression. (In this table and subsequently, we capitalize MENTAL, EMOTIONAL, and PHYSICAL whenever we refer to the principles in their transpersonal expression.)

The terms for the transcendental characteristics may need some further explanation. Vision, as the transpersonal expression of the MENTAL principle, refers to the kind of exalted vision that in some way serves humanity. Nelson Mandela's vision for South Africa is an example. His high vision motivates and guides his whole life, and he dedicates his life to its service. People are not always able to articulate their individual visions as clearly as President Mandela, but they probably know whether proposed actions or decisions are in alignment with their vision and they act accordingly. Related to vision is formless "seeing"—a kind of inner knowing about the meaning of events, or an anticipation of future events, that does not depend on rational thought or concrete imagery but is intuitively sensed. In contrast with intuition at the personal level, transpersonal intuition has spiritual connotations.

The transpersonal expression of the EMOTIONAL principle—compassion, or unconditional love—refers to the expression of an open heart, a flow of loving energy that embraces everyone and everything (inclusiveness). It is unconditional because it flows at all times and under all circumstances, regardless of whether the love is acknowledged or returned.

When the PHYSICAL principle is expressed transpersonally, the person works with others to manifest visionary and compassionate goals through a qualitative and compassionate group process.

As with personality integration, achieving transpersonal development entails integrating the "third principle," though at the transpersonal level. Thus for mental-physical and physical-mental people, the key to transpersonal development and integration is the compassion of the EMOTIONAL principle. For emotional-objective (emotional-mental) people, it is the qualitative group life of the PHYSICAL principle. For emotional-subjective (emotional-physical) and physical-emotional people, it is the vision or formless "seeing" of the MENTAL principle.

PERSONAL EXPRESSION	TRANSPERSONAL EXPRESSION
Mental	**MENTAL**
thinking	VISION
detachment	FORMLESS "SEEING"
Emotional	**EMOTIONAL**
feeling	COMPASSION
personal consciousness	UNCONDITIONAL LOVE
connection	INCLUSIVENESS
Physical	**PHYSICAL**
doing	QUALITATIVE GROUP LIFE/ACTION
sensory experience	(working with groups at a transpersonal
group identity	level toward transpersonal goals)

Figure 12.2

PERSONAL AND TRANSPERSONAL INTEGRATION

PERSONALITY DYNAMIC	PERSONAL INTEGRATION	TRANSPERSONAL INTEGRATION
Mental-Physical	**Emotional** Subjective awareness Valuing feelings Personal connection Relationships	**EMOTIONAL** COMPASSION UNCONDITIONAL LOVE INCLUSIVENESS
Emotional-Objective	**Physical** Manifestation Systemic detail Teamwork Continuity	**PHYSICAL** QUALITATIVE GROUP LIFE/ ACTION (working together at a transpersonal level toward transpersonal goals)
Emotional-Subjective	**Mental** Detachment Objectivity Perspective Structure	**MENTAL** VISION FORMLESS "SEEING"
Physical-Emotional	**Mental** Detachment Specificity Perspective Structure	**MENTAL** VISION FORMLESS "SEEING"
Physical-Mental	**Emotional** Subjective awareness Valuing feelings Personal connection Relationships	**EMOTIONAL** COMPASSION UNCONDITIONAL LOVE INCLUSIVENESS

Figure 12.3

Figure 12.3 shows the components of personal and transpersonal development for each personality dynamic.

Note that although this chart may appear to suggest that development is sequential, transpersonal development does not depend on first establishing personal development and integration. Each can take place independently of the other, or they can occur simultaneously. However, the more complete the personal development and integration, the more a person will be able to put his or her transpersonal motivations and qualities to consistent, effective use.

We should also emphasize that for each personality dynamic, the development of the third principle in its transpersonal expression seems to offer a key to awakening the transpersonal dimension *as a whole*. Thus, for the mental-physical personality, activation of the EMOTIONAL principle at the transpersonal level seems to empower expression of the MENTAL and PHYSICAL principles in this dimension also. As the energy of the EMOTIONAL principle irradiates the whole person, imbuing him or her with the quality of compassion, it unlocks a far more expanded field of transpersonal expression that also includes the other principles. The spirit of compassion enlarges the vision (MENTAL) and enhances the individual's ability to work with groups (PHYSICAL).

Similarly, in the case of the emotional-objective (emotional-mental) personality, the transpersonal expression of the PHYSICAL principle activates the transpersonal dimension as a whole, and so on with all the groups.

Regardless of their personality dynamic, people in whom both the personal and transpersonal dimensions are integrated share at least one fundamental attribute: their lives are focused on serving the collective good. In fact, as people attain this degree of development, the functioning of their personality becomes less and less the point. Their personality is merely an instrument through which they consistently express transpersonal qualities. Mother Teresa provides an example—her emotional-subjective personality is a vehicle through which she expresses exalted vision in acts of deep compassion.

Although this degree of development may be quite rare, the potential for consistent transpersonal expression lives in all of us, waiting only to be acknowledged and nourished. Indeed, many people have undoubtedly achieved a high degree of personal and transpersonal mastery and integration, their existences unknown except to those whose lives they have directly touched.

Although the personal and transpersonal dimensions are in fact an integral part of us all, often the conflicts and difficulties that come with being human can keep these worlds apart. On the one hand, there are well-functioning, integrated personalities who seem out of touch with any deeper purpose; and on the other, there are people who have glimpsed their true transpersonal potential, yet are unable to make their gifts effective in the world because their personalities are to some degree dysfunctional. In the former case, the well-integrated person may be "stuck" at the level of personal ambition or achievement and therefore blind to his or her latent transpersonal qualities. In the latter, the dysfunction prevents transpersonal awareness and qualities from being consistently and usefully expressed. For this reason, we define personal mastery *as including both personal and transpersonal development and integration.*

Developmental Stories

The developmental story of each personality dynamic is characterized by a unique core theme. We might say this theme constitutes what Joseph Campbell has called "the hero's journey."[1]

Before describing these thematic journeys, we should make a few points. First, for the sake of clarity, we again present each developmental path in a linear form. However, developmental unfolding is rarely a steady, straight-line process; instead, it features many tacks and turns, gains and retreats. Our purpose is to illustrate a general direction of development for each personality dynamic and indicate some major milestones along the way.

Second, an individual's place along the continuum of development does not necessarily reflect chronological age. For example, as every parent with more than one child knows, some infants seem more mature than others from the beginning. Conversely, adults may grow more experienced, more

---

[1] Joseph Campbell expounded on the significance for modern humanity of ancient mythological themes, including that of the hero and the hero's quest. His personality dynamic was physical-emotional. As those who viewed his public television series will recollect, he was an extraordinary storyteller with an apparently limitless memory for the details of myths and legends.

knowledgeable, and more sophisticated with the passage of time, but without necessarily advancing in wisdom, compassion, generosity of spirit, or dedication to leaving the world a better place than when they entered it.

Thus, in these pages, the beginning point identified in the development of each personality dynamic is not necessarily the starting point for everybody of that dynamic. It is a point of vulnerability, however, to which people of that personality dynamic tend to regress under conditions of stress, whether momentarily or for hours, days, or weeks, until either the stress eases or the person regains balance. Generally, the further people have moved along their developmental paths, and the more stable their personal and transpersonal integration, the less often they will revert to the beginning point, and the more quickly they will recover when they do regress.

The beginning point identified in the development of each personality dynamic is not necessarily the starting point for everybody of that dynamic. It is a point of vulnerability, however, to which people of that personality dynamic tend to regress under conditions of stress.

In the following pages, we outline the major developmental theme for each personality dynamic. Then we illustrate each developmental journey with descriptions of two people at different stages of personal and transpersonal development and integration. These descriptions are based on real people whom we have known, and who represent readily recognizable types of people. In each case, the first description portrays someone who might be termed a well-integrated personality, but lacks transpersonal awareness or integration. The second description is of someone who possesses a degree of transpersonal awareness, but whose lack of personal development and integration prevents him or her from expressing transpersonal qualities consistently in daily life. In some of the latter cases, we describe people who have had some form of "peak experience." Such experiences expand awareness, but they do not necessarily presage transpersonal development, nor are they necessary *for* transpersonal development.

In the second "story" for each personality dynamic, we could have chosen to describe someone who has achieved both personal and transpersonal integration. However, having read about a well-integrated personality in the first story, readers will easily be able to imagine the same person at the transpersonal level. The difference would be one of a finer quality of expression and a life consciously dedicated to realizing visionary and compassionate goals.

Telling the story, instead, of someone who has some access to the transpersonal dimension but cannot use those qualities effectively has a number of advantages. First, it demonstrates the vital significance of pursuing personal as well as transpersonal development if we are to realize our full potential. Second, it provides the opportunity to describe characteristics of each personality dynamic when the third principle remains unintegrated. And finally, it reinforces the point that development does not necessarily occur in a line from personal development and integration to transpersonal development and integration. It can take place in both realms simultaneously and be present, to any degree, in each.

 ## Mental-Physical

The Developmental Continuum

| Isolation | Abstract sense of connection | Sense of self as a feeling individual | Sense of others as feeling individuals | Personalized caring Subjective awareness | UNCONDITIONAL LOVE COMPASSION INCLUSIVENESS |

Figure 12.4

For the mental-physical personality dynamic, personal development progresses from relative isolation to personal connection. Transpersonal development involves awakening and integrating unconditional love. The state of isolation early in the development of some mental-physical people is not the same thing as a periodic need for time alone or chosen solitude. People at this point have no choice, but simply exist in a world cut off from others. After emerging from this state, they may not even have a language to describe that private existence.

As mental-physical people develop, they begin to connect with people, things, and events, at first by observing more than participating. As they increasingly participate in the world of events and human interaction, they strengthen their sense of themselves as individuals with a capacity to influence their environments, but their relationships with others may still be quite impersonal.

As the emotional principle comes into play, the world of personal relationship opens up, perhaps initially through a more intimate connection with one other person. As they build and sustain an increasing number of personal relationships, probably on the basis of shared values, mental-physical people increasingly value the development of their self-awareness and engage in more personal dialogue with selected people. Although they may not *speak* about caring, their *actions* express caring. Gradually they become more comfortable with expressing feelings. As they mature further, love becomes predominant in their value system. Development of the transpersonal capacity for *unconditional* love brings the ability to articulate those unifying principles that bond humanity. All-inclusive love and compassion transfuse the personality and are expressed in their every action and interaction.

Let us look now at two differing examples of "combinations" of personal and transpersonal integration. Rob represents a mental-physical person who is well integrated but has little access to the transpersonal dimension; Sally represents a mental-physical person who has some connection to transpersonal experience, but whose lack of personal integration prevents her from consistently expressing transpersonal qualities in her daily life.

Rob's mental, emotional, and physical principles are well integrated. His thinking, feeling, and actions are consciously aligned. In the case of mental-physical people, alignment entails integration of the emotional principle, which catalyzes the development of conscious relationships. Rob is focused, grounded, objective, and well balanced. In any group, whether at home or at work, he can create clear plans designed to serve the needs of all involved. Though not particularly expressive of his feelings, he maintains good relationships with everybody, connects well with people, exhibits a great deal of patience, and is nonjudgmental. On a team, Rob listens carefully and, though he is usually quiet except when he feels he has something of value to say, ensures that the discussion remains clear, purposeful, and focused on the long-term goal.

Rob's value system is quite open. Because he is essentially objective and nonjudgmental, he is a natural diplomat. In a situation of conflict, he hears both parties fairly, helps clarify their essential positions, and tries to identify common ground. He has a quiet, steady, reliable presence. The "space" in which he operates, however, is relatively limited. His life as a whole is not so much guided by a deep compassion for humankind as by the desire to perform satisfactorily at work and to relate well with his family and friends.

Sally is rather withdrawn. She rarely initiates a relationship or a new idea at her workplace; rather, she waits to be handed work, which she then carefully pursues. She is a good worker, but too uncomfortable with other people to be fully effective in groups. On a team, she almost never says a word unless someone prompts her. She limits herself to her own sphere of activity.

Sally is judgmental of others. Her value system is rather narrow; her points of view, rigid. She does not enjoy anything of a psychological nature; going to seminars on team building or personal development is painful for her. She is seen as a loner, and she would agree that she would usually much rather read a book than engage in conversation.

Her avocation is mountain-climbing. In fact, she has climbed many of the tallest mountains in the world. As she approaches a summit, she feels greater and greater freedom. Her motivation is not so much pride in accomplishment as the exalted feeling of being at one with the universe that she experiences at the mountaintop. The high perspective, the sense of space, the 360-degree vista, and the panoramas of breathtaking beauty fill her with indescribable joy. Here, she has a sense of being fully "at home."

At these times, Sally feels connected with everything and everyone, and she does not judge. She feels that she dwells "in love," and that purpose and destiny exist for all people. She deeply wishes to live this quality of life when she returns home. Her sense of mission stirs, and she wants to help others make the connections she has experienced. But back in her everyday environment, she is not sufficiently at ease in relating to others to maintain and express the quality of love she feels at the top of the mountain. She cannot connect personally. She falls into old judgmental patterns, which alienates others and aggravates her tendency to self-isolation. Her transpersonal sensibility and experiences remain unintegrated and unexpressed in her daily life.

Emotional-Objective

The Developmental Continuum

Controls the environment	Expands boundaries	Greater subjectivity	EMPOWERMENT OF OTHERS THROUGH QUALITATIVE GROUP LIFE/ACTION
Takes power for self	Includes others	Personal consciousness	
		Teamwork	Figure 12.5

For the emotional-objective group, the developmental theme begins with feeling independent of environmental influences. Emotional-objective people at the "young" end of the continuum habitually exert an impact *on* the environment, rather than respond *to* it. They feel themselves to be quite invulnerable, their confidence in themselves is absolute, and they have no difficulty making their needs known. Because their personal will is strong and they have definite feelings about what they want, a constant issue in their life journey is the right use of power. Early in their development, their only authority is themselves; life exists only to serve them, and others may feel at their mercy.

As they mature, they begin to recognize the need for expanding their boundaries to include the rights, needs, and desires of others. For example, a salesperson at this stage might say to himself, "I want to make that sale, but a colleague has made the first contact. If I want it, I'll at least have to communicate with her. . . . Maybe my relationship to that person is more important than getting what I want. I might have to forget about that sale if I want to keep our friendship strong." At this stage, emotional-objective people begin to share power. They are sensitive to others' ambitions and needs as well as their own. Other people grow increasingly important to them.

As they grow ever more sensitive to the feelings and needs of others, they gain awareness of their own subjective lives. Asking deeper questions about the inner life of other people leads to yet more questions about themselves. For example, the question, "Who is that person, *really?*" might lead

281

to the more self-reflective question, "How do I feel when I am with him?" And the desire to improve a relationship with someone in order to accomplish a task or achieve a goal might lead to self-examination along these lines, "Did I say what I *really* felt and thought?" or, "Could I have handled that differently?" Gaining understanding of themselves and other people becomes a deep need and constant practice for maturing emotional-objective people.

They also take on greater responsibility, but they come to learn that although it may be appropriate to take responsibility *for* others, sometimes it may be more appropriate to give responsibility *to* them. Rather than direct others, they increasingly collaborate *with* others to bring ideas to realization.

At some point along the way, they recognize that any achievement depends on group participation, and their primary focus becomes the development of working groups infused by a spirit of cooperation. As their transpersonal life blooms, they seek a quality of group interaction that transcends personal needs, and the purpose of their work becomes the realization of goals that serve the collective good. It is in this kind of endeavor that they find inspiration, and their spirits soar.

Let us illustrate different stages of development with accounts of two distinct emotional-objective personalities. Francine represents an integrated emotional-objective personality with little transpersonal awareness; Juan represents the less integrated personality who, nevertheless, does have a genuine connection to the transpersonal dimension.

In **Francine's** case, the three principles are well integrated. Thinking, feeling, and action are consciously aligned. Alignment, in the case of emotional-objective (emotional-mental) people, includes the integration of the physical principle. Thus, Francine is not only enthusiastic and innovative; she is also grounded. She is committed to ideas that can be *realized*. She has learned to value deeply the world of the pragmatic and is willing to work with details to manifest her ideas. At the least, she will ensure the completion of a task by seeing that it is assigned to someone who has a gift for detail.

Francine enjoys the creative interactions of teamwork. Her teammates appreciate working with her because her nature is primarily optimistic and she brings a spirit of innovation to the team. She is deeply committed to the people and projects she values. She is hard-working, focused, and available to her colleagues. Her attention, however, is totally consumed by her work, personal goals, interests, and family. She is not given to expanding the boundaries of these territories. They engage her fully.

With **Juan**, on the other hand, the physical principle is not yet integrated into his personality. He is often in trouble with other people because he moves too quickly to build an understanding relationship with them. He focuses so much on moving events forward that he is unaware of the impact he has on others. They may experience him as brusque and assertive, whereas he feels that he is simply being enthusiastic. Because he can jump from one idea to another and is impatient with details, some people judge him as irresponsible. It is not that he lacks a sense of responsibility, but that he has not yet learned to take the time to think through his ideas, to work carefully and collaboratively, to listen to what others have to say, and to ensure that he is being clear. As a result, he is often shocked by confrontations with others, unaware of the hurt feelings or miscommunications that led up to them.

Nevertheless, Juan has a deep sense of mission. He spends quiet time alone almost every morning before going to work. In this meditative period he experiences a qualitative dimension which is boundless, finer, and loving. In these private times of quiet contemplation, he relaxes, time slows down, and he breathes more easily. He is fully at peace. Inspired by these moments, he feels the deep need to contribute to building something enduring that will serve others. But he cannot realize this need, as he does not yet have sufficient mastery of his own personal "instrument" to work effectively with others.

Emotional-Subjective

The Developmental Continuum

At the mercy of the environment	Creates boundaries	Gains objectivity and detachment	EMPOWERS VISION THROUGH EMPOWERMENT OF SELF
Gives power away	Values self		

Figure 12.6

An emotional-subjective person at the earliest stage of development is exquisitely vulnerable to his or her environment. It is as if the membrane between the self and the outer world is exceedingly permeable, so that the physical body directly absorbs the impact of the environment. At this point, there is no definition of self because there are no boundaries to separate the self from whatever is around. If the environment is in any way abusive or uncomfortable, the emotional-subjective person at this stage of development, even as an adult, feels utterly helpless; if the environment is agreeable, he or she can feel comfortably dependent.

With time, emotional-subjective people begin to create boundaries between themselves and others. This progression may begin simply with the expression of personal preferences. For example, a child may say, "I like the color green; I don't like blue so much." Or an adult may begin to express preferences that he or she knows are not shared by others present. The next step is conscious differentiation from the immediate *emotional* environment. At this stage, if a colleague is angry, the emotional-subjective person needs neither to be traumatized by the anger nor to react with anger. If someone is depressed, the person need not become depressed also. The person's own feelings are differentiated from those of other people.

Each time someone who is emotional-subjective *consciously* identifies a personal feeling or a need and is able to assert, "This is *my* feeling or *my* need," the self grows more defined, and boundaries are created. This internal focus on personal feelings and needs is not being self-centered in the negative sense. Rather, it reflects the process of growth for this personality dynamic group: toward self-understanding, self-definition, and consequent self-empowerment. Developing self-defining parameters does not limit the emotional-subjective personality or diminish the ability to be open to others—it expands the available range of choices and decisions. There is empathy both for others *and* for the self.

Emotional-subjective people's process of distinguishing themselves from the environment, especially the emotional environment, is usually a journey of many years. For some, it may take a lifetime. For others, especially those who seem mature or "old" for their age from the beginning, the time may be much less.

As they establish their boundaries, emotional-subjective people slowly gain objectivity, clarity, and detachment (mental principle), until one day they realize that they simultaneously feel *and* "see"; participate *and* observe; are attached *and* detached. From this position of "detached attachment," they are freer to choose their responses and can express their love with even greater effectiveness, offering to others an objective as well as empathic heart. They can also see more clearly the role that they *and* others play in situations, without being in a constant state of self-blame whenever something goes wrong. Guilt and vulnerability wane.

As emotional-subjective people grow increasingly empowered, they learn that empowering themselves is their greatest gift to others. They are able to bring the light of discovery from their detailed self-explorations to illuminate the human condition for everyone. Because they have tracked their own journey consciously, they can assist others in theirs.

When the emotional-subjective personality is transfused by the MENTAL principle at the transpersonal level, the individual is guided by a higher vision, which he or she is now empowered to serve.

Let us conclude this section with examples of two distinct variations on this theme. Sarah represents an emotional-subjective person with an integrated personality, but little access to the transpersonal dimension. Moshe represents a less integrated personality, but with some connection to the transpersonal.

In **Sarah**, the mental, emotional, and physical principles are well integrated. That means that her thinking, feeling, and action are consciously aligned. Because the mental principle is integrated, she has developed a capacity for detachment and focus. This growth allows her to "see" as well as feel. Rather than simply reacting to situations, Sarah now has sufficient objectivity to examine her feelings and consider her responses. She can "see" that in some instances, if she accommodates someone's request, she may be infantilizing or in some other way harming the person. In these cases, saying "no" would actually express a more mature love.

Sarah is highly empathic, and enjoys satisfying relationships with others. With her keen intuition, she has learned to trust her "gut" feelings. She is affable, spontaneous, funny, dramatic, caring, and involved. She is an efficient and capable worker who is in touch with the pulse of the people. Relationships with others form the center of her life.

At this point in her development, Sarah is clearly a well-functioning, integrated emotional-subjective personality. However, she lacks the sense that she is in service to something higher than herself. Her ambitions are essentially personal. She does not yet have a larger, guiding vision that she uses her gifts to serve.

Moshe, on the other hand, reacts highly emotionally in most situations. He is at the mercy of whatever emotional environment he is in. He is unable to protect himself from absorbing the pain of the world, and his mood shifts constantly. He personalizes everything. He is only occasionally able to integrate detachment with his sensitivity. His self-esteem is frequently threatened by his sense of guilt—his relentless companion.

Moshe is highly personal in his caring for others; he wears his heart on his sleeve. In his deep need to be available to others, he plays many roles. He becomes what is needed. This empathic fluidity frequently blurs his sense of identity. "Who am I really?" he sometimes wonders.

And yet, at the same time, Moshe is tuned to something finer. When he is alone and his emotions are quiet, he glimpses a vision of loving service in which he has a specific role. But in his everyday life he cannot hold that vision. He becomes caught in the turbulence of his emotions and cannot align himself with the sense of mission that stirs. His energies are bound up in the events and relationships of the moment. Sometimes he feels desperate because he senses that he is somehow missing his calling. Will these two parts of himself ever come together?

Physical-Emotional

The Developmental Continuum

Immersed in the environment	Creates boundaries	Subjective awareness	VISION
			FORMLESS "SEEING"
No boundaries	Expresses personal	Capacity for perspective,	
No personal voice	voice	structure, specificity	

Figure 12.7

For the physical-emotional person, the developmental continuum begins with immersion in one's group and physical environment. There are no boundaries between the individual and his or her surroundings. There is no personal voice—only a collective voice.

Physical-emotional people at this end of the continuum have little awareness of their individual identity, including their personal feelings, thoughts, and aspirations. They exist as part of the "living history" into which they have been thrust. As long as this kind of condition is maintained, they feel a comfortable sense of unity and belonging. The group provides their primary identity.

Developing sufficient self-awareness to establish a boundary between themselves and their communities of family, friends, classmates, colleagues, and so on, may take considerable time. The beginning of the process may be accompanied by discomfort as the person senses the separation occurring between him or herself and the group or groups with which he or she is identified. These feelings may sharpen painfully as the personal voice emerges and the sense of individual identity unfolds. He or she takes a momentous step when able to view the group objectively and give voice to his or her own needs and opinions while maintaining respect for the group and valuing consensus and unanimity.

As time passes, physical-emotional people absorb massive amounts of factual data. Because their physical and emotional worlds are directly linked, they internalize the unsorted data with all its connections and relationships.

To "rise above" this mass of data and be able to see it clearly, organize it, and use it effectively, they need to develop and integrate the capacities for *specific* focus and detached perspective of the mental principle.

For example, imagine that a physical-emotional individual has inwardly stored 2,565,112 pieces of data. As the capacities for a more detached view and single focus develop, he or she can "see" that this mass of data can be sorted into, say, five themes; for example, people, technologies, history, crafts, and nature. The person can now organize the two million plus pieces of data into these five thematic structures—and also take in new data more selectively and sort it more immediately. As the inner process of organizing information becomes more simple, the person can more easily retrieve and use the accumulated knowledge. He or she can also communicate with enhanced clarity and simplicity.

As their capacities for perspective and structure (mental principle) and self-awareness (emotional principle) continue to develop, physical-emotional individuals handle ever more complex responsibilities with increasing skill. When the transpersonal MENTAL principle eventually transfuses an integrated physical-emotional personality, the person experiences both the clarity of a detached perspective and the inspiration of a guiding vision, which the personality is now dedicated to realizing.

Let us provide examples of two different physical-emotional personalities. Katrina represents the integrated personality with little access to the transpersonal dimension. Tim represents the less integrated personality who, nevertheless, has a real connection to this dimension.

Katrina's mental, emotional, and physical principles are well integrated. This means that her thinking, feeling, and actions are consciously aligned. In the case of physical-emotional people, alignment includes the integration of the mental principle, which adds the capacities for structure, focus, and perspective. Being physically centered, Katrina retains a deep connection to groups, but with time she has become increasingly self-aware and able to express her own feelings and opinions. She is articulate, and her verbal presentations are methodical and precise.

Katrina is highly competent. She astounds people with her incredible memory for detail. Her colleagues call her "the corporate memory bank." She excels at sustaining methodical work and keeping a whole operation working systematically. She is thorough and totally reliable. Although she takes in masses of detailed information, she knows when overload threatens and takes breaks when she needs to. She may need only five or ten minutes for quiet reflection, but she has learned that this short respite can be crucial for maintaining her effectiveness. She has also learned to take time alone each evening to sort, organize, and gain perspective on the day's events. Recognizing that she adapts to whatever environment she is in, she is learning to be selective about where she places herself.

Katrina is a well-functioning personality who deals efficiently with the concrete and pragmatic affairs of her work and everyday life. However, she has little awareness of the transpersonal dimension and has no call to serve an inspirational vision.

Tim, on the other hand, has not yet learned how to detach himself from the total environment. Immersed in a world of details, he frequently feels overwhelmed. He has difficulty saying "no," because in his view it violates his deep need to accept "what is" uncomplainingly. Acceptance, adaptability, and perseverance mark his character. He is often tired but strives to contribute further whenever he is asked. Tim is very intelligent, but the lack of integration of the mental principle keeps him from speeding up his responses to meet the requirements of a specific situation and impedes his ability to communicate clearly and succinctly.

Because Tim has not differentiated himself well from the group, he is generally unaware of individual distinctions in people. Although people have often disappointed him, he rarely tries to figure out what went wrong in a personal interaction; he accepts people as they are. Occasionally, however, he vents long-accumulated frustrations in an explosion of anger, as if every cell in his body is angry. He does not hold onto the anger, but neither does he know how to prevent the pattern from repeating.

Nevertheless, Tim has had many awareness-expanding experiences, especially in nature. For him, being in nature has a meditative quality. He is sensitive to the movements of the wind and the messages it brings; he feels the life of the rocks; he experiences himself as an integral part of the living system of the universe. Sometimes he has transcendent experiences. An example occurred early one morning at sunrise when, as the sun came up, Tim felt suddenly "tuned" to it. He *became* the sun. It was as if he merged into the rays and in doing so "heard" their "sounds" and "colors." On such occasions, his understanding of "what is" expands beyond the concrete and pragmatic, and he glimpses another dimension that he yearns to integrate into his personal life. But the two worlds remain separate. He is so embedded in the texture of his daily existence that he cannot consciously direct his life. This prevents him from living the quality of his transpersonal experience and serving a higher vision.

Physical-Mental

The Developmental Continuum

Immersed in the collective value system	Creates boundary between value system of group and self	Subjective awareness	UNCONDITIONAL LOVE
Rigid values and structures	Expresses personal voice	Personalized caring	COMPASSION
No personal voice			INCLUSIVENESS

Figure 12.8

For the physical-mental group, development moves from immersion within a group's *collective* value system to expressing *individual* values, which increasingly include awareness and valuing of the world of personal feelings and relationships (emotional principle).

At the beginning of the continuum, physical-mental people have little awareness of their individual identity. The group provides their identity. They have no personal voice, only a collective voice. They never question the primacy of the group and its value system. This state of affairs may feel comfortable at first, until personal consciousness begins to dawn, and they begin to feel the tension between their growing sense of self and their identification with the group.

As physical-mental people distinguish themselves more and more from the collective, life becomes both more conscious and more complex. Up to this point, they have used their natural gifts for precision, order, and efficiency in the service of their group(s). Now they no longer accept without question a group's values and purposes but develop and bring forward their own views, which may diverge from those of the group.

As physical-mental people develop self-awareness, they engage in more personal dialogue with selected people. As the subjective world becomes more known to them, they begin to realize that their data gathering is incomplete without clear information about people and their individual values, needs, and feelings. They increasingly consider issues related to people, and take people's feelings and personal reactions into account in formulating their systemic plans.

With development of the transpersonal dimension, they devote their capacity for systemic planning and building to the compassionate service of the collective good.

Let's look at two examples of distinctly different physical-mental personalities. Dave represents the integrated personality with little access to the transpersonal dimension; Rose represents the less integrated personality who does have a connection to the transpersonal.

Dave's mental, emotional, and physical principles are well integrated. This means that his thinking, feeling, and actions are consciously aligned. In the case of physical-mental people, alignment involves the integration of the emotional principle, which catalyzes the development of self-awareness and *conscious* relationships. Dave is objective, grounded, and also at ease with people. He is an adept problem-solver. He creates purposeful and efficient systemic models and plans, to which all parties can subscribe. He communicates with others a great deal and actively seeks information about people as he collects his data. Although he is attuned to practical purposes and required actions in any discussion, he also concerns himself with the emotional comfort of his colleagues. On a team, Dave often remains quiet except when purposes and values are unclear, or when proposed models and structures in his view are inadequate. He can supply a great deal of relevant information if called on to do so. Otherwise, he listens carefully, making certain that consensus is honored and that the discussion stays on target.

Dave's value system is open and broad. In a situation of conflict, he will hear both parties fairly and help reframe their expressed needs to ensure complementarity and synergy. He usually does not talk about what he might do on someone else's behalf—he just does it. The transpersonal dimension, however, remains outside his experience. His realm is the physical world of concreteness and practicality.

Rose, on the other hand, is very set in her ways. She makes personal judgments, often unconsciously, that create division between herself and others. Her value system is narrow; her points of view rather rigid. She does not believe in psychology and does not value the world of emotions and feelings. She is factual and concrete, objective and focused. She takes pride in these capacities. Her systematic way of working, unalleviated by emotional flexibility, has led to her having rules for everything and everyone (including herself). Therefore, although she works hard, she doesn't achieve as much as she could because she cannot develop comfortable working relationships with others. She would much rather be alone in her garden than engage in most conversations.

In her garden, Rose experiences unity with nature and feels herself in creative partnership with nature's laws. She feels in harmony with the life of the plants and vegetables she tends, and she maintains the garden as if it were a sacred temple. She feels herself to be in service to something invisible, yet alive and immensely intelligent. Cultivating her garden, she feels serene and in a loving relationship with all that is.

However, she cannot transfer the love she feels in the garden to her other activities and relationships. The worlds of her garden and of her daily life interacting with people are totally distinct. The personal and transpersonal dimensions are not yet integrated.

In Summary

In this chapter, we have presented our understanding of the process of personal and transpersonal development and integration for the different personality dynamics. The question remains: How do we *achieve* mastery? First, cognitive understanding of the developmental needs of the different personality dynamic groups provides some guidelines. However, cognitive understanding alone is never sufficient. Personal mastery requires commitment to consistent practice with specific tools.

Over the years, we have developed many tools and practices for personal and transpersonal development, some of which are included in Chapter 10, "Communication and Team Learning: Beginning Tools and Practices." However, while practical exercises can be readily taught in the experiential context of seminars, they are less easily conveyed in the context of a book. Providing instructions for them in print also takes considerable space.

Our solution, therefore, has been to create audiotapes that include exercises for the personal and transpersonal development of each of the personality dynamics. Audiotapes also enable us to facilitate use of the exercises through specifically selected music. The exercises and music are differentiated for enhancement of each of the mental, emotional, and physical principles, and for meeting the specific needs of each personality dynamic. The tapes are accompanied by an explanatory booklet.

These exercises have been used by thousands of people over many years and in many cultures, and have profoundly influenced the lives of those who have practiced them consistently. Interested readers can find additional details at the back of the book.

Visions: Looking Ahead

O ur vision for Human Dynamics is succinctly expressed in the following statement of purpose: *The development, empowerment, and sustainment of individual and collective human potential, the world over.*

In Chapter 11, we described some of the ways in which this vision is beginning to be realized in business and healthcare. In this chapter, we focus on work in progress in research, education, and bridging Eastern and Western cultures, and on future plans and intentions in these areas.

Basic Research

The Link Between the Personality and Physiological Functioning

Because the personality dynamics are *living systems* rather than theoretical constructs, we believe they can be validated scientifically through a variety of means. The fundamental characteristics of each personality dynamic surely have underlying physical manifestations. The neural pathways of each personality dynamic, for example, are presumably unique. If these complex underlying physical processes could be teased out, we would have further ways of identifing individual personality dynamics, and be able to understand their functioning more completely.

Just as we are certain that the personality dynamic patterns are encoded in the voice, we believe that they are also encoded in the brain and in the DNA. As Chapter 2 stated, we launched a research project on voice-spectrum analysis in 1981, with promising early results. We plan to resume this exploration in the near future. We would also welcome the opportunity to collaborate in research linking the personality dynamics to brain functioning and genetic mapping.

Research of this kind can do more than simply validate our perception of the existence of these distinctions in systemic functioning; it can make early identification of the personality dynamic possible by technological means, providing invaluable information for parents, teachers, and health-care workers, in supporting the development of children.

Another kind of basic research interests us, which to some readers may seem more "far out." This is study of the centers of energy associated with each of the personality dynamics. Actually, it is now commonly recognized that people (like all other forms of life) constitute energy systems; and of course from ancient times systems have been developed and utilized for understanding the functioning of people in terms of energy flow.

It has been the experience of ourselves and others that the central energy location is different with the different personality dynamics. One can clearly sense, for example, that the main center of energy of mentally centered people is around the head, of emotionally centered people in the area of the chest, and of physically centered people in the abdomen (the Japanese "hara"), with subtleties of distinction depending upon whether an individual is emotional-mental or emotional-physical, and so on. While we can train people to be sensitive to these quite apparent distinctions, we would like to explore any way in which they could be registered through technology.

Health

We know a great deal about the needs of the different personality dynamics with regard to the maintenance of mental, emotional, and physical health. We are already able to offer programs that identify the reactions to stress of the different personality dynamics, relate maintenance of wellness to the natural movement along the different developmental paths, and offer practices and exercises for supporting that movement. Wellness will be the topic of our next book. However, a wide field of additional medical research remains to be explored.

For example, some years ago, a small research study with only 12 subjects undertaken by a Swedish pharmacological lab indicated that metabolic rate varied predictably among the different personality dynamics—fastest with the mentally centered, slowest with the physically centered, with the emotionally centered in between. Confirmation of this finding through more extensive investigations would have major implications for the prescription of drug dosages.

Over the years, we have collected informal health histories that have convinced us that each personality dynamic group not only has unique requirements for maintaining wellness, but also tends toward specific patterns of illness.

Diabetes is a case in point. It has been remarkable to us how many physically centered people report that they suffer from diabetes, given that the physically centered are only 15 percent of the general population in non-Far Eastern cultures. Apart from our own observations, formal studies have shown that a high percentage of Native Americans suffer from diabetes. For example, studies of the Pima Indians in southern Arizona have shown that as many as 40 to 50 percent become diabetic. As we previously noted, the great majority of the Native American population that we have investigated is physically centered. Statistics also show that the differences in diabetes rates between native Asian populations and migrant Asian populations are quite striking—the prevalence of gender- and age-specific diabetes is about twofold higher among migrant Asians. The great majority of the Asian population is also, in our experience, physically centered.

This data suggests a hypothesis worth exploring: (1) physically centered people have a genetic predisposition to diabetes, (2) if diabetes is not so prevalent in Asia, then the stress for physically centered people of living among populations and cultures that are not primarily physically centered—the United States, for example—may trigger the predisposed condition. It would be interesting to investigate whether physically centered people who live in urban environments in Western cultures are more susceptible to diabetes than those who are more able to maintain their natural rhythms by living in rural environments.

Our feedback also suggests that emotional-subjective people are particularly susceptible to gastrointestinal disorders; and many physical-emotional people have indicated problems related to their arms, legs, hands, and feet (for example, tingling and numbness in their limbs). The susceptibility of the different personality dynamics to specific illnesses and disorders and exploring ways of correcting them seems a particularly fruitful area of research.

Education

Schools and Classrooms as Learning Organizations

Our vision for the role of Human Dynamics in education is based on extensive experience training and working with teachers in schools in Canada, Sweden, Israel, and the United States.

As one aspect of this vision, we believe that Human Dynamics can contribute to the development of schools as optimally functioning organizations. Institutions of learning have as great a need as any other organizations to function well as working communities whose members are self-aware, well trained, in a constant process of development, and able to communicate well and work cooperatively. Everything written earlier about the applicability of Human Dynamics programs to business organizations applies equally to schools and centers of educational administration.

But teachers have a special responsibility. The learning and development of the next generation are to a large degree in their hands. We believe that teacher training should be even more sustained and supportive than even the extensive training often undertaken in business organizations. Our teacher training program therefore has a triple focus. The first emphasis is the teacher himself or herself. Who is the teacher, how does he or she naturally learn and teach, and how can we help the teacher develop his or her own potential? The second emphasis is the student. Who is the student, what are his or her specific learning processes and developmental needs, and how can we help his or her own self-understanding? Only after addressing these issues do we move to our third emphasis, the point at which so often teacher preparation begins, and identify teaching approaches and how we manage our classrooms and shape delivery of the curriculum.

Our vision therefore includes the widespread training of teachers in their own development as individuals and team members, training in being sensitive to the different personality dynamics in their classrooms, and training in adjusting their approaches so that they can respond appropriately to each student's specific needs with regard to learning, motivation, communication, and development.

It may seem that we are advocating making the teacher's task more complicated, but in fact we are simplifying it by providing keys to optimal success. A teacher trained in Human Dynamics can view each new class in terms of five fundamental patterns, rather than a diverse group of 30 or so idiosyncratic individuals whose needs will become apparent only over time. This does not mean that students' individuality is not recognized. On the contrary, knowing a student's personality dynamic permits a teacher to connect with him or her uniquely, with profound insight and understanding, and in a language that will "reach" the student. Understanding the different personality dynamics also enables teachers to evaluate each student's work, behavior, and progress with far greater accuracy and understanding. Finally, trained teachers can help students along their particular paths, not only in their learning but also in their personal and interpersonal development. We have developed many processes, many of them using the arts in specific ways, to aid mental, emotional, and physical development and integration. It is part of our vision that every student in every classroom should feel individually "seen," understood, connected with, and enabled to learn and mature optimally.

One of the greatest gifts we can bestow on our children is to enable them to grow up in consciousness, with understanding of their own needs with respect to learning, development, and maintaining well-being. Students who can articulate themselves in this way are empowered for life.

Perhaps most important of all is the insight that students can potentially gain into their own processes. One of the greatest gifts we can bestow on our children is to enable them to grow up in consciousness, with understanding of their own needs with respect to communication, learning, development, and maintaining well-being. Students who can articulate themselves in this way are empowered for life.

It is also part of our educational vision that every classroom should become a model learning *community*, with the teacher as facilitator. Students can be helped to understand and appreciate others' processes as well as their own, and they can develop skills in teamwork and collaboration crucial to the future of the nation and the world. This process can be initiated at any level, but the earlier the better. Even children of preschool age can be helped to understand themselves and appreciate others, using the Human Dynamics insights, if facilitators use a language appropriate for their age level. At the junior high school level and above, when development of personal identity is so crucial, we find that students greatly enjoy and appreciate the introduction of Human Dynamics as part of their studies for self-understanding. More than ever, in a global society, training in both self-understanding and interdependent living is desperately needed. The world would be transformed if the development of self-knowledge, appreciation of self and others, and conscious empathy were an integral part of educational curricula.

Shifting Perceptions

Teachers who attend Human Dynamics programs report consistently that when they face their students again, they discover that their perceptions have shifted. Recognizing the different personality dynamics at play, they find themselves discarding negative labeling in favor of deeper understanding. A student formerly labeled "slow" may now be recognized as a physical-emotional learner who needs more time than others to assimilate new material and complete assignments, and who needs information to be presented concretely, experientially, and with considerable context. A child considered a "behavior problem" may be recognized as an emotional-objective learner who has been insufficiently challenged or who needs more opportunities to learn through experimentation. An "attention-deficit-disordered" child may be an emotional-subjective learner who needs a language to articulate turbulent inner feelings and who would benefit from training in gaining detachment from both his or her own emotions and the emotions of others, and in maintaining focus.

Probably the learning process least understood and most misinterpreted is that of physical-emotional learners. On four different occasions, each in a different culture—the U.S.A., Canada, Sweden, and Israel—we asked the teachers in a school to gather the 150 children of most concern to them. Now, although physical-emotional students are only about 5 percent of the population in these cultures, in each instance 50 to 60 percent of those selected were physical-emotional, most identified as "slow learners." In our evaluation, none had a learning disorder, but their process, being so different from that of their peers, had baffled their teachers and become a real liability for the student. At each school we were able to alter the teachers' perception of these students, and provide helpful guidelines.

This way of seeing students is a far cry from judging them as deliberately aberrant or in some way damaged or deficient, and it empowers both the students and the teacher. It enables students to maintain a positive self-image and provides teachers with a structured way to help students succeed.

For example, we would like to tell the story of Bill, an emotional-objective youngster, to illustrate how understanding his personality dynamic was instrumental in turning a "behavior problem" into a success story.

In 1986, while conducting an educational research project in Canada, we entered the classroom of a veteran teacher who had become a colleague and friend during work we had done together previously. We had come to observe one of her students, a nine-year-old boy named Bill, whom she had identified as emotional-objective, and with whom she was having difficulty. We had no difficulty recognizing him. As soon as we entered the room, he leapt from his seat to introduce himself to us. It was soon apparent that he had a tremendous amount of energy and that he might not know exactly how to channel it. He seemed to be in constant motion. Bill was to become not only a "case" about whom we consulted over a period of about six months, but also a friend.

On that first day, Sandra took him out of the classroom for a short talk. In essence, she said to him, "Bill, you have a lot of power. Now, you can do two things with power: you can use it well, or you can abuse it. Which do you do?" The question caught his attention. He pondered it seriously, then answered, "I abuse it." When asked if he knew the reason, he thought again, then replied, "I'm out of control."

In ensuing conversations, Sandra suggested that perhaps he might enjoy being in control, utilizing his wonderful energy and power in ways that would serve him and others better. His answer was a guarded "Maybe." Nevertheless, he agreed that Sandra should discuss with his teachers and his parents the possibility of finding new activities into which he could put his energy. In fact, he seemed to like the idea.

As we have said, Bill is an emotional-objective student, highly intelligent and creative. However, at that time, he was at a stage of his maturity (see Chapter 12, "The Developmental Continuum") where he so needed to establish his own authority that he was challenging the authority of his teachers and his parents. In the process, he had become identified as the worst-behaved youngster in the school, a reputation he seemed determined to uphold.

As movers and initiators, emotional-objective people face a recurring theme in their developmental journey: their *relationship to power.* How will they use it? The right use of power involves taking responsibility, which most emotional-objective people are eager to do. Therefore, we suggested that the teacher ask Bill if there was something for which he wanted to take responsibility. Bill's answer was, "The library!" (He wanted a *big* job.) With our help, the teacher and Bill "negotiated" a contract, in which both parties agreed on

- Bill's precise responsibilities in administering the library procedures for his class.
- The exact consequences should he fail to meet them.

It was agreed that, as his first job, he would rethink and re-create the procedures and policies for his class's use of the library. When these had been approved by the teacher, he would explain the policies to his class and help them understand how to follow the procedures. He requested, and was given, a pin to identify him as the library "authority." Should he fail to live up to his agreement, or abuse his authority in any way, he would lose his job for a period of time.

When emotional-objective people of any age defy authority, they need clear rules and consequences. Because the words "fair" and "respect" have profound meaning for this group, we recommended to the teacher that she frame her communications to him in these terms. She would say, "I cannot *respect* your indifference to other people's needs." "It is not *fair* to us both that you have broken our agreement." "You are being *unfair* to the class when you boss them around; if you just explain to them the *rules* for using the library, they will *respect* you."

Many emotional-objective youngsters see themselves as small adults rather than children, so the teacher spoke to and treated Bill as an adult. Bill was extremely demanding at times, determined to test his teacher's resolve to stick by the rules. She did so to the letter, always reminding him of the "fairness" of their contract; always clearly identifying how he had violated the contract; always following through with the agreed upon consequence; and never becoming trapped in a personal confrontation. She did everything she could to help him succeed and resolutely ignored his many attempts to argue when consequences were in order. Bill gradually discovered that he gained greater satisfaction from exercising his own authority responsibly than from defying the authority of others or challenging the terms of his agreement. Over time he became a model librarian who took great pride in his achievement.

We videotaped an interview with Bill shortly after we first met him, and again six months later. The change in him is clearly evident in these tapes. In the first interview, he has difficulty sitting still. His eyes dart around, he enjoys making distracting noises, and he delivers a monologue about the various devices he has created for scaring people. His energy is uncontrolled and erratic. In the second, he is calm, his gaze is steady, he engages in a dialogue, and he talks with pride of completing his homework. He has not lost his energy, but it is now focused and engaged. By approaching Bill through his inherent relish of responsibility and need for structure and rules, the teacher helped him develop both self-respect and respect for the authority of others. He thus became a cooperative and accomplished class member, who may well develop into an admirable leader. Indeed, the love of responsibility that emotional-objective people have can lay the foundation for effective leadership.

Bill also benefited from the teacher's implementation of an instructional approach tailored to his personality dynamic. He was given many open-ended assignments with small groups. (An example of an open-ended assignment would be asking students to read about education in Japan, England, and the U.S., and then to produce a plan for reforming education in one of these countries, by borrowing practices from the other two.) This format offers the opportunity for shaping and reshaping ideas through brainstorming and creative experimentation. Emotional-objective people prefer to learn in this open-ended way because it challenges their imagination and offers the opportunity to create new models. They thrive in the light of newness and change. Repetition can bore them.

When Bill and his small group had finished each creative task together, they had to present their results to the class for feedback and then return to their task to refine their presentation. Setting a structure that involves feedback, refinement, and detailing (physical principle) counters the tendency of some emotional-objective learners to stay at the level of general ideas that may not become grounded. It completes the cycle of learning and integrates the direction of growth.

We met Bill quite by accident, three years later, when he was 12 years old. He had clearly matured and sincerely thanked us for "helping him to become grown up." He particularly appreciated his teacher for her steadfast patience and belief in him.

Future Projects

We have found that the beneficial effects of Human Dynamics expand exponentially the greater the number of people who gain exposure to it in any environment. Human Dynamics helps promote cohesion. In our educational projects, we always recommend that training be provided for administrators and parents as well as teachers. It facilitates communication and collaboration between administrators and teachers, between educators and parents, and between parents and children. In this way, all share a framework of understanding through which to nurture the well-being of the children.

A project we have in progress, and one dear to our hearts, is to contribute to the self-awareness of young students by creating several sets of books. Each set will explore an issue fundamental to self-understanding, such as "How I Learn," or "How I Like to Talk with Others." Each set will contain five books—each book from the perspective of a different personality dynamic, providing information geared to that personality dynamic, and written in the language, rhythm, and tone of that personality dynamic. In fact, the authors of the books in each set will represent the different personality dynamics. Reading their "own" books will promote students' self-discovery and personal integration; reading "others'" books will, with adults' help, promote interpersonal understanding and skills.

For example, picture a classroom of young students. All the children have read (or had read to them) a book describing, in children's terms, how the emotional-subjective child can become stressed. The teacher asks, "Who do you think is like this in our class?" or "Which of you feels this way?" Then the class discusses the issue. The children learn to understand and accept each other while gaining vital information for individual well-being. Accompanying material would be available for teachers and parents. While promoting individual development and group empathy, these books would also help resolve issues of diversity; for as they learn to appreciate diversity in the form of the personality dynamics, students recognize that they share fundamental processes that cross barriers of age, race, culture, and gender.

Because the diverse personality dynamics are present in every classroom, it is part of our vision that Human Dynamics training becomes recognized as basic preparation for teachers and an accepted part of the curriculum of teacher training in colleges and universities. Parent training can also be made available through colleges, schools, day-care centers, children's hospitals— even as part of prenatal preparation.

We hope someday to sponsor child-centered conferences, created by children and teachers together. At these conferences, children would demonstrate to adults through drama, art, poetry, and exhibits the diverse ways in which they learn and grow. They could also share *their* dreams for the future.

East and West
Bridging Eastern and Western Cultures

As we mentioned earlier, approximately 80 percent of the people we have studied who live in large cities in Western cultures are emotionally centered. This contrasts strikingly with the Orient, where the great majority of the population appears to be physically centered. This discovery offers enormous insight into fundamental differences between the East and the West and, we believe, accounts for many misunderstandings between them.

Let's revisit some basic characteristics of emotional and physical centering:

EMOTIONAL CENTERING		PHYSICAL CENTERING	
Orientation:	Individual (I, me, mine).	**Orientation:**	Group (we, us, our).
Time:	Present and immediate future.	**Time:**	Continuity of past and present into the long-term future.
Learning:	Linked to individual experiences and interpretations. Requires dialogue, interaction with others, and opportunities for experiment and self-expression.	**Learning:**	Through detailed texts; hands-on experiences; in organic time; through repetition.
Movement:	Spontaneous.	**Movement:**	Deliberate.
Communication:	Expressive of individual personality, ideas, feelings, and subjective awareness.	**Communication:**	Factual; detailed; expressive of group decision-making.

Figure 13.1

The disparity between these two kinds of centering is evident, as is their potential for complementarity.

Discussing physical centering with physically centered *Western* people (communicating, of course, in English) has helped us learn much about Asians. We subsequently confirmed our insights through discussion and workshops with Asian nationals. It has become increasingly clear to us that the cultural patterns of the East reflect the physically centered characteristics of its people, just as the cultural patterns of the West reflect the emotionally centered characteristics of *its* people. In perceiving differences between East and West in these terms, we believe that Human Dynamics offers a foundation of understanding that can help bridge the two cultures.

As Asia opens up, it incorporates elements of Western culture. This can be seen as both a gift and a burden. The gift is the awakening of the emotional principle with its attributes of personal consciousness, valuing individual initiative and creativity, and sounding the personal voice. The burden is the possibility of Asians abandoning their natural capacities in favor of taking on a Western "personality." It is essential that the gifts of the physical principle continue to be honored and maintained, while the emotional principle is developed and integrated consciously and with care. To free the potentially volatile emotional principle carelessly, when it has slumbered for millennia, could be akin to opening up a Pandora's box! Schools are where this careful process can best be undertaken.

The West also needs to continue work with the emotional principle. All over the world, among individuals, groups, and nations, the emotional principle still tends to be out of control and primitively expressed. It so often takes the form of anger, hatred, fear, projection, depression, or withdrawal. There is a long journey yet to be traveled from personal awareness to the development of collective, conscious empathy. In the West, the emotional principle needs to be matured; in the East, to be birthed.

The gifts that the East offers the West are the attributes of the physical principle—systemic long-range planning, sustained building over time, respect for natural rhythms, and valuing of the group. Integration of these in the West would add complementary gifts and provide a foundation of stability to help modify imbalanced expression of the emotional principle.

The Human Dynamics programs for East/West bridge building are based on these perceptions. Rather than simply provide each group with information about the other's cultural practices, we help them to understand and, as far as possible, develop the attributes of each other's personality system. In working with Eastern managers, we expand the range of our usual corporate tools. We use art, music, poetry, and consciously directed communication not only to indicate distinctions between the emotional and physical realms, but also to promote personal awareness and elicit personal expression. At the same time, we adapt our teaching approaches to accommodate their physically centered learning processes—for example, providing more hands-on experiences, moving at a more deliberate pace, exploring fewer aspects in greater depth, and working systematically. Both Eastern and Western managers learn about the contrasting processes of their counterparts; and both practice personal development exercises to integrate the more latent principle. They internalize the experience, as far as possible, of walking in the other's shoes.

For example, in one seminar with Japanese and American managers, we demonstrated some of the differences between the physically centered East and the emotionally centered West by showing pairs of art slides that were similar in content but different in execution. For example, each of one pair of slides showed a mother bathing her child, but the manner of presentation was quite distinct. The Western picture was an emotional presentation, in which the feelings of the mother for her infant and the sense of emotional connection between them were clearly presented. Each figure was highly individualized, and the artist used vivid colors and swirling brushwork to reflect the emotional situation. The Japanese painting, by contrast, presented figures in a more detached way. Rather than individualized representations, the image captured "motherness" and "childness" through generalized figures, and it *suggested* rather than demonstrated emotion. The Japanese painting emphasized clean line and design rather than multiple shades and textures. Both images had an extraordinary aesthetic appeal, but each in a totally different way. Through a succession of such slides and discussion by both groups, we conveyed a sense of the distinction between an emotionally centered and a physically centered sensibility.

Our purpose, however, was to move beyond simple cognitive understanding of the distinctions between the two groups. We sought an experiential understanding by evoking the physical principle, primarily for the benefit of the American group, and the emotional principle, primarily for the benefit of the Japanese. Working with the emotional principle also benefited the Americans, however, for even in Western organizations in which the majority of the employees are emotionally centered, the emotional principle, as we have seen, is so often denied, unconscious, or out of control.

As a means of working with the emotional principle and evoking personal awareness, we showed a pair of slides whose images were open to subjective interpretation and asked the participants to each make up a story about one of the slides. They were to use the components of the picture as elements in, or triggers for, their story. We then paired the participants, each American with a Japanese partner, and asked them to read their stories to one another. The next step was for each participant to re-imagine and rewrite his or her story, this time including himself or herself as a participant in it. Again they were asked to share their stories with their partners. Their final step was to ask themselves what links they saw between the roles, feelings, or attitudes they had created for themselves in their stories, and their real-life roles, feelings, attitudes, or experiences. And again, they were asked to share their insights with their partners.

This enjoyable and entirely subjective process illuminated for each participant a side of themselves that might otherwise be unknown, and it engaged them in a creative process of self-discovery. For the Japanese, in particular, it engendered discovery of what was unique and individual to each member of the group—a process that paralleled the more individualized and subjective experience of the majority of their American colleagues. The Japanese were excited about their discoveries. One was inspired to create his first haiku; another said, "If opening up the emotional principle will help me to be more creative, I want more of it *now*!"

We also wanted to work directly with the physical principle to promote the Americans' communication with the physically centered Japanese. Because many Western business people need to know how to make effective presentations to their counterparts from the East, we created a detailed three-page document on how to make a presentation to physically centered people, and gave a copy to each participant. The Japanese managers were then asked to comment on the text while the Americans listened. The exercise taught the Americans an extraordinary lesson about physically centered people: the Japanese appointed someone to read the entire document aloud, pausing after each sentence for group discussion.

We allowed one hour for the exercise, but at the end of that time the Japanese had read through only about half of the text. In the end, they recommended very few changes. The accuracy of the document, however, was less significant than the process to which the Westerners were exposed. They were able to immerse themselves in the methodical process of their Japanese associates, absorb their pacing and rhythm, and note the kinds of questions they asked, their sequencing, attention to detail, and group interaction. They not only learned how to make an effective presentation to the Japanese, but also gained understanding that would be useful in pursuing any kind of connection with people from the Far East, or with physically centered people anywhere. Through this experience, the Westerners tapped the physical principle in themselves.

We believe that East/West bridging requires more than simply sharing information about distinctions in cultural practices. It also requires experience with the principle that is central to the other culture and integration of it in ourselves. We are currently training pairs of facilitators specifically for work in East/West programs, one member of each pair being physically centered, and the other emotionally centered. The physically centered person has a natural resonance with the Asian culture as it is, while the other represents its deep need and developmental direction. The emotionally centered person has a natural resonance with Western culture as it is, while the other represents one of *its* deep needs and areas of growth.

In Summary

We have taken a long journey together in this book. Our purpose has been to help raise collective consciousness about how we human beings seem to be "designed," and to offer practical examples of this new knowledge. We hope that in the process we have enabled you to share some of the wonder we feel as we contemplate and experience the full expression of the three universal principles, and see how they combine to form the distinct personality dynamic systems.

In exploring the practical applications of this new knowledge, we have used primarily examples from the world of business and organizational life. As David Marsing at Intel showed, it is possible to have—as an end in itself—a vision for an organization as a conscious community. In such a community, members have an empathic concern for one another and for the larger community; at the same time, they work efficiently and achieve spectacular results. Indeed, as David explained and as we have consistently seen demonstrated, a conscious and qualitative process engenders qualitative results. Human Dynamics offers basic tools to these ends.

We recently held a consultation with members of the senior management of a large multinational oil company. We learned that they had completed a three-year world-wide investigation into the roots of business failure and effective sources of training for business success. What were their conclusions? The results of their odyssey came down to this: It was the dysfunctional behavior of people and their difficulties in working together that led to failure; and it was the development of people *as people* that brought organizational success. This was not news to us, but we were deeply impressed by the integrity of their search, and believe that they had succeeded in finding the hidden treasure. It is encouraging to know that this fundamental realization is becoming more widespread.

Of course, the lessons of business apply to every other arena of human interaction and endeavor. Indeed, the survival of our species depends in the end on our ability to understand ourselves and develop our individual and collective capacities. This should be the main agenda in our homes, our classrooms, and our daily lives.

As we hope we have been able to show, this body of work that we term Human Dynamics brings essential insights and basic training to the fields of business, parenting, education, healthcare, and cross-cultural bridging. Above all, perhaps, it offers a framework of understanding and provides tools and practices for the pursuit of mastery of ourselves. Finally, it expresses the fullness of who we really are, individually and in our collective interactions. In mastering five "languages," we can move beyond the "confusion of tongues"; in developing conscious empathy, we can surmount divisive barriers of race, color, creed, and hierarchy; and in acknowledging and honoring a transpersonal depth in ourselves and one another, we can move toward realizing our human potential and fulfilling our human destiny.

An old man going a lone highway,
Came in the evening, cold and gray,
To a chasm vast, both deep and wide.
The old man crossed in the twilight dim,
The swollen stream was as naught to him,
But he stopped when safe on the farther side,
And built a bridge to span the tide.
"Old man," said a fellow pilgrim near,
"You are wasting your strength in labor here,
Your journey will end with the closing day,
You never again will pass this way,
You've crossed the chasm deep and wide,
Why build you this bridge at eventide?"
The laborer lifted his old gray head,
"Good friend, in the path I have come,"
        he said,
"There followeth after me today,
A youth whose feet must pass this way.
This chasm which has been naught to me,
To that young man may a pitfall be.
He, too must cross in the twilight dim,
Good friend, I am building this bridge for
        him."

—*Will Allen Dromgoole*

Human Dynamics Research Program

Since 1979, Dr. Sandra Seagal and her associates have been engaged in an ongoing research program to explore, verify, and expand their understanding of the underlying variables and attributes of Human Dynamics.

Initial research efforts (1979–1982) were exploratory, attempting to define the basic categories, the most fundamental attributes of these categories, and the scope of the observed distinctions in psychological and behavioral functioning. During this period, nine Ph.D. theses were completed, using as their theoretical framework the understandings which are now known as the Human Dynamics system. These studies were completed under the direction of Dr. Seagal, with W. Brugh Joy, M.D., serving as faculty advisor.

Since 1982, a number of studies have been conducted as part of the continuing Human Dynamics research program. In total, the studies have involved more than 40,000 research subjects representing over 25 cultures (see pp. 317–318).

Hypotheses

The hypotheses underlying the research program are as follows:

1. Three fundamental varieties of systemic human functioning can be identified.

2. These three ways of functioning ("ways of being centered") correspond to a "basic operating system" for the individual (rather than an aggregate of personality characteristics).

3. There are three variations on each of these ways of functioning, making nine possible patterns ("personality dynamics").

4. These nine personality dynamics differ from one another along a number of fundamental variables (for example: communication needs and processes, learning and problem-solving processes, memory traits, relationship to change, causes of stress, tendency to attend to detail, pacing, relationship to time, kind of interaction with others, needs for verbal communication).

5. The personality dynamics of an individual are stable across time (that is, an individual's personality dynamic remains the same throughout life).

6. The personality dynamics are nuanced but not determined by culture.

7. Identification of the personality dynamics does not require a written test, but can occur either through self-identification or through behavioral observation with minimal interaction.

8. People mature along specific lines of development which relate to their personality dynamic.

Methodologies

Methodologies used in the research program have included:

1. *Interviews: Structured and Unstructured*

Over 12,000 interviews with individuals have been conducted by the Human Dynamics research team. The majority of these interviews have been unstructured in format, but have centered on the themes of attitudes, behaviors, and perceptions related to work, education, and relationships. Additional topics have included stress and health issues.

Interviews are typically 45–60 minutes in length. Approximately 2,500 interviews have been documented through video, audiotapes, or written notes.

2. *Questionnaires*

Questionnaires have been used primarily in educational settings where teachers and parents have been asked to rate, on a five-point scale, a child's performance and capacity in a variety of situations and the adults' own attitudes toward education.

3. *Behavioral Observation*

More than half of the individuals studied (approximately 20,000 people) have been the subjects of systematic behavioral observation by trained observers. Specific observation categories documented: use of language (pace, rhythm, type and number of words used, silence, degree of dominance in conversation, etc.); use of body (hands, eyes, face); contribution to problem-solving activities.

A. Structured (videotaped) studies have set parameters, tasks, or situations for groups of two, three, and four people to respond to within a given time. One standard protocol groups either three adults or three children of the same personality dynamic and gives them the assignment of creating an "ideal recreational area for their community" using the materials provided and working within a set time frame. (Adults are given 20 minutes; children, 40 minutes.) This particular protocol has been repeated 81 times with adults and 159 times with children (ages have ranged from 5–12 years, but within a single group the ages have varied less than 10 months). Replications have included various combinations of gender and cultures. A second standard protocol, with adults, is setting a group task for individuals of different personality dynamics. This experiment has been repeated approximately 60 times.

B. Unstructured observations have measured variables similar to the structured observations, but have been conducted outside a specific assignment or time frame.

4. *Self-Identification Procedure with Groups and Individuals*

Approximately 12,000 people have participated in a three-to-four hour procedure which allows them to identify their own personality dynamic. This procedure involves viewing videotapes, group discussion, and reading text. Results of the individuals' self-assessments are then compared with the assessments of the trained observers.

5. *Projective Tests*

A "Mountain-Valley-World" guided visualization, developed by Dr. Seagal, is a procedure for assessing the relative degree of functioning and integration in individuals of the mental, emotional, and physical principles. It provides a basis for applying measures that will aid the balanced development in both adults and children of the three principles and of the specific capacities which are associated with each principle.

This visualization often reveals the individual's deepest values and inherent motivations, which are then possible to nurture and to help become manifest.

The visualization is appropriate for either children or adults (with slight changes in wording). Interpretation of the visualization is based either on self-reporting by the subject or through analysis of a drawing made by the subject.

The visualization has been administered to thousands of individuals. Documented administrations and evaluations include 1,830 to children and 550 to adults.

6. *Longitudinal Studies*

Several longitudinal studies have been conducted. One group of approximately 60 adults in the Los Angeles area was studied over a five-year period through repeated interviews, observations, questionnaires, and projective tests. A second group of 35 adults in Canada participated in a similar research project for three years. A group of children from an Arlington, Texas, school have been videotaped and analyzed at two-year intervals since 1983.

Samples

Subjects in the research program have ranged in age from two weeks to 94 years. Approximately 12 percent of the research subjects have been elementary school students; less than 1 percent have been younger than five years of age; 85 percent have been adults (ranging between 25 and 60 years of age).

Women represent about 40 percent of the sample studied.

More than 75 percent of the research subjects came from three countries—the United States, Canada, and Sweden—although they have represented diverse cultures within those countries (for example, among immigrant children in northern California or Native American women in Canada).

Specific Studies in Educational Settings

1. Jane Adams School, Lawndale, California, 1982–83.
   289 students and 26 parents; interview, observations, and projective testing.
2. Robert Muller School, Arlington, Texas, 1983–present.
   20 students and 20 parents in initial interview and observation. Follow-up by videotapes with selected children at two-year intervals.
3. Middlesex School District, Ontario, Canada, 1985–86. Two schools (K–8); total of 576 students. Interviews and administration of projective tests with all students; 90 children selected for videotaping for behavioral analysis.
4. Year-Long Study, 1987–88, in five sites: Los Angeles (urban); Sweden (suburban area of Stockholm); rural areas of northern California; urban area of London, Ontario; adjacent rural area in Middlesex County. Total of 17 classrooms (student population, 462). Assessment of students by

parents and teachers; attitude questionnaires for parents and teachers; administration of projective test to all students; collection of student performance and attendance; videotaping of student interviews.

Studies by Independent Researchers

1. Study of Individuals with Eating Disorders (Mary Hamilton, M.Ed., Faculty of Physical Education, University of Western Ontario, Canada). Funded by the Ontario Women's Directorate, 1985.

2. Learning Styles Assessment of 130 Female Students in the Technology and Trades Programs (Carol Brooks, Ph.D.). Funded by the Canadian Ministry of Skills Development, 1985.

3. Learning Styles Assessment of 206 Native American Women (Carol Brooks, Ph.D.). Funded by the Canadian Ministry of Skills Development, 1986.

4. Study of Managers in Three Cultures. Neil Abramson & Harry Lane, University of Western Ontario, 1990. Doctoral dissertation study.

Countries/Cultures Represented in Research Program

North America:

United States***	(Afro-American**)	(Native American**)
Canada***	(Asian**)	(Hispanic**)
Mexico*		

Europe/Eastern Europe:

England***	France**	Denmark**
Germany**	Holland**	Greece*
Finland**	Sweden***	Spain*
Scotland*	former Yugoslavia*	Portugal*
Switzerland**	Romania*	Poland*
Czech Rep.*	Ireland*	Italy**
Russia*		

Middle East:

Israel***	Palestine**	Turkey**
Iraq**	Iran**	
Armenia**		

South America:

Brazil*	Argentina*	Peru*
Chile*		

Caribbean:

Haiti*		
Jamaica*		Cuba**

South Pacific:

Bali*	Australia**	New Zealand*

Asia/Southeast Asia:

Japan**	China**	Thailand*
Vietnam*	Tibet*	India**
Pakistan**	Afghanistan*	Laos**
Cambodia*	Mongolia*	Philippines**

Africa:

Egypt*	Gambia*	Kenya*
Mozambique*	Morocco*	Ethiopia**

***Extensive studies

** Interviews/ observations

* Limited exposure . . . for example, in-depth study, but with only a few people from that culture

Some Well-Known People

We have identified the personality dynamics of the following well-known people through studying them on videotape, and in some cases by reading their writings. Their photographs appear either in this section or in the body of the book.

We have selected these particular individuals primarily to demonstrate that leadership and achievement take many forms and may be represented by people of any personality dynamic. There are Nobel-Prize winners among each of the five groups of people shown here.

The brief remarks about each individual indicate some traits and qualities that typically reflect his or her personality dynamic.

MENTAL-PHYSICAL

Krishnamurti

Indian-born spiritual teacher who lived and taught in the West. Detachment a central part of his message. Precise use of words. His spiritual teaching was intellectually rather than emotionally framed.

Bertrand Russell

British philosopher, mathematician, and social reformer, known for his trust in the power of the rational mind and the clarity of his writing. A highly independent thinker, twice imprisoned for upholding his pacifist principles.

Alistair Cooke

English-born journalist, radio and television commentator, and introducer of PBS' Masterpiece Theater. Known for his dry sense of humor, precise and elegant use of language, and ability to objectively interpret the English culture for Americans and vice versa.

Georgia O'Keeffe

American artist. The subjects of her paintings are often singular; e.g., one flower, or a lone animal skull. Her paintings do not include people. She spent a great deal of her life, and found much inspiration, in the space and solitude of New Mexico.

Prince Charles

We have so far found the largest number of mental-physical people to be of British descent, although even in Britain they are still a small minority—possibly 8%–10%. Prince Charles, like his father Prince Philip, is mental-physical. He is by nature rather detached (unlike Princess Diana, who is emotional-subjective and by nature highly relational).

John Cleese

British comedian, actor, director, writer. Plans his scripts with great care. His humor is rationally based—it is the humor of the absurd, of turning the rational upside down.

Katharine Hepburn

Like most mental-physical performers, she projects a persona, rather than "becoming" someone else. Known for her individualistic thinking and dry humor. Her autobiography describes events, but is extremely reticent about close personal relationships. Other mental-physical film personalities—James Stewart, Henry Fonda, Fred Astaire. Remember the essential traits of Astaire's dancing—precision, elegance.

EMOTIONAL-OBJECTIVE

Mahatma Gandhi

An outstanding example of a developed emotional-objective leader. Risked. Challenged. Embodied his ideas—willing to die for them. Able to inspire others and provide them with blueprints for action, exerting political pressure through public symbolic acts.

Martin Luther King, Jr.

Like Gandhi, an inspirational leader, committed to the principles of non-violence. He, too, used the power of his words and intensity of his commitment to give others direction and move them to action. He also lived and died embodying his teaching.

Dag Hammarskjöld

Swedish statesman and vigorous leader as Secretary-General of the United Nations, 1953–1961. His posthumously published journal of personal reflections, *Markings*, is a record of his intimate spiritual thinking.

John F. Kennedy

Responsive to and supporter of the new and challenging (e.g., the space program). Able to convey his ideas compellingly. Inspired by those who risked for their beliefs (*Profiles in Courage*). His emotional-subjective brother, Robert, conveyed more personal empathy than John did.

Eleanor Roosevelt

An active first lady who promoted social change. Played an energetic role during World War II. Acknowledged as a role model by Hillary Clinton, who is herself emotional-objective.

Ingrid Bergman

A "cool" actress—less able to take on a broad range of characters than, say, Meryl Streep or other emotional-subjective actresses. Always Ingrid Bergman—but performed with still a considerable emotional range.

EMOTIONAL-SUBJECTIVE

Mother Teresa

The depth in her eyes is remarkable. She represents the evolution of the emotional principle—pure compassion. She has taken the emotional-subjective journey to integration of greater objectivity, or she could not have endured the suffering of those she has chosen to help.

Albert Einstein

An intellectual giant, but also a man of feelings, expressed both in his personal life and fervent appeals for international collaboration and world peace. A violinist. Looked at relationships on a cosmic scale ("Theory of Relativity"). Many great physicists—e.g. David Bohm, Richard Feynman—are or were emotional-subjective.

Mikhail Gorbachev

Personal connection a characteristic of his leadership style. Showed feelings. Enjoyed mingling with people. Excellent organizer, orchestrating events on international scale in pursuit of his vision.

Isaac Stern

American violinist, known for the warmth of his personality and his playing. The award-winning documentary video "Mao to Mozart" shows him teaching "playing from the heart" to technically proficient students.

John Steinbeck

American author, whose works express great compassion for the socially disadvantaged. Created a wide range of characters, finding delight in idiosyncrasy and nobility in humble people.

Meryl Streep

Actress able to play a vast range of roles. Other outstanding examples, among so many emotional-subjective actors and actresses able to "become" others with relative ease, are Dustin Hoffman, Robin Williams, Michelle Pfeiffer, and Emma Thompson.

PHYSICAL-EMOTIONAL

Winston Churchill

Epitome of courage and tenacity. Able to hold masses of information and grasp the movement of the whole in the conduct of World War II. An eminent historian. Speeches combined telling accumulation of detail with blunt fact and concrete imagery. "I have nothing to offer but blood and sweat and tears and toil." Pastimes were nature and craft-related—landscape painting, landscaping, and bricklaying. Boris Yeltsin and Wilhelm de Klerk are current physical-emotional leaders.

Robert Frost

A poet who used images of nature to illustrate aspects of the human condition. Tone of his poetry was matter-of-fact rather than lyrical.

Margaret Mead

A pioneer in anthropology. Studied the cultural pattern of societies. Lived in them, absorbing the rhythms of the people's lives.

R.C. Gorman

Navajo watercolor artist. His paintings typically depict Native Americans in the natural landscape. The figures are stylized and representational rather than individualized.

Spencer Tracy

Physically centered actors usually do not display a wide emotional range, but typically project strength, reliability. Often seem to act by just being themselves. Spencer Tracy was one example; John Wayne and Humphrey Bogart were others.

Ralph Richardson

Again, examples of physically centered actors are relatively rare—however, in his acting, he suggested emotional depth.

PHYSICAL-MENTAL

Dalai Lama

A down-to-earth spiritual leader who describes himself as "a simple Buddhist monk." Preaches fundamental tenets. "What we need is warmth of heart." "Compassion is a universal religion." "Control your anger." "Take it easy." Takes a long view in his understanding of political events. Hobby: watch repair.

Nelson Mandela

President of South Africa. Renowned for his persistence and endurance in pursuing his vision of a just and united country. A political prisoner for 27 years, he refused to accept compromises which might have freed him. As a leader, he tries to create the societal structures that will endure in the future. Conveys enduring strength rather than variety of mood. Current public figures in the U.S. who are physical-mental: Warren Christopher, Bob Dole, and Ross Perot.

Cesar Chavez

Founder of the first successful farm worker's union in the U.S. Also characterized by persistence and endurance in a lifelong struggle seeking rights for migrant farm workers. A "man of the people."

Rachel Carson

Author of *Silent Spring*, one of the first books to draw attention to humanity's destructive impact upon the cycles of nature. The power of her writing lies in accumulation of data and compellingly detailed descriptions of the systemic outcomes if environmentally threatening practices do not change.

Yasunari Kawabata

Japanese author. As with most Japanese writers, emotion is more implicit than dramatically expressed. Precise descriptive detail.

Buckminster Fuller

Architect and engineer, interested in fundamental natural structures and "deriving maximum output from minimum input of energy and materials." A number of eminent architects have been physical-mental, including Frank Lloyd Wright.

Clint Eastwood

Roles have tended to the taciturn and minimally expressive. As a director, he is extremely efficient, completing projects on schedule and under budget. Gives actors freedom to find own emotional expression. Likes to use the same crew members—a purpose-oriented family.

Text Credits

In all cases, the publisher has made every effort to contact and get permission from the appropriate institutions for the previously published material used in this book. Nevertheless, if omissions or errors have occurred, we encourage you to contact Pegasus Communications, Inc.

Chapter 2
p. 21, Laurens van der Post: from a videotaped interview with Arianna Straussinopolous.

Color Insert
p. 2, Krishnamurti: excerpts from Krishnamurti: *The Years of Awakening,* by Mary Lutyens, 1975. Farrar Straus & Giroux; p. 3, Georgia O'Keeffe: from *Georgia O'Keeffe—Art Letters,* by Jack Cowart and Juan Hamilton, 1987, [p. 231]. National Gallery of Art. Reprinted by permission; p. 3, Bertrand Russell: reprinted by permission of Simon & Schuster from *A History of Western Philosophy,* by Bertrand Russell [p. xiii]. Copyright © 1945 by Bertrand Russell. Copyright renewed 1973 by Edith Russell; p. 4, Mahatma Gandhi: Quotations from the writings of Mohandas K. Gandhi © Navajivan Trust, Ahmedabad, India; reprinted from *The Words of Gandhi,* selected by Richard Attenborough, published by Newmarket Press; p. 5, Martin Luther King: from *The Words of Martin Luther King, Jr.* by Coretta Scott King, [p. 90]. Newmarket Press; p. 6, Mother Teresa: from *Mother Teresa,* 1986 Petrie Productions, distributed by Red Rose Gallerie; p. 7, Albert Einstein: from an address at California Institute of Technology, 1931; p. 7, Isaac Stern: from *Mao to Mozart,* Kari Lorimor Home Video, 1980, Harmony Film Group, Hopewell Foundation; p. 8, Winston Churchill: from a speech in the House of Commons, December 8, 1941; p. 9, Margaret Mead, from *Blackberry Winter,* by Margaret Mead, 1972. William Morrow & Company, New York; p. 10, Dalai Lama: from *The Heart of Tibet,* by Dalai Lama. Reprinted by permission of The Office of Tibet; p. 11, Rachel Carson: excerpt from *Silent Spring* by Rachel Carson. Copyright © 1962 by Rachel L. Carson; copyright © renewed 1990 by Roger Christie. Reprinted by permission of Houghton Mifflin Company. All rights reserved; p. 11, Nelson Mandela: from his inaugural address, May 1994.

Part II Opener
p. 57, Margaret J. Wheatley: from *Leadership and the New Science,* by Margaret J. Wheatley, 1992, [p. 80]. Berrett-Koehler Publishers.

Chapter 5
p. 67, Laurens van der Post: from a videotaped interview with Arianna Straussinopolous; p. 83, Laurens van der Post: from *A Walk with a White Bushman,* (co-author Jean-Marc Pottliez). Chatto 7 Windus Ltd., London, 1986. Reprinted by permission of Chatto & Windus.

Chapter 6
p. 89, Dag Hammarskjöld poem: "Thus It Was," from *Markings* by Dag Hammarskjöld,

[p. 5], translated by Leif Sjoberg and W. H. Auden. Translation copyright © 1964 by Alfred A. Knopf, Inc. and Faber and Faber, Ltd. Reprinted by permission of Alfred A. Knopf; **p. 90**, Martin Luther King: from *The Words of Martin Luther King, Jr.* by Coretta Scott King, [p. 90]. Newmarket Press; **p. 91**, Bill Clinton: from "Educating Bill—The President's Take on His Crash Course in the Ways of Washington," by Jack Nelson and Robert J. Donovan, *Los Angeles Times Magazine,* August 1, 1993. Reprinted by permission; **p. 95**, John F. Kennedy: from *Profiles in Courage,* by John F. Kennedy, [p. 266]. Copyright © 1955, 1956, 1961 by John F. Kennedy. Copyright © renewed 1983, 1984, 1989 by Jacqueline Kennedy Onassis. Foreword copyright © 1964 by Robert F. Kennedy. Copyright renewed. Reprinted by permission of HarperCollins Publishers, Inc.; **p. 97**, Franklin Roosevelt: from an address at Oglethorpe University, May 22, 1932; **p. 115**, Dag Hammarskjöld poem: "Forward!" from *Markings* by Dag Hammarskjöld, trans., L. Sjoberg and W. H. Auden. Translation copyright © 1964 by Alfred A. Knopf, Inc. and Faber & Faber Ltd. Reprinted by permission of Alfred A. Knopf, Inc.

Chapter 7
p. 134, Poem #1,212 "A word is dead. . ." by Emily Dickinson from *The Complete Poems of Emily Dickinson,* edited by Thomas H. Johnson, [p. 534]. Little Brown and Company; **p. 139**, Walt Whitman poem: excerpt from *Song of Myself,* 1855, by Walt Whitman; **p. 151**, Walt Whitman poem: excerpt from *Song of Myself,* 1855, by Walt Whitman.

Chapter 8
p. 160, LeRoy Littlebear: from a speech to the Constitutional Committee Hearings, in Ottawa, January 1992. Reprinted by permission of LeRoy Littlebear, professor of National American Studies, University of Lethbridge, Alberta; **p. 161**, Margaret Mead: from *Blackberry Winter,* by Margaret Mead, 1972. William Morrow & Company, New York; **p. 161**, Winston Churchill: from *The Finest Hours,* 1964, Jack Le Vien International Productions, Ltd., an MGM/Perin Inc. Productions Company; **p. 163**, Robert Frost poem: "Mending Wall," by Robert Frost, 1914; **p. 172**, Tom Joyce: from "The Language of Ironwork," by Tom Joyce, *Fine Homebuilding,* June/July 1992, [p. 78], Taunton Press. Copyright © 1992 by Tom Joyce. Reprinted by permission of the author; **p. 178**, excerpt from *The Peregrine,* by J. A. Baker, [p. 13]. Copyright © 1967 by J. A. Baker. Copyright renewed. Reprinted by permission of HarperCollins Publishers, Inc.

Chapter 9
p. 184, Rachel Carson: from *The Sea Around Us,* Revised Edition, by Rachel Carson [p. 118]. Copyright © 1961 by Rachel L. Carson, renewed 1989 by Roger Christie. Reprinted by permission of Oxford University Press, Inc.; **p. 207**, Buckminster Fuller poem: from *Buckminster Fuller to Children of Earth.* Copyright © 1972 by Buckminster Fuller. Reprinted by permission of the Estate of Buckminster Fuller.

Chapter 13
p. 311, "The Bridge Builder," by Will Allen Dromgoole, [originally written in late 1890s] published in Beta Theta Pi 1992 Convention Issue magazine.

Photo and Illustration Credits

Chapter 1
p. 2, Superstock, Inc.

Chapter 2
p. 10, The Image Bank; p. 17, Buckminster Fuller: © 1996 Allegra Fuller Snyder. Courtesy Buckminster Fuller Institute, Santa Barbara.

Chapter 4
p. 44, Nawrocki Stock Photo.

Color Insert
p. 2, Krishnamurti: AP/Wide World Photos; p. 3, Rolling hills: Superstock, Inc.; p. 3, Katharine Hepburn: Movie Still Archives; p. 3, Georgia O'Keeffe: UPI/Bettmann; p. 3, Bertrand Russell: AP/ Wide World Photos; p. 4, Mahatma Gandhi: The Bettmann Archive; p. 5, Ingrid Bergman: The Bettmann Archive; p. 5, Martin Luther King, Jr.: The Bettmann Archive; p. 5, Eleanor Roosevelt: Woodfin Camp & Associates; p. 6, Mother Teresa: AP/Wide World Photos; p. 7, Albert Einstein: The Bettmann Archive; p. 7, Meryl Streep: AP/Wide World Photos; p. 7, Isaac Stern: AP/Wide World Photos; p. 8, Winston Churchill: Woodfin Camp & Associates; p. 9, Margaret Mead: AP/Wide World Photos; p. 9, Robert Frost: The Bettmann Archive; p. 10, Dalai Lama: © 1991 Office of Tibet, London; p. 11, Escher woodcut: © 1996 M.C. Escher/Cordon Art—Baarn—Holland. All rights reserved; p. 11, Rachel Carson: AP/Wide World Photos; p. 11, Nelson Mandela: AP/Wide World Photos; p. 11, Clint Eastwood: AP/Wide World Photos; p. 12–16, Fractals: see chapters 5–9.

Chapter 5
p. 58, fractal "Knotted Field," by Michael Field and Nathan Field. *Fractals, Patterns of Chaos,* [p. 94]. Reprinted by permission of Michael Field.

Chapter 6
p. 84, fractal "Kamtorus," by Dan Farmer. *Fractal Creations,* 2nd ed., by Tim Wegner and Bert Tyler. Copyright © 1993 by The Waite Group, Inc. Reprinted by permission.

Chapter 7
p. 116, fractal by Homer Smith. *Fractals, Patterns of Chaos,* [p. 81]. Reprinted by permission of Homer Smith.

Chapter 8
p. 152, fractal by Joe Cantrell. *Fractals, Patterns of Chaos,* [p. 13]. Reprinted by permission of Joe Cantrell.

Chapter 9
p. 182, fractal by Paul Meakin. *Fractals, Patterns of Chaos,* [p. 20]. Reprinted by permission of Paul Meakin.

Chapter 12
p. 268, Corn seedling: Superstock, Inc.

Chapter 13
p. 294, Dancer: The Image Bank.

Additional Resources

Human Dynamics International and the Human Dynamics Foundation offer a variety of resources to spread, enhance, sustain, and translate into effective practice the understandings of Human Dynamics.

Currently available are:

AUDIOTAPES AND BOOKLET: *Personal Development Processes*
In this set of four audiotapes, Sandra Seagal and David Horne guide listeners through exercises for personal and transpersonal development that facilitate integration of the mental, emotional, and physical principles. Specific music selections accompany each exercise.

VIDEO PROGRAM FOR PARENTS, TEACHERS, FAMILIES
These videotapes illustrate distinctions among different personality dynamics through interviews with families and sequences with children.

Accompanying texts explore the implications for enhanced family relationships and children's optimum learning and development.

PROGRAMS
Human Dynamics International offers seminars, facilitator training, and consultation in the fields of business, education, healthcare, and parenting.

For more information, contact:
Human Dynamics International
115 S. Topanga Canyon Blvd. Ste. J
Topanga, CA 90290
(888) 546-0366
(310) 455-1149
FAX (310) 455-2057
www.humandynamics.com

Pegasus Communications, Inc., publisher of *Human Dynamics: A New Framework for Understanding People and Realizing the Potential in Our Organizations*, helps managers explore, understand, and articulate the challenges they face in managing the complexities of a changing business world. Pegasus keeps managers on the forefront of organizational innovation with leading-edge publications, conferences, and other materials about organizational learning and systems thinking.

For more information about *The Organizational Learning Resource Library*™ Catalog, *The Systems*

Thinker™ Newsletter, *Leverage®: News and Ideas for the Organizational Learner,* or the *Systems Thinking in Action®* Conference, contact:

Pegasus Communications, Inc.
One Moody Street
Waltham, MA 02453-5339
(800) 272-0945
(781) 398-9700
FAX (781) 894-7175
www.pegasuscom.com

PEGASUS
COMMUNICATIONS